Gendered Spaces

Gendered

The University of North Carolina Press

Chapel Hill and London

Spaces

DAPHNE SPAIN

The paper in this book meets the guidelines for permanence
and durability of the Committee on Production Guidelines
for Book Longevity of the Council on Library Resources.

96 95 94 93 92   5 4 3 2 1

Library of Congress Cataloging-in-Publication Data
Spain, Daphne.
  Gendered spaces / by Daphne Spain.
    p. cm.
  Includes bibliographical references and index.
  ISBN 0-8078-2012-1 (cloth : alk. paper). —
ISBN 0-8078-4357-1 (paper : alk. paper)
  1. Sex discrimination against women—History.
2. Space (Architecture)—History. 3. Sex role—
History. 4. Social status—History. 5. Women—
Dwellings—History. 6. Sexual division of labor—
History. 7. Sex role in the work environment—
History. I. Title.
HQ1150.S68   1992
305.3—dc20   91-25057
                                           CIP

Frontispiece. A woman entering a traditionally masculine
space symbolized women's suffrage in 1877. Library of
Congress.

To Dolores Hayden

Contents

Tables

Figures

Preface

When I was young, it seemed natural that women stayed in the kitchen to clean up after a meal while men went into the living room. The women talked about kids, recipes, illness, friends, and relatives, while the men talked about jobs, politics, and sports or watched television. Few women then had jobs outside the home, and few men spent much time inside the home. Now, as an adult, I am struck by the relative absence of such "gendered spaces" in American homes, schools, and (to a lesser extent) workplaces. Women may still choose the company of other women, and men of other men, but it is more by preference than by convention. The implications of changes in such spatial arrangements for women's status—over time and across cultures—are the subjects of this book.

I started thinking about the relationship between space and gender as a result of a joint appointment in sociology and urban planning. Planning is in the School of Architecture at the University of Virginia, and my colleagues there all used the language of design. My sociology colleagues talked of power and theories of stratification. I began searching for ways to integrate my sociological and planning interests and found that housing, which I have previously studied from the standpoint of racial inequalities, was also ame-nable to gender analysis. I then had the good fortune to discover the work of Dolores Hayden, Eugenie Birch, Susan Saegert, and Gerda Wekerle, all of which led me to think about architectural and planning issues from a feminist perspective.

Further reading unearthed several references to the observation that women's status is lowest in societies in which housing is sexually segregated. I began to speculate whether such a hypothesis could be tested empirically and whether there were other types of gender segregation that might be associated with women's status. From there I formulated the concept of "spatial institutions," matching the social institutions of the family, education, and the labor force with their respective spatial corollaries of the dwelling, the school, and the workplace. Each of these spatial institutions, I found, had varying degrees of gender segregation across cultures and over time.

xiv

The process of collecting examples of segregated and integrated dwellings, schools, and workplaces revealed the importance of access to knowledge. The original hypothesis about the relationship between segregation in the home and gender stratification thus was expanded to specify how the association of segregation with women's status is mediated by the limits placed on women's access to knowledge. In essence, spatial segregation does more than create a physical distance; it also affects the distribution of knowledge women could use to change their position in society.

The pursuit of examples of the relationship between space and status took me to a number of disciplines. The anthropology literature provided numerous accounts of dwellings and women's status in nonindustrial societies. Architectural history informed much of the work on housing, while histories on women's labor force participation were culled for the information on workplace segregation. Theories in sociology and geography, in turn, were integral to the development of the model of reciprocity between space and status.

To demonstrate the pervasiveness of spatial institutions and their association with gender stratification over time and across cultures, I was interested in a wide range of examples. The book is thus broader than it is deep in any one field. A conscious choice was made to investigate the interrelation of gender, status, and space across a multitude of cases in order to argue for the importance of the connections. While some details are admittedly lost through this approach, the sacrifice is worth the corresponding gain in relevance and significance. I leave it to other researchers to pursue individual cases in greater depth.

No book focusing on gender can avoid being positioned within a feminist literature. This study belongs in that category for at least three reasons. First, it questions the structure of status differences between women and men and proposes possible ways in which that structure might be changed. Second, the concept of "gender" designates here the socially constructed, mutually dependent nature of femininity and masculinity rather than the biological differences associated with women and men. Finally, the book incorporates an ongoing feminist concern with "private" and "public" spheres.

Possibly more controversial from a radical feminist standpoint is that I advocate spatial integration as a route to higher status for women. This, of course, taps directly into the current feminist debate about equality versus difference. Further, I rely on traditional "male" measures of status: control of labor, control of property, and participation in public life. While post-structural feminists are correct to question not only male privileges but the criteria by which those privileges are defined, "male" rules still apply until a totally egalitarian society emerges. My use of such traditional measures of status is therefore meant to conform with current stratification research practices rather than to endorse their legitimacy. **xv**

I share the feminist hope for a future society that equally values caretaking and moneymaking, one that attaches as much importance to the activities occurring in private spaces as to those occurring in public places. The reality is that nonindustrial and industrial societies attribute greater value to the public forms of status defined as masculine. This system is not likely to change until women occupy the same space as men, and occupy it in ways that redress the existing distribution of knowledge and balance of power.

Acknowledgments

As the dedication indicates, I owe the greatest intellectual debt to Dolores Hayden. Her scholarship introduced a generation of architects and planners to gender issues. Also important were the encouragement and support for this solo venture from colleagues on two previous projects, Shirley Laska and Suzanne Bianchi. I was in a position to write this book largely as a result of collaborations with them earlier in my career. Comments from architect K. Edward Lay, planner William Harris, and sociologist Donald Black, all at the University of Virginia, contributed to useful revisions early in the writing process. Robert A. Beauregard of the University of Pittsburgh introduced me to the work of feminist geographers and read several chapters.

Conversations with Thomas Guterbock, Murray Milner, Gianfranco Poggi, and Patricia Taylor refined the ideas presented here. To Carl Trindle I owe the observation that secretaries now work in "reverse Panopticons." Classes I audited, taught by colleagues Robert Vickery and Michael Bednar in the School of Architecture, introduced me to the architectural perspective on social issues. Numerous discussions with Maryanne Ferme, a University of Chicago doctoral student in anthropology and Carter Woodson Fellow at the University of Virginia, helped clarify gender issues for nonindustrial societies. The usual disclaimers apply to any errors resulting from misunderstanding the guidance of others.

Professor Martin Whyte of the University of Michigan generously provided the Human Relations Area Files data set on which part of the book is based, and John Jarvis helped convert the files to a user-friendly form. Steve Ainsworth coded additional data on spatial segregation, and other research assistants—Marian Borg, Mary Madden, Dasretta Sapp, and Claudette Grant—performed numerous hours of library work and proofreading. Joan Snapp accurately and with good humor processed endless versions of the manuscript.

xviii   Financial support for preparation of the book was granted by the University of Virginia in the form of a semester's leave from teaching and two summers of research grants. I owe special thanks to chairmen David Phillips and Donald Black for coordinating leave time between two departments when I held a joint appointment in sociology and planning.

The publication process was simplified by timely comments from Catharine Stimpson and by Paul Betz's faith in the project. Several anonymous reviewers also deserve credit for improving the final product.

Finally, the greatest thanks are due my husband and colleague, Steven Nock, who read many drafts and helped clarify my thoughts on numerous decompression walks through the woods. His encouragement was crucial to the successful completion of the manuscript.

Gendered Spaces

1

Space and Status

A whole history remains to be written of spaces—which would at the same time be the history of powers— . . . from the great strategies of geo-politics to the little tactics of the habitat.

—Michel Foucault, *Power/Knowledge*

Throughout history and across cultures, architectural and geographic spatial arrangements have reinforced status differences between women and men. The "little tactics of the habitat," viewed through the lenses of gender and status, are the subjects of this inquiry. Women and men are spatially segregated in ways that reduce women's access to knowledge and thereby reinforce women's lower status relative to men's. "Gendered spaces" separate women from knowledge used by men to produce and reproduce power and privilege.

Sociologists agree that, whether determined by the relationship to the means of production, as proposed by Marx, or by "social estimations of honor," as proposed by Weber, status is unequally distributed among members of society and that men as a group are universally accorded higher status than women as a group (Blumberg 1984; Collins 1971; Huber 1990; Whyte 1978a). Status distinctions among groups of people constitute the stratification (social ranking) system of a society. Women's status is thus a component of gender stratification, as is men's status. "Women's status" and "gender stratification" are used interchangeably throughout this book to designate women's status in relation to men's. "Gender" refers to the socially and culturally constructed distinctions that accompany biological differences associated with a person's sex. While biological differences are constant over time and across cultures (i.e., there are only two sexes), the social implications of gender differences vary historically and socially.

Women and men typically have different status in regard to control of property, control of labor, and political participation. A variety of explanations exists for the persistence of gender stratification. Most theories are based on biological, economic, psychological, or social interpretations (Chafetz 1990). Our understanding of the tenacity of gender inequalities, however, can be improved by considering the architectural and geographic spatial contexts within which they occur. Spatial arrangements between the sexes are socially created, and when they provide access to valued knowledge for men while reducing access to that knowledge for women, the organization of space may perpetuate status differences. The "daily-life environment" of gendered spaces thus acts to transmit inequality (Dear and Wolch 1989, 6). To quote geographer Doreen Massey, "It is not just that the spatial is socially constructed; the social is spatially constructed too" (Massey 1984a, 6).

The history of higher education in America provides an example of the spatial contexts with which gender relations are entwined. Colleges were closed to women until the late nineteenth century because physicians believed that school attendance endangered women's health and jeopardized their ability to bear children (Rosenberg 1982, 5; Rothman and Rothman 1987). In 1837 Mary Lyon defended her creation of the first college for women, Mt. Holyoke, by citing its role in "the preparation of the Daughters of the Land to be good mothers" (Watson 1977, 134). Mt. Holyoke was built in rural Massachusetts to protect its students from the vices of big cities (Horowitz 1984).

An initial status difference (the fact that few women were physicians and none sat on college admissions boards) translated into the exclusion of women from colleges. Spatial segregation, in turn, reduced women's ability to enter the prestigious medical profession to challenge prevailing assumptions about the suitability of educating women. The location of knowledge in a place inaccessible to women reinforced the existing gender stratification system that relegated women to the private sphere and men to the public sphere.

A few pioneering women gained access to higher education, initially through segregated women's colleges. They entered a different world from that of men's colleges such as Harvard, Amherst, and the University of Virginia, which consisted of separate buildings clustered together around common ground. Male students moved from chapel to classroom to their rooms; dormitories had several entrances; rooms were grouped around stairwells instead of on a single corridor; and faculty lived in separate dwellings or off the campus entirely. In contrast, the first women's colleges were single large buildings that housed and fed faculty and students in addition to providing space for classrooms, laboratories, chapel, and library under the same roof. Compared to the relative freedom of dispersed surroundings enjoyed by men, women were enclosed and secluded in a single structure that made constant supervision possible (Horowitz 1984, 4–22).

Women eventually entered coeducational institutions with men. Initially, though, they were relegated to segregated classrooms (Woody [1929] 1974, 2:285) or to coordinate (i.e., "sister") colleges on separate campuses (Newcomer 1959, 40). Spatial barriers finally disappeared as coeducation became increasingly acceptable. As women attended the same schools and learned the same curricula as men, their public status began to improve—most notably with the right to vote granted by the Nineteenth Amendment in 1920.

Thus, both geographic distance and architectural design established boundaries between the knowledge available to women and that available to men. The existing stratification system depended on an ideology of women's delicate health to deny them access to college. These resultant spatial arrangements, in turn, made it difficult for women to challenge the status quo. Once spatial barriers were breached, however, the stratification system began to change.

The Social Construction of Space

Geographic. Geographers have been the most vocal advocates of the integration of space into social theories. It is not sensible, they argue, to separate social and spatial processes: to "explain why something occurs is to explain why it occurs where it does" (Sack 1980, 70). Space is essential to social science; spatial relations exist only because social processes exist. The spatial and social aspects of a phenomenon are inseparable (Massey 1984a, 3; Dear and Wolch 1989).

Among sociologists and geographers who have addressed the spatial perspective are Durkheim (1915) on the social construction of space, Goffman (1959) on the presentation of front-stage versus backstage behavior, Reskin (1988) on the devaluation of women's work, and Harvey (1973) on urban planning. Harvey identifies the city as a crucible in which the sociological and geographical imaginations become most compatible. The tendency to compartmentalize the shape of the city from the activities that constitute it should be avoided, since spaces and actions are different ways of thinking about the same thing (Harvey 1973, 26). The difficulty in achieving a synthesis is that social scientists do not yet possess a language adequate to the simultaneous occurrence of spatial form and social processes.

Part of the difficulty in establishing a common language is the tendency to think in causal terms: do spatial arrangements *cause* certain social outcomes or do social processes create spatial differentiation? Geographers are the first to point out the folly of "spatial fetishism," or the idea that social structure is determined by spatial relations (Massey 1984b, 53; Urry 1985, 28). Yet it is also true that once spatial forms are created, they tend to become institutionalized and in some ways influence future social processes (Harvey 1973, 27). Although space is constructed by social behavior at a particular point in time, its legacy may persist (seemingly as an absolute) to shape the behavior of future generations.

Rather than thinking in terms of causality, Harvey proposes that space and social relations are so intricately linked that the two concepts should be considered complementary instead of mutually exclusive. Although it is necessary to break into the interactive system at some point to test hypotheses, whether one chooses spatial form as the input and social processes as the output or vice versa should be a matter of convenience (Harvey 1973, 46). Harvey suggests that instead of talking about either space or society causing certain outcomes, or the continuous interaction of space and society, efforts be made to "translate results generated in one language (say a social process language) into another language (the spatial form language). It is rather like translating from a geometric result to an algebraic result . . . both languages amount to different ways of saying the same thing" (Harvey 1973, 46–47). In other words, it is fruitless to try to isolate space from social processes in order to say that one "causes" the other. A more constructive approach is to acknowledge their interdependence, acknowledge how one tries to separate the two for analytic purposes, and then reintegrate the two. A geographer might emphasize a *spatial*-social language, while a sociologist might emphasize a *socio*-spatial language of explanation.

My hypothesis is that initial status differences between women and men create certain types of gendered spaces and that institutionalized spatial segregation then reinforces prevailing male advantages. While it would be simplistic to argue that spatial segregation causes gender stratification, it would be equally simplistic to ignore the possibility that spatial segregation

6

reinforces gender stratification and thus that modifying spatial arrangements, by definition, alters social processes.

Feminist geographers have been pioneers on the frontier of theories about space and gender. In an article titled "City and Home: Urban Housing and the Sexual Division of Space," McDowell (1983) argues that urban structure in capitalist societies reflects the construction of space into masculine centers of production and feminine suburbs of reproduction (see also Mackenzie and Rose 1983; Saegert 1980; and Zelinsky, Monk, and Hanson 1982). The "home as haven" constituting a separate sphere for women, however, becomes less appropriate as more women enter the labor force. **7**

According to feminist geographers, a thorough analysis of gender and space would recognize that definitions of femininity and masculinity are constructed in particular places—most notably the home, workplace, and community—and the reciprocity of these spheres of influence should be acknowledged in analyzing status differences between the sexes. Expectations of how men and women should behave in the home are negotiated not only there but also at work, at school, and at social events (Bowlby, Foord, and McDowell 1986). The power of feminist geography is its ability to reveal the spatial dimension of gender distinctions that separate spheres of production from spheres of reproduction and assign greater value to the productive sphere (Bowlby, Foord, and Mackenzie 1982).

Architectural. Architectural space also plays a role in maintaining status distinctions by gender. The spatial structure of buildings embodies knowledge of social relations, or the taken-for-granted rules that govern relations of individuals to each other and to society (Hillier and Hanson 1984, 184). Thus, dwellings reflect ideals and realities about relationships between women and men within the family and in society. The space outside the home becomes the arena in which social relations (i.e., status) are produced, while the space inside the home becomes that in which social relations are reproduced. Gender-status distinctions therefore are played out within the home as well as outside of it (Hillier and Hanson 1984, 257–61).

The use of architecture to reinforce prevailing patterns of privilege and to assert power is a concept dating from the eighteenth century with Jeremy Bentham's Panopticon (from the Greek, for all-seeing). A circular building of cell-like partitions, the Panopticon had at its center a tower allowing a supervisor to observe the occupants of each room. A window at the rear of each cell illuminated the occupant, and side walls prevented contact of occupants with each other. Such surveillance and separation inhibited the contagion of criminal behavior (in prisons), disease (in hospitals), or insanity (in asylums) (Foucault 1977, 200; Philo 1989).*

The Panopticon was "polyvalent in its applications," an architectural system that existed independently of its specific uses. Foucault described it as a machine which could produce the relationships of power and subjection. **8** "It is a type of location of bodies in space, of distribution of individuals in relation to one another, of hierarchical organization, of disposition of centers and channels of power . . . which can be implemented in hospitals, workshops, schools, prisons" (Foucault 1977, 202; see also Evans 1982, 198–206).

Prisons are the clearest examples of space being used to reinforce a hierarchy and to assert power, yet some schools of the eighteenth century were also built on panoptic principles. The École Militaire, designed by the architect Gabriel, was "an apparatus for observation": rooms were small cells distributed along a corridor so that every ten students had an officer's room on each side. Every room had a chest-level window in the corridor wall for surveillance, and students were confined to their rooms through the night. Teachers dined at raised tables to supervise meals, and latrines had half-doors so the heads and legs of students could be seen. Side walls were sufficiently high, however, that students could not see each other (Foucault 1977, 173).

Bentham also was concerned with those "melancholy abodes appropriate to the reception of the insane." He proposed that madhouses erected according to his guidelines could have beneficial effects on the mentally ill (Philo 1989, 265). Architect William Stark's proposal for the Glasgow Asylum (in 1816) followed Bentham's design, adding distinctions by gender, class, and

---

*Speaking tubes between the central tower and each cell, a feature of the first "Penitentiary Panopticon" drawn by Willey Reveley in 1791, eventually were abandoned because they allowed two-way communication. Such a system was contrary to the control of information intended to flow only from the less powerful inhabitants at the periphery of the building to the powerful at its center (Evans 1982, 208).

Fig. 1.1. William Stark's preliminary panoptic plan for the Glasgow Asylum divides space by gender, social class, and degree of illness. Reproduced from "Third Report from the Committee on Madhouses in England," *Parliamentary Reports* 6 (1816): 361, by permission of the Syndics of Cambridge University Library.

level of illness. Men and women were separated, by social rank, into separate wings of the asylum depending on whether they were in an "ordinary" or "convalescent" state (Philo 1989, 268).

Panoptic principles could be applied to schools, prisons, and asylums; Bentham also recognized their application to the workplace. From the central tower a manager could supervise all his employees, whether they were nurses, doctors, foremen, teachers, or warders (Foucault 1977, 204). The manager could judge workers, alter their behavior if necessary, and deliver new instructions. One of the design's special advantages was that "an inspector arriving unexpectedly at the center of the Panopticon will be able to judge at a glance, without anything being concealed from him, how the entire establishment is functioning" (Foucault 1977, 204). The manager had full view of the workers, while workers did not know if they were being observed. In this way the Panopticon reinforced the prevailing relationship between management and labor.

In the creation of new products, and in order to improve productivity, steps in the process of manufacturing were divided into components with a corresponding division of the labor force. The ability to compartmentalize labor *and* workers enabled managers to control the entire process of production, while workers understood only their own contribution rather than the entire process. Spatial control reinforced control of knowledge, which operated to deter labor from organizing against management.

Spatial Institutions

Over the course of the life cycle, everyone experiences one or more of the institutions of family, education, and the labor force. If we are to understand the systemic nature of gender stratification, it is to the interplay of these institutions that we must look (Brinton 1988). Equally important are the spaces within which institutional activities occur. Families must be analyzed in the context of dwellings, education in the context of schools, and labor in the context of workplaces. These "spatial institutions" form barriers to women's acquisition of knowledge by assigning women and men to different gendered spaces. Masculine spaces (such as nineteenth-century Amer-

10

ican colleges) contain socially valued knowledge of theology, law, and medicine, while feminine spaces (such as the home) contain devalued knowledge of child care, cooking, and cleaning.

An institution, in sociological terms, refers to a patterned set of activities organized around the production of certain social outcomes. For example, the family is an institution because it is organized to reproduce future generations. Certain institutions are universal and evolve to fill requirements necessary to the maintenance of society. All societies must have the ability to biologically reproduce themselves, convey knowledge to members, produce goods and services, deal with the unknown, and preserve social order. Thus, some form of family, education, military, economy, religion, and system of legal justice exists in every society.

11

The activities that constitute institutions, of course, occur in specific places. Families live in homes, while education and religion are carried out in schools and churches. There is some overlap in institutions and the spaces they occupy. Educational and religious instruction, for example, may take place in the home, as does economic production in nonindustrial societies. Yet if one were to assign a primary spatial context to each major institution, the family would occupy the dwelling, education the school, economy the workplace, religion the church, and the legal system a courthouse. This book addresses the relationship between gender stratification and the spatial institutions of the family/dwelling, education/school, and labor force/workplace.

The Family and Segregated Dwellings. Nonindustrial societies often separate women and men within the dwelling (P. Oliver 1987). In a typical Purum house, for example, domestic space is divided into right/left, male/female quarters, with higher value attributed to areas and objects associated with right/male and lower value associated with left/female (Sciama 1981, 91). Dwellings of the South American Jivaro Indians demonstrate a similar pattern, with the women's entrance at the left end of the rectangular hut and a men's entrance at the right end; women's beds and men's beds are arranged at their respective ends of the *jivaria* (Stirling 1938). The traditional courtyard pattern of the Nigerian Hausa (used by both Muslim and non-Muslim families) also differentiates men's from women's spaces (Moughtin 1985, 56). Traditional Muslim households are divided into the *anderun* at the back for the women and the *birun* at the front for men (Khatib-Chahidi 1981).

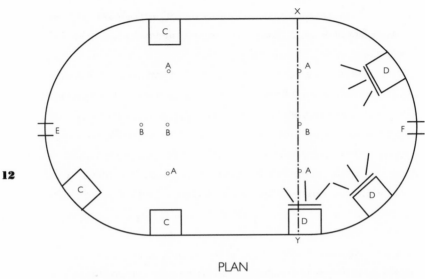

PLAN

A = LATERAL POSTS   B = CENTRAL POSTS   C = WOMEN'S BEDS
D = MEN'S BEDS   E = WOMEN'S ENTRANCE   F = MEN'S ENTRANCE

Fig. 1.2. The men's and women's entrances are at opposite ends of the South American *jivaria*. Adapted from Stirling (1938).

A variety of cultural, religious, and ideological reasons have been used throughout history to justify gender segregation. Muslims, for example, believe that women should not come into contact with men who are potential marriage partners. The system of purdah was developed to keep women secluded in the home in a space safe from unregulated sexual contact, yet it also served to restrict women's educational and economic opportunities. Muslim women therefore have lower status outside the home, compared with women in less sexually segregated societies (Mandelbaum 1988).

Nineteenth-century America and Great Britain had less overt forms of sexual spatial segregation than nonindustrial societies. They were still characterized, however, by gendered spaces. The ideal Victorian home contained a drawing room for ladies and smoking and billiard rooms for gentlemen; the "growlery" was the husband's retreat from domesticity (Franklin 1981; Girouard 1979; Kerr [1871] 1972; Wright 1985). Contemporary American society has been characterized by reduced levels of gender segregation within the dwelling. An era of open floorplans was ushered in by Frank Lloyd Wright's "Usonian" home, and today many high-priced suburban houses are built with "great rooms" in which men, women, and children all share the same space during part of each day.

Education and Segregated Schools. In nonindustrial societies, ceremonial men's huts are the locus of formal education. The huts are places in which men teach boys the techniques of hunting, fishing, warfare, and religious rituals. Initiation rites accompanying passage through the age-set require the proper execution of a series of tasks set forth by the elders. Since girls and women are not allowed to enter the hut, they are excluded from avenues of formal education (Bateson 1958; Hogbin 1970; Maybury-Lewis 1967).

13

For example, secret musical instruments are kept in men's houses and represent a source of power over women. The Iatmul and Wogeo men of New Guinea (Bateson 1958; Hogbin 1970) and the Suiai of the Solomon Islands (D. Oliver 1955) possess flutes or slit-gongs, while Brazilian Shavante men learn songs not taught to women (Maybury-Lewis 1967). During initiation into the men's club of the Wogeo Islanders, boys are told they are hearing monsters that will swallow them. Once the boys pass their initiation rites, they are told by the men: "There were no supernatural beings, only flutes. . . . These were the mysteries that must be hidden from the women. In a few years the boys would be taught how to play the tunes. The entire affair had been invented long ago by the culture heroes to turn children into men—*to separate them from their mothers*" (Hogbin 1970, 110; emphasis added). The power of the musical instruments is insured only as long as they are kept secret from the women. Ceremonial huts create the geographic distance between men and women that facilitates preservation of musical knowledge for men.

Schools are the loci of formal education in American society. Just as ceremonial men's huts are places in which boys learn to hunt and fight in nonindustrial societies, schools are the places in which, until relatively recently, occupational skills were conveyed only to boys. Excluding girls from schools—elementary through college—insured that, as a group, women would be less able than men to read, write, and cipher. Paths to public status therefore were limited. Elementary and high schools became sexually integrated as industrialization proceeded, but American colleges did not become coeducational until the late nineteenth century. Women did not begin to enter places of higher education in large numbers until the mid-twentieth century (Solomon 1985).* Spatial segregation thereby reduced women's access to knowledge and likely had a greater negative association with women's status than the form of dwellings.

The Labor Force and the Segregated Workplace. The division of labor in nonindustrial societies is simultaneously spatial and gendered. Men and women tend to perform different tasks divided fairly consistently along gender role stereotypes: men hunt, and women cook and care for children (Murdock and Provost 1973). Since hunting typically occurs far from the dwelling, while cooking and child care occur close to it, spatial distinctions are an integral part of the gender division of labor.

Such spatial arrangements may also be related to gender stratification. Men's labor is more universally valued because men tend to distribute excess goods (from a successful hunt, for example) to families outside the immediate household, while women prepare food primarily within the family (Friedl 1975). To the extent that women do not accompany men to learn hunting skills, the reciprocity between spatial segregation and gender stratification is reinforced. The initial reason for women not learning to hunt—immobility due to responsibility for child care—becomes obscured as spatial segregation insures that few women acquire the ability to hunt.

Segregated workplaces also exist in industrialized societies. When American women began to enter the labor force in the nineteenth century, the relatively few jobs open to them were highly segregated by gender. Domestic service and teaching were acceptable female occupations, but factory and clerical work were controversial because they placed women in the same spaces as men. Women in typically male occupations, however, earned more and had higher status than women in typically female occupations (Aron 1987).

Today, when more than one-half of American women are in the labor force, they still work in a small number of occupations and in places separate from men (Baron and Bielby 1985; Reskin and Hartmann 1986; A. M. Scott

*By 1870 approximately 200 colleges in the United States were educating almost 11,000 women, but they constituted fewer than 1 percent of all women aged 18 to 21 (Solomon 1985, 62).

1986). "Thus in modern workplaces there are not only men's and women's jobs but also men's and women's spaces" (J. W. Scott 1982, 176). In an era in which the majority of women's and men's daily lives are spent outside the dwelling, and to the extent that they do not share the same workplace, contact between the sexes is reduced. Since public status derives at least partially from occupational skills, many of which are learned on the job, workplace segregation contributes to women's lower status. Once again, access to knowledge and spatial relations mediate the status of women.

15

The present study uses comparative and historical analyses to explore the intersection of gender, space, and status in nonindustrial societies and in the United States. "Nonindustrial societies" refer to those dependent on hunting and gathering, horticulture, agriculture, or fishing as their means of livelihood. Information on nonindustrial societies is based on ethnographies provided primarily by anthropologists. The first part of the book uses quantitative cross-cultural data for nonindustrial societies and the second part uses qualitative historical data for the United States to trace changes in the relationship between gender stratification and spatial institutions. The two parts are connected by their common emphasis on spatial institutions, but no attempt is made to imply an evolutionary sequence of development. Two different approaches, one more quantitative and comparative, the other more qualitative and historical, help address the complexity of the relationship between gender stratification and spatial arrangements. Neither of these approaches proves a theory of space and status in the empirical sense. Rather, a combination of data from a variety of sources and quite different analytical techniques are used to construct a plausible and rich interpretation of the confluence of status, gender, and space.

Space, Knowledge, and Secrecy

Spatial segregation is one of the mechanisms by which a group with greater power can maintain its advantage over a group with less power. By controlling access to knowledge and resources through the control of space, the dominant group's ability to retain and reinforce its position is enhanced. Thus, spatial boundaries contribute to the unequal status of women. For women to become more knowledgeable, they must also change places.

Many types of knowledge exist, only some of which is highly valued. "Masculine" knowledge is almost universally more prestigious than "feminine" knowledge. Men's ability to hunt in nonindustrial societies is therefore more highly valued than women's ability to gather, although women's efforts actually provide more of the household's food (Friedl 1975). In advanced industrialized societies, math and science skills (at which men excel) are more highly valued than verbal and relationship skills (at which women excel).

Shared knowledge can bind the members of society together. Well-known origin myths, for example, create solidarity around a group identity. Knowledge can also separate the members of society, however. Every society restricts some types of knowledge to certain members. Successful hunting techniques are known only to a few men in nonindustrial societies, just as medical expertise is known only to an elite few in advanced industrial societies. Sometimes the distribution of knowledge is controlled through institutionalized gate-keeping organizations (such as a men's hut or the American Medical Association). Thus, every society possesses differently valued knowledge that theoretically is available to all members but in reality is not.

Use of language among the Endo of Kenya is a case in point. Women and men are thought to have a different relation to language, with women having less mastery and control of what they say. To be male among the Endo means being in command of language. Anthropologist Henrietta Moore (1986, 164–65) identifies knowledge, like language, as a male attribute. Although some older women may be regarded as knowledgeable, they do not possess the special social knowledge which is the preserve of men. Adult status is achieved only by the acquisition of esoteric knowledge through rites of passage. Language and knowledge together "construct a discourse of power" regulating gender relations. Since women possess neither language skills nor social (male) knowledge, they are excluded from political and ritual power.

The group with less-valued knowledge may contest the legitimacy of its

16

unequal distribution. Nineteenth-century American feminists, for example, fought vigorously to open medical colleges to women. Many other examples exist of women (both white and black) organizing to open schools, achieve the vote, and join labor unions (Foner 1988; Kessler-Harris 1982; Flexner 1975). The long battles accompanying each of these efforts demonstrate how contentious acquiring access to knowledge can be. Those with valued knowledge are the most powerful, which buttresses their ability to define their knowledge as the most prestigious and to maintain control of it. Knowledge thus forms the basis for a stratification system.

17

Moore (1986, 83, 120) recognizes the relationships among knowledge, power, and space in her analysis of domestic space as the "text" within which movement and action are analogous to speaking and reading (i.e., interpreting) a literary text. The organization of space is "both product and producer" of existing social and economic relations: "Spatial representations express in their own logic the power relations between different groups; they are therefore active instruments in the production and reproduction of the social order. The ability to provide interpretations of a spatial text . . . is political, because the power to impose the principles of representation of reality—which is no more than the construction of those principles—is a political power" (H. Moore 1986, 89).

Spatial barriers become established and then institutionalized for reasons that have little to do (manifestly) with power, but which tend to maintain prevailing advantages. This is because space is a "morphic language," one of the means by which society is interpreted by its members (Hillier and Hanson 1984, 198). The reciprocity between space and status arises from the constant renegotiation and re-creation of the existing stratification system. Bourdieu (1977) proposes that the power of a dominant group lies in its ability to control constructions of reality that reinforce its own status so that subordinate groups accept the social order and their own place in it. The powerful cannot maintain their positions without the cooperation of the less powerful. If a given stratification system is to persist, then, both powerful and less-powerful groups must be engaged in its constant renegotiation and re-creation. Women in nonindustrial societies who observed taboos barring them from ceremonial men's huts and women in nineteenth-century America who accepted the medical opinion that they should not attend college were as engaged in upholding gendered power differentials as were men. From Moore's perspective, "the dominated are as involved in the use and maintenance of power as the dominant, because there are no available forms of discourse which do not appeal to the given categories, divisions and values which simultaneously produce and expose the relations of power" (H. Moore 1986, 194).

Thus, women and men together create spatial segregation and stratification systems. Both sexes subscribe to the spatial arrangements that reinforce differential access to knowledge, resources, and power: men because it serves their interests, and women because they may perceive no alternative. In fact, greater and lesser degrees of cooperation exist within stratification systems. Some women may believe in the legitimacy of their lower status due to strong ideological pressures or religious creeds. Other women may participate in a stratification system because they have little choice (e.g., if they have not received the training necessary for more prestigious status). Still other women struggle against the prevailing system, calling for the right to vote, equal pay for equal work, and reproductive freedom. Most status differences are reinforced by subtle forms of spatial segregation. Instead of being visibly manifest in spatial barriers, status hierarchies often are determined in secret. Secrets, in turn, are preserved often through spatial boundaries.

The Role of Secrecy. Place, power, and knowledge interact to create secrecy. In "The Secret Society," Georg Simmel made the following observation: "The secret is not only a means under whose protection the material purposes of a group may be furthered; often, conversely, the very formation of a group is designed to guarantee the secrecy of certain contents. This occurs in the special type of secret societies whose substance is a secret doctrine, some theoretical, mystical, or religious *knowledge*. Here, secrecy is its own sociological purpose: certain insights must not penetrate into the masses; those who know form a community in order to guarantee mutual secrecy to one another" (Wolff 1950, 355; emphasis in original).

Simmel did not specifically address the relationship between secrecy and spatial segregation, although he acknowledged the role of seclusion in reinforcing secrecy's effects. He singled out "certain secret orders among nature peoples" as an example of a secluded secret society. Such societies were characterized by separate huts that were symbolically different from the

18

surrounding dwellings. They were composed only of men and their essential purpose was to emphasize the differentiation of men from women (Wolff 1950, 364). Members of the secret order wore masks, and women were forbidden to approach them. If women discovered that the actors were their husbands, the orders lost their "whole significance" and became "harmless mummeries" (Wolff 1950, 364). In other words, spatial distance reinforced knowledge differences between women and men. When that distance was breached, men lost some of their power over women.

In *Economy and Society*, Max Weber recognized explicitly this relationship **19** between spatial segregation and gender stratification. His study of nonindustrial societies identified men's houses as repositories of power from which women were excluded (Weber [1921] 1978, 907). Men gathered there for religious ceremonies and initiation rites and to make major decisions affecting the village. Women were barred from participation—and thereby barred from training in the practical and symbolic skills necessary for leadership positions.

Among the Taos Pueblo Indians, the link between men's clubs, secrecy, and power is equally explicit. The *kiva* is an underground chamber used as a meeting place by secret societies; it is the training ground for leaders in religious and political ceremonies crucial to the transmission of the Indians' oral culture. Women may hold auxiliary *kiva* membership and enter the chambers to cook and clean, but they do not have access to the esoteric information shared by men. The *lulina* ("The Old People") control the behavior of others through their knowledge and use of *kiva* secrets. The system of *kiva* apprenticeship "denies major political participation to those who do not have the proper religious training and bars them from access to religious knowledge. In other words, religious knowledge is a prerequisite for secular office-holding at the senior level. Nontraditionalists cannot gain technical or formal power, and secrecy prevents them from learning the underpinnings of certain political acts because the rationale of such acts is frequently attributed to religious reasons" (Brandt 1980, 139).

Knowledge, Secrecy, and Women's Status. Several examples of spatially segregated institutions in American history exist to illustrate how separating women from sources of knowledge influences women's status. The first is the college, in which very few women were enrolled until after World War II.

When higher education first opened to women, it took the form of spatially segregated women's colleges. Women did not gain the training necessary for careers outside the home until the end of the nineteenth century, when professional programs became coeducational. Bitter controversy ensued over women's rights to share the same space and the same knowledge with men. The battle over coeducation in state universities began in 1862 and did not end for over a century. Such intense resistance to gender integration reflects the perceived costs to the powerful group of sharing space and knowledge with the less powerful.

The second "men's club" was the labor union. When the Knights of Labor (organized in 1869 as a secret society) opened its doors to women in the 1880s, about 10 percent of its membership was female. The proportion of women in unions declined after the Knights of Labor disbanded in 1886 (Kessler-Harris 1982, 86). Women constituted approximately 2 percent of union membership in 1900, although 18 percent of the labor force was female at that time (U.S. Bureau of the Census 1975, 127). One reason for the decline in the proportion of female participation was that union meetings were often held in saloons that excluded women (Kessler-Harris 1982, 152, 158).

Labor unions served one of the same educational functions for blue-collar workers that colleges did for white-collar workers, as the following passage suggests: "Skilled trades had traditionally been a province of unionized craftsmen who jealously guarded access to training in their fields. Though women frequently taught each other, and occasionally managed to 'steal' a trade from a willing male relative, they were rarely admitted to the requisite apprenticeships. Where they managed to acquire skills and posed a threat to male workers, craft unions sometimes grudgingly helped women to form separate, affiliated unions" (Kessler-Harris 1982, 171). In both Great Britain and the United States, labor unions have actively discouraged women from gaining technical expertise crucial to success in blue-collar jobs (Bradley 1989; Cockburn 1983).

Predominantly male unions, like predominantly male colleges, retained control of information until their "secrets" were discovered by a few pioneering women. When that happened, separate organizations—*separate places*—were created in which women were segregated from men. Whether

20

that contributed to a different curriculum, as it did in colleges, or in lack of access to apprenticeships, as it did in unions, the result was a lack of female access to masculine knowledge and status. Lack of status, in turn, reduced women's ability to sexually integrate places of knowledge.

Information control is thus a way to control prestige, power, and wealth. The role of secrecy in maintaining social control is suggested by the following passage: "Social divisiveness which is generated by conflicting interests creates the social conditions under which secrecy thrives. To the extent that secrecy denies social actors information which might reveal that they are **21** exploited, or manipulated by others, to that extent then secrecy promotes order" (Tefft 1980, 67). As long as the medical profession was closed to women, for example, men like Dr. Edward Clarke could warn women that higher education would damage their health (Rosenberg 1982, 5). Only after numbers of women had risked becoming educated and continued to lead healthy lives was the ill-health myth abandoned. The period in which that assumption was being challenged was a period of turmoil in regard to gender stratification, however. Dr. Clarke's ideas existed side by side with the ideas of the first feminist convention at Seneca Falls and women's entry into the labor force. Once the "secrets" of higher education were released to women, their suspicions of the causes of their lower status were confirmed, threatening the social order that dictated private spheres for women and public spheres for men.

Theories of Gender Stratification

The numerous theories of gender stratification proposed by anthropologists, economists, psychologists, and sociologists shed light on the relationship among knowledge, place, and power. From an institutional perspective, the majority of theories can be classified into those that focus on the family and those that look to the economy for explanations. Simply stated, the former argue that characteristics of individuals (supply) contribute most strongly to gender-status distinctions, while the latter claim that economic structure (demand) shapes gender-status distinctions. Marxist-feminist theories bridge family and economic explanations.

The Family. Family-centered explanations for nonindustrial societies are grounded in lineage descent patterns and marital residence. There have been conflicting interpretations of the effects of postmarital residence and type of descent on women's status (Whyte 1978a). Generally, matrilineal descent and matrilocal residence are associated with higher status for women since the bride continues to live near her female kin, who can provide economic and political support. Patrilineal descent and patrilocal residence require the woman to move to her husband's kin group after marriage, thus allowing **22** men to appropriate women's labor and solidify male dominance (Blumberg 1984).

In both nonindustrial and industrialized societies, socialization takes place primarily within the family and contributes to different life options for girls and boys (Maccoby and Jacklin 1974; Stockard and Johnson 1980). Whether due to men's psychological need to distance themselves from women (Mead 1949), to the internalization of gender-appropriate roles resulting from different parent-child interaction (Chodorow 1978), or to developing a different ethic of relationships over rules (Gilligan 1982), women and men are socialized in ways that reproduce lower status for women.

Closely tied to socialization is women's responsibility for domestic tasks. Cooking, cleaning, and child care—the "messiness" of daily life that exposes women to continuous interruptions—have been proposed as one reason women occupy the private sphere while men dominate the public arena (Lamphere 1987). Nonindustrial societies in which fathers are regularly involved in domestic life and spend time with children are less rigidly stratified by gender than societies with absent fathers (Coltrane 1988). In advanced industrial society, moreover, the traditional division of labor inside the home reduces the probability that women will earn high wages outside the home (Berk 1985; Boulding 1976).

The effects of socialization and responsibility for domestic tasks, of course, can be interpreted in a number of different ways. The functionalist approach to gender stratification, represented by Parsons and Bales's (1955) theory of instrumental and expressive roles within the family, proposes that men are the instrumental providers of wealth (forming the primary link with the economic system), while women are the expressive caretakers of emotional needs within the home. The theory does not explain why such gender differentiation should lead to unequal prestige for men and women.

Gutentag and Secord's (1983) sex-ratio theory is essentially a demographic explanation with origins in fertility differences. They argue that women's social status is highest in societies where the sex ratio is low (i.e., when there is a surplus of women) and lowest in societies where the sex ratio is high (i.e., when women are in scarce supply). When there are "too many women" to find husbands and adopt traditional roles as wives and mothers, alternatives such as higher education and labor force participation become more socially acceptable for women.

Sherry Ortner (1974) proposes that the ideological basis of gender strat-   **23**
ification is the almost universal identification of women with natural reproductive processes and men with cultural processes. As long as societies value culture (in the form of technological manipulation of the environment) over nature, masculine attributes will be valued over feminine attributes and women's status will be lower than men's. Thus, reproductive roles of women in the family create archetypes of gender relations outside the family.

The Economy. Economy-centered explanations for gender inequalities in nonindustrial societies are those dealing with women's contribution to subsistence. Recent ethnographic studies have verified the importance of women's economic control of property and labor in regard to their social status. Sanday's (1981) study of 156 cultures, Blumberg's (1984) research on sixty-one nonindustrial societies, and Friedl's (1975) review of six cultures all stress the importance of women's contributions to economic production as predictors of their status.

The type of economic subsistence characteristic of a culture also has been shown to affect gender stratification. According to numerous studies, women's status in nonindustrial societies is highest where hunting and gathering takes precedence and lowest in agricultural societies (Blumberg 1984; Chafetz 1984; Huber and Spitze 1983). The degree of gender inequality is low in hunting and gathering societies because little surplus exists on which to base a stratification system. Through gathering, women contribute a large share of food to the household more routinely than do men, who are only sporadically successful at hunting. To the extent that women distribute food only within the household and men distribute any surplus outside the household, however, men have higher status than women (Friedl 1975). By the time societies develop through the horticultural stage and into the agricultural, technology (in the form of the plow and heavy draft animals) reduces women's contribution to production in relation to men's. Women's lower subsistence contribution to the household and the evolution of land as the major form of wealth interact to increase the level of gender stratification (Huber and Spitze 1983).

Among industrial societies, human capital and occupational segregation explanations trace women's lower status to their position in the labor force. Human capitalists argue that women and men invest differently in market skills and thus reap differential rewards (Mincer and Polachek 1974). Men, for example, are more likely to invest many years in training to become surgeons, while women are more likely to invest fewer years to become nurses. This interpretation of women's lower wages relative to men's has been challenged by researchers, most notably on the issue of "depreciation" of human capital (i.e., on the length of time it takes to regain skills on reentry into the labor force) (Corcoran and Duncan 1979; see Bianchi and Spain 1986, 188–95).

Another explanation for women's lower earnings and occupational status relative to men's is occupational segregation that creates "men's jobs" and "women's jobs." According to this explanation, women are paid less than men because they enter more poorly paid occupations. High levels of occupational segregation by gender exist in all industrialized societies and perpetuate earnings differences (Reskin 1984; Reskin and Hartmann 1986; Roos 1985).

A purely demographic explanation of women's lower status in the workplace is Kanter's (1977) theory of the "token woman." She proposes that women who are in a significant minority in their work organizations will suffer predictable losses of status relative to men who are in the majority. Token women face performance pressures (e.g., higher visibility of errors and attention to discrepant characteristics such as dress) that highlight their lack of organizational power. Kanter suggests that when women and men are more proportionately balanced in the workplace, women's status will improve.

Marxist-Feminist Interpretations. Marxist-feminist analyses link familial and economic explanations of gender stratification. Frederick Engels ([1884] 1942) traced the "world historic defeat of the female sex" to changes in economic production that allowed men to acquire private property. The concept of "paternity" was established to include the possession of women and children so that private goods could be passed from one generation to the next. According to Engels, with the advent of private property and the patriarchal family, women were transformed from independent household managers to subordinate workers in privately "male-owned" families.

Marxist-feminists argue that patriarchy and capitalism interact to insure that women are oppressed because of both their gender and class (Beneria and Roldan 1987; Crompton and Mann 1986). Radical feminists define **25** patriarchy as a male hierarchical ordering of society, based on biological differences, which is manifested through men's control of women's labor and sexuality (specifically in regard to reproduction) (Eisenstein 1979; Hartmann 1981). Patriarchy is institutionalized in the nuclear family and becomes the model for men's power in other realms (Clawson 1980; Rowbotham 1973). In capitalist societies, the material basis of patriarchy consists of men's control of well-paid jobs (Hartmann 1976). Nonetheless, Marxist-feminists argue that patriarchy precedes capitalism as a form of women's oppression (Eisenstein 1979, 25), even though patriarchy and capitalism cannot be separated as explanations for women's status in industrial societies.

Steven Goldberg's *Inevitability of Patriarchy* (1974) attributes male dominance to biological factors. Goldberg argues that hormones make men more aggressive than women and thus more successful in a competitive world. Collins (1971) also proposes that biology operates to men's advantage: their physical strength helps men gain and maintain a dominant position, while women must rely on personal attraction to bargain in the marriage market for higher-status males. Both Goldberg and Collins perceive men's higher status to be grounded in biology translating into power on the societal scale. Patriarchy is based on social advantages derived from men's physical strength. Those advantages influence the negotiation of power within the family, thus forming a model for male alliances and dominance outside the family.

In sum, most explanations of gender stratification identify the family and/or the economy as the foundation from which status differences arise. No existing explanations, however, consistently incorporate the spatial context in which the activities constituting these institutions occur. Adding the spatial dimension of institutions helps form a new perspective on gender stratification by grounding abstract concepts in physical space.

The Spatial Perspective. Other social scientists have examined space in relation to gender, but few have focused on the interplay between spatial arrangements and women's status. Goffman (1977) proposed that gender segregation is fluid: men and women periodically separate into different places, but regroup in integrated spaces to carry out shared goals. Thorne (1989) cites gender segregation in schools as a component of childhood development for boys and girls. Ardener's (1981) edited volume titled *Women and Space* is an extensive collection of anthropological articles highlighting the importance of spatial arrangements. Finally, Rosaldo (1974) proposed nearly twenty years ago that women's status is lowest in societies with highly differentiated private and public spheres.

Emphasis on space and status weaves the threads of inquiry begun by other researchers into a common cloth. Thinking about gendered spaces meets a goal of feminist theory to reveal "how gender relations are constituted and experienced and how we think or, equally important, do not think about them" (Flax 1987, 622). This includes exploring gender relations in concrete situations that have spatial attributes. Space often is taken for granted or ignored, and not solely by theorists. Those who benefit from existing arrangements are particularly prone to this blind spot. Daniels (1975, 343) points out that ritual, manners, language, and separation of activities all are mechanisms by which systems of dominance and subordination are maintained: "Those in the superordinate status will find this structure undergirding their privileged condition natural or even virtually invisible." Those in the subordinate status may (or may not) recognize the disadvantage of the system.

This argument about space and status enables us to think more clearly about previously invisible relationships. I propose three hypotheses as plausible explanations for the maintenance of gender stratification over time and across cultures:

1. Varying degrees of gender segregation characterize social institutions.

2. Gender stratification is reinforced by spatial segregation.

3. The greater the distance between women and sources of valued knowledge, the greater the gender stratification in the society.

Emphasis on access to knowledge is a critical component of the argument. Spatial arrangements would make no difference to stratification if all resources and knowledge were divided equally between "women's spaces" and "men's spaces." Yet that seldom happens. Stereotypically masculine knowledge in spatial institutions such as the workplace is accorded higher status **27** than feminine knowledge associated with the home. The accessibility of valued knowledge is thus a central requirement of gender stratification theory (Brinton 1988). Spatial institutions sustain status inequalities when they regulate access to knowledge and resources differentially by gender. As geographers Bowlby, Foord, and McDowell (1986) point out, gender relationships are defined in particular places in ways that cumulatively reinforce status distinctions between women and men. Women's responsibilities for child care in the home influence ideas about appropriate "women's work" (e.g., teaching and nursing), which in turn contribute to women's lower wages relative to men's. Gendered spaces that create the greatest distance between women and sources of masculine knowledge therefore have the strongest association with gender stratification. We would thus expect that segregation within the home, a feminine space with the least socially valued knowledge, would be less clearly associated with women's status than segregated schools or workplaces.

A spatial approach forms one of the links between micro and macro levels of sociological analysis. Huber (1990, 1) proposes that a basic challenge of sociological theory is to explain "how persons affect collectivities and how collectivities affect persons over time." If one substitutes the word "space" for "collectivity," the question becomes "how do people constitute the spaces in which they carry out daily activities and how do those spatial arrangements affect their activities?"

The perspective of space and status does *not* attempt to explain the origin of gender stratification or how men initially occupy positions of higher status than women. Neither does it address why men try to retain their positions of power. Finally, this argument remains silent on whether the relationship between spatial segregation and stratification results from the conscious efforts of individuals to dominate others, or even whether men and women are aware of gendered spaces. Rather, the perspective of space and status addresses the ways in which status differences are maintained (once in place) by the spatial relationships between men and women.

Conclusion

28

Over two decades ago, geographer Edward Soja lamented that "there has been no attempt to explore the spatial dimension of societal organization on a level equivalent to the extensive examination of kinship and contract relations" (Soja 1971, 8). He proposed that analysts study how location affects status and how status affects location. By 1989 Soja was more strident in his demand for the geographical dimension: "We must be insistently aware of how space can be made to hide consequences from us, how relations of power and discipline are inscribed into the apparently innocent spatiality of social life" (Soja 1989, 6).

The proposed relationship between space and status is grounded in the "structuration" approach, whereby the properties of a social system express themselves through daily activities at the same time those activities generate and reproduce structural properties of the social system. Institutions simultaneously shape individual behavior and are shaped by individuals' (intentional and unintentional) behavior. In this way, institutions are constantly created and re-created (Bourdieu 1977; Giddens 1979; Pred 1981).

Human geographer Allan Pred attempts to integrate structuration theory with time-geography by conceptualizing the production, reproduction, and transformation of social relations (especially power) in the context of specific locations in time and space (Pred 1981, 37). He argues that the daily behavior creating (and created by) institutions must take place within temporal and spatial boundaries. Spatial institutions such as dwellings, schools, and workplaces form these boundaries within which social relations interact with social structure.

Gendered spaces themselves shape, and are shaped by, daily activities. Once in place, they become taken for granted, unexamined, and seemingly immutable. What *is* becomes what *ought* to be, which contributes to the maintenance of prevailing status differences (see Berger and Luckmann 1967; Pred 1981). Status often depends on the power to control some form of knowledge, whether it is scientific, religious, entrepreneurial, political, or psychological. "The possession of such knowledge by institutional power holders . . . is built up and modified through the details of everyday life" in specific places at specific times (Pred 1981, 47). To the extent that spatial arrangements buttress an unequal distribution of knowledge between women and men, they contribute to the maintenance of gender stratification.   **29**

The following examples of the relationship between spatial segregation and gender stratification are presented from a variety of sources. The status of an individual woman or man is not as critical to a study of gender stratification as the structures established to insure that men as a group or women as a group exercise power. Women's status relative to men's differs across cultures and over time, creating a continuum of power relationships rather than a dichotomy (Chafetz 1990; Huber and Spitze 1983; Lamphere 1987). The current work explores that continuum in relation to spatial segregation by gender, in particular to the reciprocity between the social construction of space and the spatial construction of social relations.

PART ONE

Spatial Institutions in Nonindustrial Societies

he three chapters constituting Part 1 describe spatial institutions in nonindustrial societies. The family, education, and the division of labor are examined cross-culturally for evidence of geographic and architectural segregation of the sexes and for the relationship of this segregation to status differences. Qualitative data from ethnographic accounts are supplemented by quantitative analysis of data from the Human Relations Area Files (see appendix A for a description of this data set).

Chapter 2 reviews women's status according to the absence or presence of segregated dwellings. Chapter 3 analyzes women's status with regard to the presence of ceremonial men's huts, and chapter 4 considers the relationship between women's status and sexually segregated work groups. Each chapter provides both examples of societies that fit the predicted relationship between space and status and examples that may be exceptions. The measurement of women's status varies depending on the detail available in ethnographies, but the three variables used consistently in quantitative analyses are those measuring women's control of labor, control of property (via inheritance rights), and degree of participation in public life outside the dwelling (via power in kinship networks).

Most of the descriptive information about nonindustrial societies has been gathered by anthropologists in the last fifty years. Because these societies had come into varying degrees of contact with Western culture at the time they were studied (Schrire 1984), they should not be equated with *pre*industrial or primitive societies of centuries ago. The term nonindustrial refers only to the type of economic organization (i.e., hunting/gathering, agricultural, horticultural, or fishing) characteristic of small village or tribal societies. In order to further avoid the implication of an evolutionary sequence between this and the second part of the book, I use the present tense in describing all nonindustrial societies.

The Mongolian *Ger* and the Tuareg Tent

[Russian] women's status reached a low point in the seventeenth century, when an extreme segregation of the sexes prevailed and was a matter of family honor. . . . Moscow women lived in harem-like *terema*, sequestered on the upper-most floors of their houses; they ate separately from men, and were rigorously shielded from the public view.

—Francine du Plessix Gray, "Reflections: Soviet Women"

History holds many examples of sexually segregated dwellings associated with women's lower status. Ancient Greek houses consisted of a series of apartmentlike *megarons* surrounding separate women's and men's courtyards (Newmark and Thompson 1977, 59), and women's status in Greece was similar to that of slaves (Gutentag and Secord 1983). Purdah has specified the seclusion of women in particular places within the home for many centuries, and Islamic women's status is relatively low (Khatib-Chahidi 1981).

Numerous anthropological and architectural studies have documented "controlled intimacy" in the spatial institution of the family/dwelling. The black tent (*ghezhdi*) of the nomadic Ghilzai, the fortresslike *qala* of Afghanistan (Hallet and Samizay 1980, 25, 123), and the *Haveli* of India (Anderton 1989) are each internally differentiated by gender, as are the Bedouin tents of the Sudan (Faegre 1979; Verity 1971), the domed *indlu* of the African Zulu (Biermann 1971), the Tibetan tent (Faegre 1979), and the reed houses of coastal Yemen (Varanda 1982, 140).

Gender divisions within the dwelling typically reflect religious beliefs about the proper order of the world. The vision of the external world is thus re-created within the internal world as a means of maintaining social order. Hillier and Hanson (1984, 180) identify the Turkish *yurt* as "one of those striking cases where the interior of the dwelling is seen as a microcosm of the universe." The structure of the *yurt* parallels the global structure of society; "it builds its local relationships in the image of society as a whole." Since disorder—anything or anyone out of its proper place—becomes polluting (Douglas 1966), a great deal of social effort goes into defining proper places. Moreover, the correct use of space by men and women in many nonindustrial dwellings is closely controlled by taboos. In the Mongolian *ger*, for example, family members may move about the tent freely but have to sit, eat, and sleep in their proper places. Moving an object from the male to the female side (or vice versa) is a sin that requires ceremonial purification. Men are forbidden to touch "female" things, and women are forbidden from stepping over "male" objects. Such restrictions often remove women from

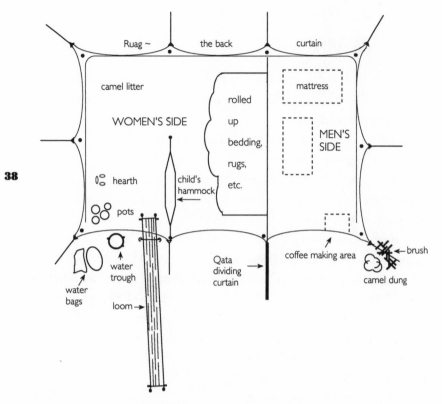

Fig. 2.1. The women's and men's sides of the traditional Bedouin tent are divided by a curtain. Adapted from Faegre (1979, 24) by permission of Doubleday.

knowledge in nonindustrial societies. This chapter clarifies the association between gendered dwelling spaces and women's status.

Sexually Segregated Dwellings

The Mongolian Ger. Dwellings in nonindustrial societies may be divided internally by physical partitions, but more often the divisions are symbolic. The tents of Turkish, Afghani, and Mongolian nomadic tribes provide examples of symbolically differentiated gendered spaces. Known in Turkey as the *yurt*, in Afghanistan as the *kherga*, and in Mongolia as the *ger*, the

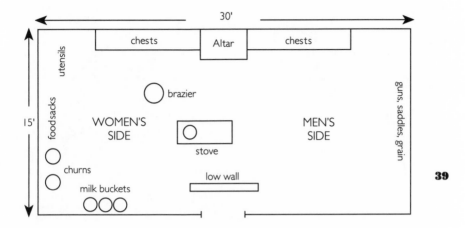

Fig. 2.2. The women's and men's sides of the Tibetan tent are divided only by symbolic boundaries. Adapted from Faegre (1979, 59) by permission of Doubleday.

dwelling consists of a circular frame covered with woolen felt mats. The entrance varies from a simple flap to elaborately carved portable doors.

Each of these single-room dwellings is characterized by separate spaces for women and men. In the traditional *ger*, the male (ritually pure) half is to the left of the door and the female (impure) half to the right of the door. The male section contains the possessions of the head of the household and honored guests; the female section contains cooking utensils and children's possessions (Humphrey 1974).

Books are kept in the male part of the traditional tent with the highest status—the *xoimor*. Because books contain religious and historical knowledge, Mongolian women historically have been forbidden to read them. The fear that women would destroy the social order if they became literate was expressed in the proverb, "For a woman to look at a book is like a wolf looking at a settlement" (Humphrey 1974, 275). Symbolic spatial distinctions within the tent thus reinforce Mongolian men's control of written knowledge and reduce women's access to positions of religious authority.

The socialist revolution in 1921 transformed Mongol social structure more rapidly than it transformed the *ger*. Mongols still have culturally designated places for people and objects within the dwelling, but the objects

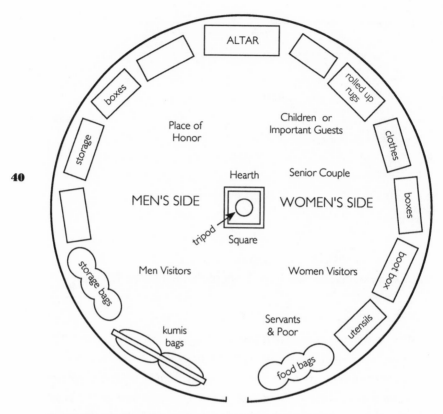

Fig. 2.3. The traditional Mongolian *ger* places women to the right of the hearth and men to the left. Adapted from Faegre (1979, 91) by permission of Doubleday.

have changed. For example, when a Mongol woman buys a sewing machine, she places it in the same sector where her bridle and saddle would have been placed in the nomadic tent. Pictures of revolutionary heroes now replace Buddhist deities on the altar. The most honored guest still sits in the male *xoimor*, but now the guest may be an official of the collective rather than a herdsman (Humphrey 1974).

Social changes have broken down traditionally gendered spaces as well. Female literacy was a goal of the revolution, so the sacred books were moved from the *xoimor* to the woman's side of the parental bed. A public health campaign introduced the washstand, for which a new space—neither male nor female—was created (Humphrey 1974). Books that were once restricted to the male side of the *ger* became available to women in the modern tent, and access to the sacred texts increased the probability that women could improve their public status by learning to read.

Algerian Berber Houses. Berber houses of Kabylia, Algeria, are simple spaces divided both symbolically and physically into male and female domains. The traditional dwelling is a rectangular room partitioned by a wall to separate a dark, lower-level stable from the living quarters on a higher, lighter level. The male entrance is on the east wall and the female entrance on the west. The light, southern end of the house is linked with culture (the **41** male half) and the dark, northern end with nature (the female half) (Bourdieu 1971; Ortner 1974).

The low, dark part of the house is opposed to the higher, lighter part, as feminine is to masculine: "The opposition between the upper part and the lower part reproduces within the space of the house . . . the opposition between female space and male space . . . on the one hand, the privacy of all that is intimate, on the other, the open space of social relations; on the one hand, the life of the senses and of the feelings, on the other, the life of relations between man and man, the life of dialogue and exchange" (Bourdieu 1971, 100).*

The traditional Berber house is organized according to a set of dichotomies: fire-water, cooked-raw, high-low, light-dark, day-night, male-female. Bourdieu interprets those distinctions as symbolic of the opposition between the house and the rest of the world: the female, intimate sphere opposed to the masculine sphere of public life. Part of the fabric of feminine and masculine gender role behavior revolves around the relationship to the house. Men are expected to leave the home at daybreak and keep the company of other men in public. Women almost never leave the home and are hidden within its walls. When a male guest enters the house he gives the mistress of the house a sum of money called "the view" to compensate for the invasion of privacy. The extent of women's seclusion within the home is

---

*In contrast to the negative associations with the female part of the Berber house are the positive associations with the nourishing and life-giving properties of the equally dark female side of the Savunese house of Indonesia (Waterson 1990, 189–91).

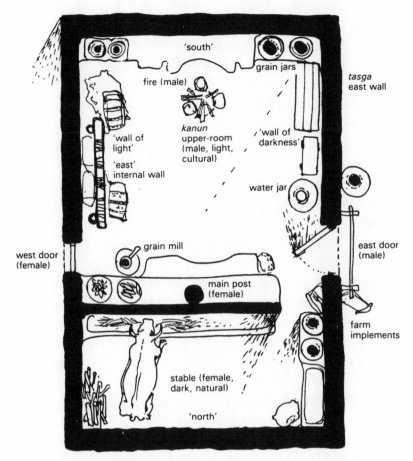

Fig. 2.4. In the Algerian Berber house, the female side is associated with the dark and nature, while the male side is associated with light and culture. Reproduced from P. Oliver (1987, 162) by permission of the University of Texas Press.

reflected by the proverb that "woman has only two dwellings, the house and the tomb" (Bourdieu 1971, 104).

Berber men control women's space inside the home as a way of maintaining their own power to define the world: "The orientation of the house is fundamentally defined from the outside, from the point of view of men and, . . . by men and for men, as the place from which men come out. The house is an empire within an empire, but one which always remains subordinate because, even though it presents all the properties and all the relations which define the archetypal world, it remains a reversed world, an inverted reflection. 'Man is the lamp of the outside and woman the lamp of the inside'" (Bourdieu 1971, 110).

Relegating women to the separate sphere of the home—and to separate spheres within the home—is an effective mechanism for eliminating female competition for public status. The proverbs quoted by Bourdieu suggest that Berber women play no role in the public sphere and are subordinate within the private sphere.

The Barasana Maloca. A third example of an association between sexually segregated dwellings and women's lower status comes from the Barasana Indian tribe of Colombia, South America. Barasana families live in longhouses called *malocas* and are separated from neighbors by several hours of land or river travel. The household consists of brothers or close patrilineal cousins together with their wives, children, and sometimes one or more parents. The largest structures are eighty by forty feet and house several families. The *maloca* has two doors: one at the front used by men and one at the back used by women and children. The front of the house is associated with men's public social life, while the rear of the house is associated with women's cooking and family life (S. Hugh-Jones 1979, 26–28).

Barasana daily life is strictly segregated by gender. Men and women carry out different subsistence activities in different places, use different areas within the *maloca*, enter and exit through different doors, eat at separate times and in separate groups, and take part in different conversations. Gender segregation becomes overtly enforced at ceremonies when secret instruments are used. The ritual known as *Fruit House*, which is performed at the ripening of each important edible fruit, is carried out within the *maloca* and accompanied by men playing the *He* flutes. Hugh-Jones describes preparation for the ceremony as follows: "Soon after first light, when the beer is all made, the women sweep the house clean and sprinkle water on the floor. A thick screen of woven palm leaves is moved across the house beyond the posts . . . completely shutting off the rear end. Women, children, and pets are then confined in this screened-off area whilst the *He* are played into the house. Later on the women may leave the house to go to the gardens" (S. Hugh-Jones 1979, 51).

The major initiation rite, known as *He House*, is characterized by the same gender segregation. Women and children are first screened at the rear of the

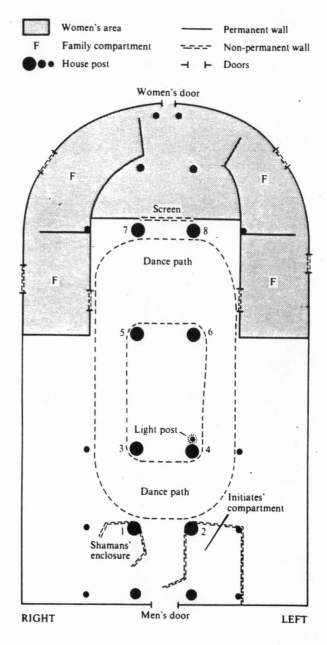

44

Fig. 2.5. Women's spaces are separated from men's spaces by permanent walls in the Barasana *maloca*, or longhouse. Reproduced from S. Hugh-Jones (1979, 50) by permission of Cambridge University Press.

house and later driven from the house into the surrounding shrub as the men play flute tunes translated in part as "don't let the women see me." Failure to leave the house on command has potentially drastic consequences for Barasana women: one myth maintains that when they become pregnant, they will miscarry and die, while another specifies that women caught stealing the instruments will be gang-raped (S. Hugh-Jones 1979, 73, 131). The violence associated with women's transgressions of their proper space in relation to the *He* instruments reflects the importance attached to male control of harvest rituals and musical instruments.

45

The status of Barasana women is relatively low by nonindustrial standards. Only males are chiefs, and women do not participate in the political organization of the tribe. Other important social roles, such as dancers, chanters, and shamans, are occupied only by men. Shamans hold the greatest knowledge of myths and therefore the highest status in Barasana society. During certain religious ceremonies, participants entrust shamans with their lives; such crucial positions are not occupied by women (S. Hugh-Jones 1979, 37).

Men's dominance over women is incorporated into Barasana myth. One myth tells how the women stole the *He* flutes from the men and completely reversed the social order, "the men becoming like women and the women achieving political dominance over the men"; "normal" relations were restored only after men retrieved the sacred flutes (S. Hugh-Jones 1979, 6). Hugh-Jones identified the control of the *He House* ritual and the instruments as a central form of control over women: "As the main expression of a secret men's cult, focussed on the *He* instruments that women are forbidden to see on pain of death, [the *He House* ritual] establishes and maintains a fundamental division between the sexes. This division implies the power and dominance of men over women and a measure of antagonism between the sexes which is expressed in myth" (S. Hugh-Jones 1979, 38).

For the Barasana, then, the physical form of the *maloca* reduces women's access to knowledge. The spatial segregation of the longhouse excludes women from the ceremonies and rituals in which men share information crucial to the acquisition of public status. The powerful effects of spatial segregation are reflected in the Barasana women's cooperation in maintaining gender stratification. Hugh-Jones, whose wife stayed behind the screen with the other women while he participated in the *He House* ritual with the men, reports that most Barasana women know exactly what the flutes look like and what goes on in the ceremony—even to the names of the instruments played by specific men. The women say they are not so much afraid of seeing the *He* flutes themselves as of the reaction of the men if they do (S. Hugh-Jones 1979, 129). Even when missionaries exposed the instruments, the women did not want to see them. They see the successful completion of the *He House* and *Fruit House* rituals as essential to the integrity of the community. Women believe, as do men, that if they let men know they can see the sacred flutes, social chaos would ensue. The power of the ideology of male domination, in this case reinforced by spatial segregation, is reflected in the women's active cooperation in maintaining their own subordinate status (C. Hugh-Jones 1979; see also Murphy and Murphy 1985 for a similar account of the Mundurucu).

Islamic Purdah Societies. Islamic nations represent the world's fastest-growing religious group; Muslims are projected to account for nearly one-quarter of the world's total population by 2020. Currently, Islam is the majority religion in forty nations; sixteen others have significant Muslim minorities (Weeks 1988). These developing countries form a "purdah zone" that extends throughout the Middle East and Northern Africa. Purdah refers to the veiling and seclusion of Muslim women to minimize their contact with men* (Caplan 1985; Mandelbaum 1988; Papanek 1973). To the extent that the purdah countries of India and Iran are developing nations, their economic and sociopolitical systems more closely approximate nonindustrial than industrial societies.

Segregation from men is the cornerstone of purdah, and Muslims believe that purdah is divinely ordained. Muslim women cannot enter the male sanctum of the mosque but must pray at home. Muslims impose purdah when a girl reaches puberty, and women veil themselves in front of family members and strangers (Mandelbaum 1988). These customs strictly dictate women's behavior and the space in which it occurs. Purdah commands women to cover their faces, avoid eye contact with men, abstain from displaying finery, and remain in their homes (Maududi 1972).

---

*Purdah is also an integral part of the Hindu religion. To simplify the discussion, however, only Islamic purdah is reviewed.

Adherence to purdah is simplified by the layout of the dwelling. Within the Indian household, men and women often sleep in separate rooms or on separate sides of a hut and sit apart at social or religious gatherings. Men spend most of their time in their own quarters, talking, smoking, or working; women rarely enter the male sanctum (Mandelbaum 1988, 4). Indian women carry out domestic work in the courtyard or inner rooms that men may enter only to take meals or perform chores. Muslim women keep strictly to their own part of the house (the *zenana*); larger Muslim houses have a room at the front for entertaining visitors that the women do not enter; their **47** space is in the courtyard (Mandelbaum 1988, 4, 80).

One of the manifest functions of purdah is to protect the family's "honor" (*izzat*). A woman brings dishonor to the family if she fails to observe purdah properly (by talking to strangers, for example). The higher a family's status (their *izzat*), the more able they are to relieve women from economic duties and place them in seclusion. Thus, Indian women and men see the seclusion of women as a status symbol to which families aspire. While *izzat* carries a positive connotation about what a man can do to attain honor, purdah carries a negative connotation about the activities a woman should avoid. The active pursuit of *izzat* is enhanced by the passive observance of purdah, and purdah becomes stricter the greater the family's *izzat* (Mandelbaum 1988, 24, 35).

Seclusion (in one's own house or the houses of female relatives) comprises the ideal life of traditional Iranian women. The conventional house of a wealthy Iranian family fifty years ago would have consisted of two sectors organized around separate courtyards. Figure 2.6 demonstrates the layout of the *anderun*, or female and more private half, and the *birun*, or male and more public half of the house. Contact between the sexes was dictated by the etiquette of *mahram* (kin not eligible for marriage) and *na-mahram* (eligibility for marriage). Only *mahram* males were admitted to the *anderun*; *na-mahram* men were entertained only at the front of the *birun*. If female visitors entered the *anderun*, family members who were *na-mahram* would withdraw. Because their wealth enabled the household to create gendered spaces, women in such households often led more secluded lives than women in poorer families.

More modest dwellings of the middle class have fewer partitions but keep the basic layout of an entertainment area at the front and family quarters at

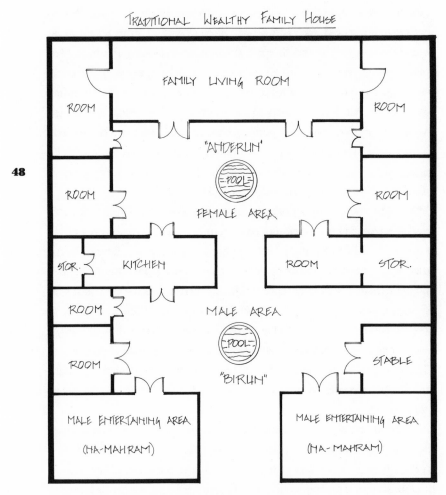

Fig. 2.6. Wealthy Muslim families can afford gendered spaces, such as the *anderun* for women and the *birun* for men. Adapted from Khatib-Chahidi (1981, 121).

the rear of the courtyard (see figure 2.7). The entertainment area is used by men and women if guests are members of the extended family; if *na-mahram* visitors are present, men and women are entertained separately.

The modern Iranian urban apartment replaces the courtyard with a central hall with rooms opening onto it (see figure 2.8). The hall becomes the *anderun* or family quarters of the more traditional dwelling, where television watching and meals take place. Placement of the formal entertainment area

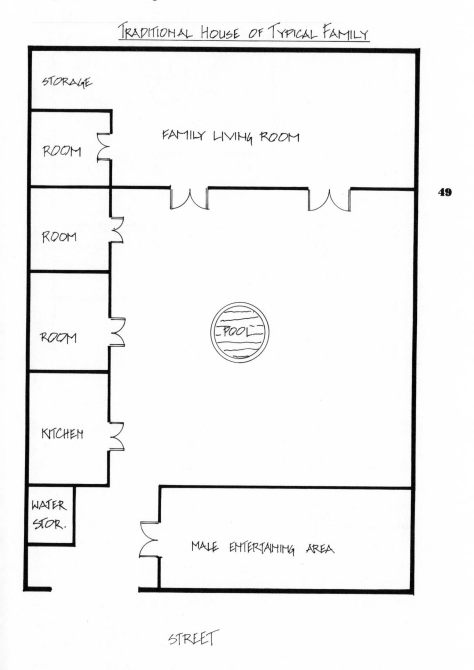

TRADITIONAL HOUSE OF TYPICAL FAMILY

STORAGE

FAMILY LIVING ROOM

ROOM

ROOM

ROOM

POOL

KITCHEN

WATER STOR.

MALE ENTERTAINING AREA

49

STREET

Fig. 2.7. A typical Muslim house traditionally has one courtyard, but with a separate entertainment area for men. Adapted from Khatib-Chahidi (1981, 122).

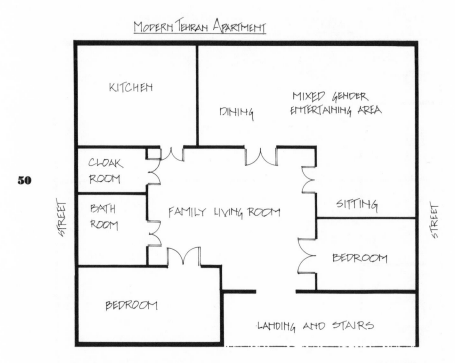

Fig. 2.8. The modern Tehran apartment is likely to have a gender-neutral entertainment area. Adapted from Khatib-Chahidi (1981, 123).

at the back of the apartment reflects weakened prohibitions against shared male and female space: the traditional courtyard allows women to see a visitor without the visitor seeing them, whereas the family living area of the hall means that women and men can see each other regardless of *mahram* status. Further, friends as well as relatives now share the *anderun* space. (In a particularly religious household, older women may still retire from the hallway into a bedroom to avoid seeing a *na-mahram* male [Khatib-Chahidi 1981, 124].)

Although Iranian society was moving toward modernization by the early 1970s, the fundamentalist revolution of 1979 emphasized a return to more segregated lifestyles. The new Islamic Constitution of the Republic of Iran states that women's "pioneering mission" is within the home raising children. Immediately after the revolution, a kindergarten teacher in Tehran was censored for not segregating three- and five-year-olds in class, and educated women had trouble finding government employment (Khatib-Chahidi

1981). With Ayatollah Khomeini's advocacy of marriage for girls before their first menses, women's status in postrevolutionary Iran seems destined to decline; it also may be accompanied by greater attempts at gender segregation.

Purdah stipulates that women's sphere is the home. Only with a man's permission and under special circumstances does the Koran allow women to leave the home to visit the mosque or travel alone. Islam specifies women's **51** rights of inheritance and the value of education, yet in reality women often relinquish inheritance to avoid rivalry with brothers (Mandelbaum 1988, 34). Education for women is limited to that which prepares them to become good wives. In short, "the Islamic civilization segregates men and women and employs them respectively for the purposes Nature has created them for, affording them equal opportunities of attaining success and honour and progress in their own natural spheres" (Maududi 1972, 161).

The status of women is typically low in countries with high birth rates, and Islamic societies have very high fertility by international standards. The total fertility rate among Islamic nations in 1988 was 6.0, compared with 4.5 for other developing nations and 1.7 for developed nations such as the United States (Weeks 1988, 13). This means that Islamic women have an average of six children throughout their childbearing years, compared to an average of less than two for American women. Purdah encourages high fertility by secluding women in the home and by giving them few options other than motherhood.

Compared with other developing and developed nations, Islamic nations have the highest proportion of teen-aged women who are married (over one-third) and the lowest proportion of married women using contraception (approximately one in five). Islamic women also are less likely to receive a formal education than Islamic men and have the lowest average female attendance rates at secondary schools of all nations (Weeks 1988, 23). Such early marriage, childbearing, and lack of formal education limit the ability of Islamic women to achieve public status.

Indian women's status outside the home also is low. The only property a woman owns is her jewelry, and even that can be sold without her consent.

Before Independence in 1950, women could not vote, and women's literacy rates are still significantly lower than men's. In 1971, 20 percent of all women, compared with 40 percent of all Indian men, qualified as literate. (The census of India counts as literate anyone with the "ability to read any simple letter either in print or in manuscript and to write a simple letter" [Sopher 1980, 131].) There is some evidence that female literacy is lower in rural areas of the country with strict adherence to purdah (Sopher 1980, 186). Islamic law stipulates that court evidence must be given by two **52** women, compared with one man. It is primarily men who own property, control earnings, conduct outside transactions (including marketing), perform public ceremonies, participate in public discussions, and hold public office (Mandelbaum 1988, 43–46, 71, 124).

Sexually Integrated Dwellings

Not all nonindustrial societies are characterized by ideological or religious beliefs dictating gender segregation within the home. The architecture of many societies reflects status hierarchies based on other ascriptive factors such as age or kinship. The Balinese, for example, have a traditional house-yard layout that represents a close connection between the spatial distribution of households and their relationship to the prince. Traditional Balinese dwellings do not differentiate internal space by male and female areas.

Balinese Houseyards. Descriptions of houseyards from four locations in Bali reveal that husbands, wives, children, and assorted kin sleep together in one house within a compound containing other families' houses, a temple, kitchen, and rice barn. The number of structures within the houseyard varies by size of the kinship group (the *dadia*), as figure 2.9 illustrates.

The spatial layout of the houseyard delineates relationships among the inhabitants, so that the physical ground plan reflects social distinctions laid out in the same pattern:

The construction of such a yard is not a matter left to individual taste but follows exact prescriptions in the ancient Balinese palm-leaf law books, the *lontar*. These sacred writings distinguish between different types of buildings, give the proper dimensions, methods of construction, and uses of each, prescribe their spatial relation to one another within the houseyard on the basis of traditional cosmological ideas, relate who is permitted and who is not (for reasons of status) to build various kinds of them, outlines the ceremonies attendant on their construction, and so on. Consequently all houseyards are laid out on a fundamental pattern. (Geertz and Geertz 1975, 49)

Such detailed instructions in other cosmologies (e.g., the Hindu *Man-* 53 *asara*) specify separate male and female spheres. The Balinese house lacks such distinctions, however, and inhabitants move about freely (Waterson 1990, 187). We would expect that Balinese women have higher status relative to men than women living in sexually segregated nonindustrial societies. This appears to be the case: Balinese wives "have full rights and responsibilities [and] . . . the relationship between husband and wife is one of equality" (Geertz and Geertz 1975, 56). The most important political and religious events in Balinese life require the joint participation of husbands and wives; husbands and wives also make household decisions together. The men who make up the hamlet council (*krama banjar*) must have female partners to perform the women's tasks of preparing temple offerings. If a man does not have a wife, sister, mother, or daughter to fill this function, he cannot be a member of the council. In general, the Balinese make no sharp distinctions between feminine and masculine roles, and this weak identification by gender is reflected in their architecture (Geertz and Geertz 1975, 17, 56). That architecture, in turn, makes it easier for women to maintain their relatively high status by integration into commonly shared space with men.

The Yakan Dwelling. Another nonindustrial society with integrated living quarters and relatively high status for women is the Yakan on the island of Basilan off the southwestern point of Mindanao in the Philippines. They are a small Muslim tribe that numbered approximately 70,000 when an ethnography was conducted in the early 1960s (Wulff 1982). Many Yakan traditions survived the introduction of Islam prior to the sixteenth century, including the spatial arrangement of the dwelling.

The Yakan are agriculturalists. Their main crop, rice, is supplemented by sweet potatoes and other vegetables for consumption and copra for cash.

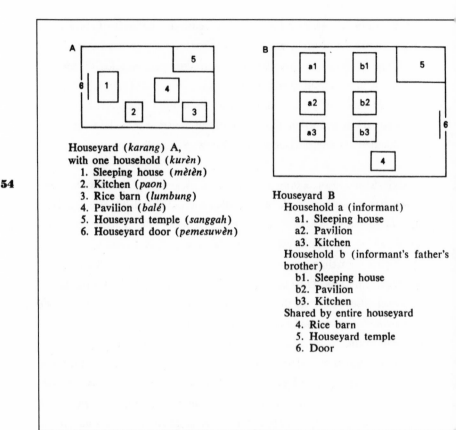

Houseyard (*karang*) A,
with one household (*kurèn*)
1. Sleeping house (*mètèn*)
2. Kitchen (*paon*)
3. Rice barn (*lumbung*)
4. Pavilion (*balé*)
5. Houseyard temple (*sanggah*)
6. Houseyard door (*pemesuwèn*)

Houseyard B
    Household a (informant)
      a1. Sleeping house
      a2. Pavilion
      a3. Kitchen
    Household b (informant's father's
brother)
      b1. Sleeping house
      b2. Pavilion
      b3. Kitchen
    Shared by entire houseyard
      4. Rice barn
      5. Houseyard temple
      6. Door

Fig. 2.9. Dwellings in the Balinese houseyard are arranged by relation to the chief, not by gender of residents. Reproduced from Geertz and Geertz (1975, 50, 51) by permission of The University of Chicago Press.

Crop rotation allows the Yakan to be sedentary. Fields are privately owned, and individual houses are scattered throughout the fields rather than located in villages. The Yakan house consists of three parts: the main building, the kitchen, and the porch. The dwellings are typically occupied by one family, consisting of a husband, wife, and unmarried children. The lack of gendered spaces in a Muslim society was remarkable enough for the ethnographer to give it special attention:

> When it comes to the main part of the house one feature is noteworthy: considering that the Yakan are Muslims, one would expect a division of the house so that there was a special closed part for women. This,

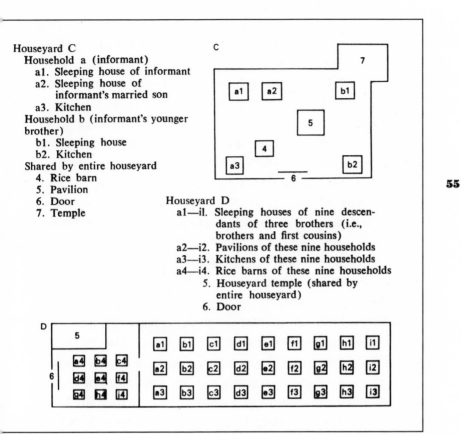

Houseyard C
Household a (informant)
  a1. Sleeping house of informant
  a2. Sleeping house of
      informant's married son
  a3. Kitchen
Household b (informant's younger
brother)
  b1. Sleeping house
  b2. Kitchen
Shared by entire houseyard
  4. Rice barn
  5. Pavilion
  6. Door
  7. Temple

Houseyard D
  a1—i1. Sleeping houses of nine descen-
      dants of three brothers (i.e.,
      brothers and first cousins)
  a2—i2. Pavilions of these nine households
  a3—i3. Kitchens of these nine households
  a4—i4. Rice barns of these nine households
    5. Houseyard temple (shared by
      entire houseyard)
    6. Door

55

however, is not the case. Usually the main building consists of one room only, which is used by men as well as women, not only residents but guests as well. Recently some people have made one or a few small rooms by putting up low bamboo walls, but this is rare, and does not really change the pattern, as the greater part of the building will still be taken up by one big room where people—men and women—may gather. (Wulff 1982, 143–44)

Yakan society is characterized by relatively low levels of gender stratification. Both women and men can own land, and at marriage a new house is built on either the husband's or wife's property. In the case of divorce, the spouse on whose land the house has been built keeps the house, and the other spouse has to leave (Wulff 1982, 139). Thus, Yakan women clearly retain control over property. Another indicator of women's status is that teachers of the Koran are most often women, and both girls and boys study the Koran (Wulff 1982, 146). This indicates both women's access to religious knowledge and their status as teachers (i.e., controllers of knowledge). Yakan women's access to such information kept secret by men in other societies should be facilitated by the sexual integration of the dwelling. (Other reports of Philippine cultures, although not describing the spatial organization of dwellings, support the conclusion that Philippine women have relatively higher status, compared with women in other nonindustrial societies; see Bacdayan [1977] and Rosaldo [1974, 39].)

56

The Tuareg Tent. A third example of a society in which dwellings are sexually integrated and women's status is relatively high is the Tuareg nomadic society of the Sahara desert in Africa. The Tuareg, who number approximately 286,000, make their living herding camels (Murdock 1959, 405). Although thoroughly Islamized, the Tuareg have reversed the Muslim custom, and it is the *men* who wear striking indigo veils (Murphy 1964).

The Tuareg also depart from Islamic tradition by not secluding women. Although other Bedouin tents have clearly demarcated male and female sides (Faegre 1979, 24), Tuareg mat tents contain no internal symbolic or physical partitions separating women from men. In *Ecology and Culture of the Pastoral Tuareg*, Danish ethnographer Johannes Nicolaisen documented no indigenous instances of sexually segregated tents—mat or skin, barrel-shaped or T-shaped. Nicolaisen acknowledged that the Northern Tuareg had recently adopted the Arab form of black tent which is divided into female and male sides, but he concluded that the T-shaped black tent was "foreign to traditional Tuareg dwellings" and had been introduced by contact with the Arabs. The majority of Kel Ayr and Kel Geres Tuareg live almost exclusively in barrel-vaulted mat tents that do not differentiate sides by gender (Nicolaisen 1963, 391).

Hillier and Hanson (1984, 178, 179) note that the system of space surrounding the Tuareg tent exhibits a minimal degree of the structure that characterizes most dwellings by differentiating inhabitants from visitors. The internal space does not differentiate *among* inhabitants (e.g., by gen-

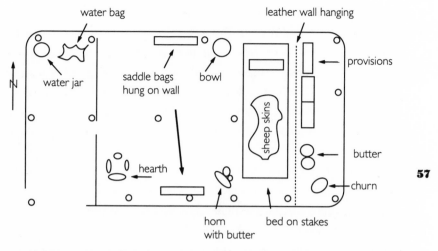

Fig. 2.10. The traditional Tuareg tent does not distinguish between male and female sides. Adapted from Faegre (1979, 74) by permission of Doubleday.

der), and both internal and external spaces are equally controlled by women and men.

Tuareg women enjoy high status, compared with their Arab counterparts. In contrast to other Berber tribes, the Tuareg are matrilineal; social status is transmitted through women, and residence is often matrilocal. Whereas only a few men are literate, most women can read and write in a script derived from a fourth-century Libyan alphabet. Music, poetry, and leather-work are exclusively female accomplishments, since men devote themselves to herding and raiding caravans. Most importantly, livestock and movable property are owned by Tuareg women. All personal property, whether owned by husbands or wives, is inherited by children regardless of gender (Hillier and Hanson 1984; Murdock 1959, 406–8). Thus, Tuareg women have very high status by standards of other nonindustrial societies.

Exceptions to the Pattern

From the evidence presented in the previous two sections, it may appear that spatial segregation within the dwelling and gender stratification are highly correlated in nonindustrial societies: that women who live in societies with sexually segregated dwellings tend to have lower status than women who live in societies with sexually integrated dwellings. Yet exceptions to the pattern exist. Women living in societies with spatially segregated quarters sometimes have relatively high status. The Navajo of North America represent a society in which women hold positions of power, yet the one-room Navajo *hogan* is symbolically differentiated by gender (Jett and Spencer 1981).

58 How might the proposed relationship between space and status account for such exceptions? Among the Navajo, segregation represents an ideology of duality and complementarity between the sexes, rather than dominance and subordinance. Their housing both reflects and contributes to a segregated social order in which women do not have access to male knowledge and do not challenge male authority. The following example demonstrates the apparent anomaly and suggests the difficulty inherent in distinguishing between duality and dominance.*

The Navajo of North America. On the continuum from patriarchal to matriarchal societies, the Navajo are closest to the matriarchal end. Descent is determined through the mother's line, and residential patterns tend to be matrilocal. A mythology of First Man's and First Woman's creation of Navajo culture provides precedent for women's relatively high public status (Kluckhohn and Leighton 1946, 180–83). It also reflects the duality at the center of Navajo religious thought.

Women hold a range of important positions in Navajo society, although not that of chief. Women have access to religious and magical lore and can become practitioners ("medicine men"). There are reports of early female warriors, and either men or women may be witches with the power to harm others (Downs 1972, 23, 109). Compared to other nonindustrial societies in which women are barred from all realms of public life, the participation of Navajo women in religious and medicinal ceremonies places them toward the high end of the women's status scale.

*The Atoni of Timor are another example of the association between spatially segregated dwellings and a duality (rather than hierarchy) of gender relations (Waterson 1990, 171–75).

The relatively undifferentiated nature of Navajo society may account for women's higher status. Historically, there have been no priests, but only a group of religious practitioners. Chanters, singers, and medicine men do not constitute a separate class of people; rather, they engage in normal household production when their services are not needed. Finally, traditionally, no chief has held authority on more than a local or transitory basis. Within the domestic realm, women influence household decisions and can obtain a divorce easily. Still, Navajo women tend to have indirect political influence, while men are more likely to hold leadership positions (Downs 1972, 23, 29, 96, 101, 122). **59**

We might predict, then, that traditional Navajo dwellings are sexually integrated. Yet the *hogan* is symbolically divided into male and female spheres. The floor represents the (female) earth and the roof represents the (male) sky. The four house posts symbolize the four poles that support the sky and represent female deities: Earth Woman, Water Woman, Corn Woman, and Mountain Woman. Men are expected to sit on the north side of the *hogan* and women on the south side; the woman's loom and cooking supplies are kept on the south side as well (Kluckhohn and Leighton 1946, 90; P. Oliver 1987, 155).

How can this discrepancy be reconciled with previous findings on the relationship between spatial segregation and gender stratification? One possibility is that the argument still applies because Navajo women do not hold community leadership roles and therefore have lower status than men. However, their access to religious and mythical knowledge is greater than for women in other nonindustrial societies, and there are no societies in which women occupy all positions of status and power. Rather, the initial argument is based on a relationship between dominant and subordinate groups. When concepts of dominance and subordinance are replaced by the concepts of duality and complementarity—and practiced in daily life as with the Navajo—sexually segregated housing may not be associated with lower women's status as clearly as when it is based on a hierarchical ideology.

These descriptions, then, suggest the range of segregation and stratification characteristic of nonindustrial societies. There are cases in which the hypothesized negative association between spatial segregation and women's status appears to be supported, and there are exceptions to the predicted pattern. In order to examine the relationship between dwelling segregation and gender stratification for a wider array of cultures, a sample of societies from the Human Relations Area Files (HRAF) has been analyzed. This quantitative approach summarizes the hypothesized relationship more succinctly than repeated descriptions of case studies. Both qualitative and quantitative analyses are useful in establishing patterns in the data.

60

Empirical Analysis

Because ethnographic reports may be written without explicit reference to spatial differentiation, it is difficult to assess with certainty the interior layout of dwellings in nonindustrial societies. The ethnographer may assume that educated readers know the culture being described is Muslim and that Muslims invariably segregate men and women. Or the anthropologist may bring certain expectations to a study and incorrectly interpret symbolic distinctions within a one-room hut. Lack of reference to internal differentiation therefore does not necessarily mean lack of gender segregation.

For example, the edited volume *The House in East and Southeast Asia* (Izikowitz and Sorensen 1982) contains six articles on Lao and Thai dwellings. Five of those articles describe the interiors without reference to spatial segregation by gender; one with diagrams of the house shows no separate male and female quarters (Charpentier 1982). Yet the sixth article mentions partitions for men and women and separate stairs for women, with no further elaboration or diagrams (Clement 1982). How does the analyst know if all other authors overlooked that architectural feature or if the sixth author identified it incorrectly?

Using more than one source of information is the only safeguard against making an error in classifying dwellings by presence of separate quarters for women and men. When possible, more than one reference was consulted in the current research; if any one of them mentioned separate male and female spaces, the society was coded as having sexually segregated dwellings. This technique reduces the likelihood that more than one ethnographer would fail to mention an important physical feature of the dwelling. The technique does not, however, control for an ethnographer's incorrect identification of interior spaces as gendered when they are not. Thus, potential exists for two types of error in the data: falsely positive and falsely negative identifications.

Among the ninety-three cultures in the present sample, data on dwelling segregation could be coded for seventy-nine. Of those, seventeen (22 percent) had some form of sexually segregated dwelling. Table 2.1 reports the distribution of nonindustrial societies by the presence of sexually segregated dwellings and women's status.

61

Three measures of women's status are used in this and subsequent analyses of nonindustrial societies. *Power within kinship networks* is a measure of women's leadership for societies in which there are few positions of political and religious authority (Ross 1986). The ability to influence people outside the immediate family demonstrates participation in the public sphere. *Inheritance of property* is a common measure of women's ability to control wealth, and *control of labor and property* is a scale most heavily weighted toward the control of male, female, and joint labor. Higher values on these measures indicate higher status for women. (Each of these variables is described in detail in appendix A.)

Table 2.1 shows that sexually segregated dwellings are most strongly associated with women's power in kinship networks. Societies lacking segregated dwellings are those in which women have the greatest kinship power. Among these societies, approximately one-quarter are those in which women's kinship power is greatest, compared with only 6 percent for societies with segregated dwellings. The average (mean) score on the three-point kinship power scale is 2.08 for societies without segregated dwellings and 1.65 for those with segregated dwellings. The Gamma value of $-.59$ indicates a fairly strong negative relationship.*

Less strong, but still in the predicted direction, is the relationship between segregated dwellings and women's inheritance of property. Societies with-

*Gamma is a measure of association appropriate for use with ordinal data. Its value ranges from -1.00 to $+1.00$. Typically, values lower than .20 indicate a weak association between two variables; values between .20 and .50 indicate a moderate association; and those over .50 a strong association.

Table 2.1. Distribution of Nonindustrial Societies by Spatial Segregation within the Dwelling and Women's Status

Measures of Women's Status		Percent of Societies with Spatially Segregated Dwellings	
		Absent	Present
TOTAL (N=79)		78%	22%
Power in kinship networks (N=79; Gamma = −.59)			
Least female power		14%	41%
Moderate female power		63	53
Greatest female power		23	6
		100%	100%
	X̄ value	2.08	1.65
Inheritance of property (N=62; Gamma = −.24)			
Male predominance		24%	19%
Male preference		28	62
Equal treatment		41	12
Female preference		6	6
		99%	99%
	X̄ value	2.30	2.06
Control of labor and property (N=79; Gamma = .20)			
Least female control		3%	6%
Less female control		23	12
More female control		63	65
Greatest female control		11	18
		100%	101%
	X̄ value	2.82	2.94

Source: Whyte's (1978a) Human Relations Area File data for measures of women's status and sources cited in appendix B for data on segregated dwellings.

out segregated dwellings are more likely to grant women and men equal inheritance rights than those with segregated dwellings. Nearly half (47 percent) of societies without segregated dwellings grant equal treatment or female preference in inheritance, compared with fewer than one-fifth (18 percent) of societies with segregated dwellings. The mean score on the four-point inheritance scale is 2.30 for societies in which dwellings are sexually integrated and 2.06 for societies in which dwellings are sexually segregated.

The final measure of women's status, control of labor and property, fails to operate in the predicted direction. Instead of a negative association with segregated dwellings, women's control of labor is positively associated with segregated dwellings. That is, women's control of labor is *greatest* in societies with segregated dwellings. Although segregation may create collective solidarity for women that enhances their economic power (Chafetz 1984; Whyte 1978a, 101), segregated dwellings do not create the kind of group separation conducive to such solidarity. Rather, segregated dwellings might not remove women from knowledge of economic activities to the same extent as other types of segregation. Since much of the labor carried out in nonindustrial societies occurs in the dwelling—particularly that performed by women and by women and men together—women could retain control of labor regardless of dwelling design. This possibility is supported by the lack of variance on this measure of women's status: nearly three-quarters of all societies are coded as "more (or greatest) female control" of labor. In other words, when women are already at the locus of labor by virtue of occupying the dwelling, their segregation from men is less crucial to their status than when the dwelling and workplace are separate places.

63

Conclusion

Women and men in nonindustrial societies can be separated from one another in environments as small as one-room huts. Case studies of the Algerian Berbers, South American Barasana, Mongolians, Indians, and Iranians suggest that sexually segregated dwellings are associated with lower status for women. Descriptions of Balinese, Yakan, and Tuareg cultures reveal sexually integrated dwellings and higher status for women. A seeming exception to the hypothesized relationship is represented by the ambiguous status of women among the Navajo, a society with segregated living arrangements based on an ideology of gender complementarity.

The dwelling is only one of three spatial institutions examined in this research. The design of dwellings is expected to be less strongly associated with women's status than segregation in other institutions because this type of architectural separation creates less distance between women and sources of knowledge than geographic segregation (such as that between dwellings and a ceremonial men's hut). The importance of dwellings should not be underestimated, however. Because women traditionally have spent so much time in the home, its design has greater consequences for women than for men, who spend less time within its walls. The dwelling is also important because it connects women's location in the spatial institution of the family to their location in the larger stratification system.

Approximately one-quarter of nonindustrial societies in the HRAF sample have gendered dwelling spaces. Among those with gender-segregated dwellings, women demonstrate less power outside the immediate household and are less likely to inherit property than in those societies with integrated dwellings. The reverse is the case for control of labor: women in societies with gendered dwellings have *more* control of labor than women in societies with integrated dwellings. Perhaps when much of the total household labor is performed within the dwelling, as it is in nonindustrial societies, architectural separation from men does not present the obstacles to knowledge acquisition that geographic segregation imposes.

Gendered spaces within the dwelling are the least visible types of segregation. Not only is their existence hidden from public view by exterior walls, but internally differentiated spaces may be invisible to occupants within the walls because of their "taken for granted" nature. By comparison, the presence of an entirely separate place of learning for men—a ceremonial hut—creates highly visible distinctions between masculine and feminine spaces in nonindustrial societies.

64

3

Ceremonial Men's Huts

The [Iatmul] men are occupied with the spectacular, dramatic, and violent activities which have their centre in the ceremonial house, while the women are occupied with the useful and necessary routines of food-getting, cooking, and rearing children—activities which centre around the dwelling house and the gardens.—Gregory Bateson, *Naven*

Anthropologists have labeled the separate living arrangements of men in some nonindustrial societies with a variety of names. Whether called a ceremonial house, bachelors' hut, or clubhouse, all serve a similar function: they are places where men congregate to the exclusion of women. In some societies men sleep in the houses apart from their wives and children, while in others they use such huts only for informal meetings or formal initiation rites. The design of the men's houses varies from being more elaborate than typical dwellings to being simpler in appearance. Whatever their built form, men's houses are places in which men gather for religious ceremonies, for initiation rites, and to make major decisions affecting the village (Bateson 1958; Herdt 1982; Hogbin 1970; Maybury-Lewis 1967; Mead 1949; Newman 1965; Read 1965). They are also places in which knowledge important to public status is passed among men and from one generation of men to the next.

Men's Huts as Institutions of Learning

The primary way in which knowledge is conveyed from one generation to the next is through initiation ceremonies. These typically take place in ceremonial men's huts. The initiation rites of African tribes are often referred to in the anthropological literature as schools for the transmission of knowledge in secular and religious matters (Hogbin 1970, 102). Wogeo boys are taught to play sacred flutes when admitted to the clubhouse (Hogbin 1970, 101), as are Gahuku boys (Read 1965, 116). Shavante boys learn practical and ceremonial skills they will need as adults, such as the construction of weapons, production of ritual regalia, the tunes of tribal songs, and the steps to traditional dances (Maybury-Lewis 1967, 111–13).

Women and girls are excluded from participation in activities of the men's huts. Although girls learn from their mothers the domestic skills necessary for maintenance of the household, these skills are less valuable as routes to public status. According to anthropologist Kenneth Read:

[Men's clubhouses] symbolized the basic division of Gahuku society, in which the men were the continuing core of every village. Men monopolized the religious symbols and the esoteric rituals associated with them, controlled subsistence activities, settled disputes, and decided the appropriate time to hold the great festivals. Women were only second-class citizens whose rights in the community were conferred by marriage rather than birth and were dependent to a large extent on their bearing sons who would carry on the corporate interests of men. (Read 1965, 96)

In *Economy and Society*, Weber drew a direct link between men's houses and the monopoly of education. The communal houses of warriors were organized around the transmission of combat knowledge, and warrior was the highest status a man could achieve. In fact, Weber reported that "he who does not pass the heroic trials of the warrior's training remains a 'woman,' just as he who cannot be awakened to the supernatural remains a 'layman'" (Weber [1921] 1978, 1144). The men's house thus reinforces the definition of warrior status as the most important, while reducing women's ability to learn combat skills.

The Iatmul of New Guinea have no formal warriors or chieftains. Instead, status is achieved by "sorcery and esoteric knowledge," by age, and by conspicuous behavior exhibited in the men's house (a "splendid building" nearly 120 feet long with a towering gabled roof) (Bateson 1958, 123). Men may win competitive debates in the ceremonial house by two methods: a demonstration of erudition by reciting thousands of totemic names or boisterous pantomime. Iatmul boys are bullied and punished during initiation rites in the ceremonial house in ways that reproduce the ideal Iatmul man—one who displays histrionics in the company of other men. A junior ceremonial house for boys allows them to mimic activities carried out in the senior house and imitate their elders by clowning for others (Bateson 1958, 125).

Societies with Men's Huts

The Akwĕ-Shavante of Brazil. In contrast to the splendor of the Iatmul ceremonial house described by Bateson is the bachelors' hut of the Brazilian

Shavante tribe. Maybury-Lewis reported that the bachelors' hut is "an uncomfortable place to live . . . badly covered, so that the sun scorches its inmates by day and the moon keeps them awake by night, and it is frequently infested with insects" (Maybury-Lewis 1967, 110). Despite its different appearance, the bachelors' hut serves a function in Shavante society similar to that in Iatmul society. It secludes young boys from females while the male adolescents acquire the knowledge necessary for adulthood.

Induction into the bachelors' hut occurs among boys united in the same age-set, a type of cohort identification that separates its members hier-archically from other members of the society and forms the central core of the Shavante stratification system. During their five years in the hut, boys are taught practical and symbolic skills in the making of weapons, ceremonial regalia, songs, and dances. The seclusion serves both to develop a "corporate spirit" and to expose the boys to older men for leadership training through example and emulation (Maybury-Lewis 1967).

Although the Shavante have no formal mechanisms for appointing chiefs, they are essentially men who exercise leadership, claim the title, and have the support of the men's council. The age-set system plays an important role in the identification and recruitment of future leaders. While still living in the bachelors' hut, two boys are appointed by the chief to lead their age-set in all its activities. Expectations for these boys are high: they learn to organize hunting, fishing, and gathering trips, lead rituals, and bear the sacred flutes and lances during initiation rites (Maybury-Lewis 1967, 191).

Shavante girls are excluded from the age-set system and thus from the training necessary to become future chiefs. Women are also barred from par-ticipation in the nightly village meetings in which the affairs of the commu-nity are discussed and in fact are not "supposed to approach the mature men's council *nor to hear its debates*" (Maybury-Lewis 1967, 143; emphasis added). Overhearing discussions of the men's council is considered disrespectful behavior for women and younger men. The taboos preventing women from listening to the men also serve to reinforce a knowledge differential between the sexes. The importance of these men's councils cannot be overestimated. Everything happening in the community (and in other communities) is discussed there, disputes are reconciled, and decisions affecting communal life are made. The men's council is so important that it often overrules the chief on a variety of issues (Maybury-Lewis 1967, 144, 199, 200).

Shavante women have little control over their own lives. Girls marry between the ages of eight and ten and typically have sexual intercourse before their first menses. Traditional Shavante society is a polygynous one in which wives are considered economic assets. Divorce is rare since men do not need to divorce one wife in order to marry another. Women who divorce are required to leave the community, a severe penalty since it means leaving an extended kinship network (Maybury-Lewis 1967, 76, 82, 94). Women who are married as children, banished from their communities if divorced, **70** and hold no positions of political power have relatively low status by standards of nonindustrial societies.

The Wogeo of New Guinea. The most imposing building in the majority of Wogeo villages when Ian Hogbin conducted his fieldwork in 1934 was the men's club (*niabwa*). The *niabwa* serves as a meeting place, male dormitory, and storage place for sacred objects (flutes, dancing masks, and ancestral remains) (Hogbin 1970, 11).

In adolescence a boy is removed from his mother and sent to sleep in the men's club, thus minimizing female influences that could sap his strength. Initiation ceremonies that attend the boys' entry to the clubhouse stress the physical and social distance between women and men. The playing of magical *nibek* flutes accompanies initiation and is a symbol of masculinity. Wogeo mythology states that although women first discovered flutes, they ceded control to men and have never played them since. The adage that "men play flutes, women bear infants" summarizes Wogeo expectations of appropriate gender role behavior. Once initiated into the clubhouse, boys are cautioned never to reveal the secrets of the flutes to women (Hogbin 1970, 101, 107).*

The position of leadership among the Wogeo, the headman (*kokwal*), is buttressed by an extensive knowledge of mythology. Every village has a pair of headmen, each of whom is a specialist in some magical system. For example, the canoe magician directs trading expeditions, while the war magician is in charge of raiding parties and the garden magician organizes

---

*Another, more extreme, example of male rejection of women symbolically associated with flutes is represented by the homosexual practices occurring in the men's hut of the Sambia of New Guinea (Herdt 1981, 1987).

horticulture. Headmen hold their positions by virtue of birth, passing them down to the eldest son, and each Wogeo headman has a "virtual monopoly within his residential cluster on the magic relating to group tasks and group well being" (Hogbin 1970, 190).

Women are excluded from positions of leadership both by birth and by lack of knowledge of the mythology handed down in the men's house. Neither do Wogeo women control property. Land is typically inherited by sons, and if a wealthy father leaves land to a daughter, she is expected to spend her entire life in his village with her husband. Wives do not exercise **71** cultivation rites but entrust them to their husbands (Hogbin 1970, 19–21).

The relationship between spatial segregation and gender stratification among the Wogeo is summarized by Hogbin as follows: "The social separateness of men and women in ordinary life is constantly underlined, and generally when working or at leisure, they remain apart. They carry out different tasks, are called on to accept different family responsibilities, and have different jural obligations. Women . . . in the wider political sphere are powerless" (Hogbin 1970, 86).

Societies without Men's Huts

The Yoruba of Nigeria. Unlike other nonindustrial societies, the Yoruba are highly urbanized. Large towns were mentioned by Portuguese travelers as early as 1505, and by the 1930s a majority of the Yoruba lived in towns of 5,000 persons or more—a proportion comparable to that in the United States (Bascom 1955, 447). The Yoruba are predominantly farmers, and their towns are rural settlements composed of family compounds. Ibadan, the largest urban area, has been called a "city-village" because its large size has not altered its village structure (Lloyd 1965, 555).

The typical Yoruba town is organized so that the family compounds face the traditional palace (*Afin*) where the chief (*Oba*) lives. Other than the *Afin*, which covers several acres, Yoruba towns have few public buildings (Ojo 1966, 132; Lloyd 1965, 555). The lack of a men's house is accompanied by fairly open housing design as well. Each compound (called *agbo ile*, or "flock of houses") forms a square enclosing an open space. A veranda circles the entire interior, connecting all exterior rooms and allowing residents to walk from one end to the other under cover. The veranda is the most commonly used part of the house: children play there, guests are entertained, meetings are held, and domestic chores are carried out under its roof. During the hottest months family members may sleep on the veranda. Rooms opening onto the veranda are used occasionally for privacy and for storing property, but the life of the compound is carried on outside (Ojo 1966, 147; Fadipe 1970, 101).

72   This openness leads to continual contact between the sexes—through lack of a men's house and presence of integrated dwellings—and suggests relatively high status among Yoruba women. Indeed, they have numerous rights not characteristic of women in other nonindustrial societies. Yoruba women are skillful traders whose profits are their own. A large majority are self-employed in agriculture, trade, or crafts and are independently wealthy. For example, nearly one-fifth of wives receive nothing from their husbands and are entirely self-supporting (Boserup 1970, 42). Most women earn enough to buy their own clothes, many provide food and household goods from their own earnings, and many wives are wealthier than their husbands. Yoruba women control property as well as their own labor. According to Lloyd: "Women are more likely to invest their profits in house property or further trading, whereas a man spends his in achieving political office. A woman's public status is determined not so much by that of her husband as by her own position in her market guild or social club" (Lloyd 1965, 566).

Although it is true that Yoruba women cannot hold the chief position of *Oba*, oral histories of traditional culture identify significant female religious and political leaders (Awe 1977; Calloway 1981). The institutionalized position of *Iyalode* ("mother in charge of external affairs") was an achieved status awarded to the village woman with the greatest leadership ability, economic resources, and popularity. It was the job of the *Iyalode* to represent women's interests in local government and to coordinate markets and trading. She held, like male chiefs, the insignia of office: a special beaded necklace, straw hat and shawl, personal servants, and special drummers and bell-ringers to call the women together. The *Iyalode*'s title gave her authority over all women (Awe 1977, 147, 148).

The *Oba* and the *Iyalode* were responsible for men's and women's activities, respectively: male chiefs conducted the business of war and received foreign visitors, while female chiefs settled disputes between women and insured smooth functioning of the market. Thus, Yoruba women had traditional sources of status unlike women in many other nonindustrial societies.

The Iroquois of North America. The Iroquois have been cited by anthropologists as one of the few societies approaching a true matriarchy (Murdock 1934). Iroquois women have rights of control over property and labor, and they are politically active in community decision making. Traditional Iroquois culture is matrilineal and matrilocal. According to Morgan (1962): **73** "Not least remarkable among their institutions, was that which confined transmission of all titles, rights, and property in the female line to the exclusion of the male. . . . If the wife . . . inherited orchards, or planting lots, or reduced land to cultivation, she could dispose of them at her pleasure, and in case of her death, they were inherited . . . by her children" (quoted in Brown 1970, 155).

Perhaps most important to the status of Iroquois women is their ownership of land. Although the Iroquois do not "own" land in the Western sense, women govern the allocation of its use, and "the lands, fields, and all their harvest belong to them" (Bonvillain 1980, 50). Women also control access to food. Stored food is a major form of wealth among the Iroquois and is distributed by elderly matrons along with the symbolic wealth of wampum, quill works, and furs. It is their ability to influence men's labor as well as their own that gives traditional Iroquois women more economic power than women of other nonindustrial societies have (Brown 1975; Bonvillain 1980).

The role of Iroquois women in political life is equally remarkable. Although women cannot hold the position of chief, women's councils are responsible for both appointing and deposing male rulers. Women are included among the *agoianders* who advise the chief and speak routinely at local councils. Accounts from the seventeenth century suggest that a woman served as a peace emissary to the French (Bonvillain 1980, 56). Declarations of war and the fate of prisoners are also decisions to which women contribute (Brown 1970, 154, 155).

Although Brown (1970, 157) identifies the Iroquois as a society spatially segregated by sex, this reference is made with regard to the spatial separation introduced by the division of labor, which took men away from camp for long periods of time. The Iroquois are remarkably spatially integrated, however, within their settlements. There is no ceremonial men's house, nor are dwellings segregated by gender. The typical Iroquois settlement of the seventeenth century consisted of villages of 300 to 600 persons living in bark longhouses distributed in linear formation (Fenton [1951] 1985, 41). The longhouse was home to several families related through the women and ruled by a matron. The Iroquois referred to themselves as "people of the longhouse," and it is possible that the longhouse was the analogy on which **74** the federated Iroquois League was built: the figurative longhouse of the league was divided into geographical compartments occupied by different tribes, just as the literal longhouse was divided into compartments for families (Brown 1970, 156).

Although there are no reports of separate men's huts among the Iroquois, certain ceremonies exist in which women's participation is restricted. "Men's feasts" are theoretically segregated by sex, but they take place in one of the family's lodges rather than in a ceremonial men's house and are sometimes attended by women. Lafitau's early-eighteenth-century account of these feasts related that women were not usually invited but often satisfied their curiosity by placing themselves at the ends of the cabin (cited in Bonvillain 1980, 51). This passage indicates that women were present even at men's functions and that the proceedings were not secret, nor were they disrupted by female contact.

Exceptions to the Pattern

In addition to those societies in which the presence of a men's hut appears to be associated with women's lower status are those in which the connection is less clear. This section describes possible exceptions to the relationship between space and status. Societies exist in which relatively high status for women accompanies a men's hut.

The Bemba of Zambia. The Bemba of Zambia (formerly Northern Rhodesia) have been identified as a matrilineal/matrilocal society with relatively high status for women (Richards 1939, 1956; Brown 1970). However, the Bemba also have a men's shelter where men gather and eat together separately from women; the women remain grouped around the verandas of their individual dwellings. This spatial segregation characterizes both the work and recreational patterns of the Bemba (Richards 1956, 50).

Women who are princesses play an important role within the hierarchical and authoritarian social structure of the Bemba. Princesses rule over small territories in the king's district and are considered subchiefs with ritual functions at tribal ceremonies. Princesses are typically sisters or maternal nieces of the chief, however, and as such occupy an inherited status not open to all women (Brown 1970, 156). Further, one of the special duties of a **75** princess is to "bear fine children in order to provide the country with chiefs" (Richards 1956, 39), a role which places primary importance on the reproductive capacity of women. Finally, princesses typically have male advisers (Richards 1956, 48).

Bemba society has no permanent form of property (such as land or cattle) that can be accumulated and inherited by succeeding generations. Thus, neither men nor women exercise control of property. Instead, social status rests on the exchange of services. A chief may demand service from subjects, a headman from villagers, or a father from family members. In this exchange hierarchy Bemba women have no power. Neither do they have control over food production or domestic authority (Brown 1970; Richards 1956). In sum, a few women occupy positions of power by virtue of their kinship with the chief, but the majority of Bemba women have relatively low status.

The Palauans of Micronesia. The status of traditional Palauan women of Micronesia appears relatively high. Records of a council of women chiefs (*klobak-l-dil*) in the nineteenth century document women who were independent of the male chiefs. It is also typical for daughters to inherit personal property from their mothers, while sons inherit small items from their fathers (land is held in joint ownership by kinship groups). Each male householder's spouse is considered his counterpart and called by a similar title (Force and Force 1972, 12, 15, 54). Palauan women speak in public, hold economic power, and play important roles in ceremonial rituals (Barnett 1960). Women's clubs (*cheldebechel redil*) perform public services such as cleaning village paths and preparing food for work groups. Although organizationally similar to men's clubs, women's societies have no clubhouses (Force and Force 1972, 19).

Palauan men's clubs (*cheldebechel sachal*) are places in which both married and unmarried men spend a great deal of time. They sleep in the clubhouse and engage in work and decision making there. That is where similarities to men's clubs in other nonindustrial societies end, however. Palauan men's clubs have female attendants to "aid and entertain" the men; sexual services are part of this practice. Women become attendants through three avenues: they are brought to the house to serve out family obligations, as individuals voluntarily seeking such service, or as captives. Men's clubs make various payments for the women who come to serve them, and when the custom was abolished by Christian missionaries, chiefs and families to whom payments had been made lost a substantial source of revenue (Force and Force 1972, 23).

Such use of women as objects of economic and sexual exchange make it difficult to assess the status of Palauan women. Some women apparently choose to be attendants, but many others have no choice. The structure of the men's club also makes Palauan society anomalous: most of them strictly exclude women. Ambiguities exist in both women's status and the degree of spatial segregation as represented by men's clubs. Women's partial integration with men, even under possibly coerced circumstances, is associated with higher status on some criteria.

Empirical Analysis

Of the eighty-one nonindustrial societies for which Human Relations Area Files data on men's huts are available, approximately one-quarter (27 percent) report the presence of a ceremonial men's house. Table 3.1 demonstrates the hypothesized negative relationship for all three measures of women's status.

Societies with men's huts are those in which women have the least power in kinship networks. Among societies *with* a men's hut, nearly one-third (32 percent) grant women the least power among extended kin. By comparison, only 15 percent of societies *without* a men's hut show such low levels of kinship power for women. The average value of women's kinship power is higher in societies without men's huts (2.03) than in those with men's huts (1.86 on a three-point scale).

Table 3.1. Distribution of Nonindustrial Societies by Presence of a Men's Hut and Women's Status

Measures of Women's Status		Percent of Societies with a Men's Hut	
		Absent	Present
TOTAL (N=81)		73%	27%
Power in kinship networks (N=81; Gamma = −.24)			
Least female power		15%	32%
Moderate female power		66	50
Greatest female power		19	18
		100%	100%
	X̄ value	2.03	1.86
Inheritance of property (N=64; Gamma = −.29)			
Male predominance		21%	38%
Male preference		38	31
Equal treatment		33	31
Female preference		8	0
		100%	100%
	X̄ value	2.29	1.94
Control of labor and property (N=81; Gamma = −.23)			
Least female control		3%	9%
Less female control		19	23
More female control		64	59
Greatest female control		14	9
		100%	100%
	X̄ value	2.88	2.68

Source: Whyte's (1978a) Human Relations Area File data for measures of women's status and sources cited in appendix B for data on men's huts.

77

A similar relationship holds for the presence of men's huts and women's ability to inherit property. Societies with men's huts are more likely to give men predominance in inheritance rights (38 percent) than societies without men's huts (21 percent). Female preference in inheritance is most likely in societies without men's huts, where the mean score on this four-point scale is 2.29, compared with 1.94 for societies with men's huts.

Finally, women's control of labor and property is greatest in societies without men's huts. Just over three-quarters (78 percent) of societies without such huts show greater female control of labor, compared with approximately two-thirds (68 percent) of societies with men's huts. The score on this four-point scale is higher in societies without ceremonial huts (2.88) than in those where a hut is present (2.68).

Conclusion

Men's huts represent the spatial institution of education in nonindustrial societies. The data suggest, for this sample of societies, that the geographic segregation of women and men resulting from the presence of a men's hut is more pervasively associated with stratification than gendered spaces in the dwelling.

Education is important because it bridges the private sphere of the dwelling and the public sphere of the workplace. In other words, education is an intermediate or intervening institution facilitating passage from domestic to social status. Women have more control over labor when they are integrated with men into the skill-learning process. In societies without men's huts, that learning may occur in the dwelling or in the execution of certain tasks. When the transmission of socially valued knowledge is institutionalized in a separate place, however, the degree of gender stratification is greatest.

Just as with prohibitions about women occupying forbidden parts of the dwelling, taboos restricting women's entry to ceremonial houses are often quite strong. While Barasana women are threatened with death if they do not leave the *maloca* during the *He House* ceremony, death for Siuai women may occur as a result of walking too near the men's clubhouse (D. Oliver 1955, 374). Such dire consequences of being out of one's proper place do not accrue to men. The implication here is that women's exposure to traditionally masculine knowledge has a potentially greater effect on the gender stratification system than men's acquisition of traditionally feminine knowledge.

The relationship between men's huts and women's status raises the issue of causality. Do men construct ceremonial huts in societies in which they already control the most knowledge and have the greatest status, or does the presence of a hut contribute to men's higher status? The spatial perspective concentrates on the mutual reinforcement of these processes rather than a **79** causal agent. Societies in which gender stratification is most pronounced are also those in which men have the most knowledge to protect. The geographic segregation created by men's huts helps accomplish that goal, and in turn it reinforces and reproduces prevailing status differences between women and men.

4

The Spatial Division of Labor

The men [in primitive societies], and not the women, take part in councils, war, religious rites, judicial procedures, and so forth; and their contribution to the economy of the family lies in those tasks which require not only strength but also absence from the home, while the women are tied to the daily chores of the home: preparation of food, cleansing the home, and nursing the children. . . . In primitive societies the spheres of activities of the sexes are clearly demarcated; and if a woman does not enter into male activities, neither does her husband seek to compete with her in female activities.—Edward Evan Evans-Pritchard, *The Position of Women in Primitive Societies*

S ir Edward Evan Evans-Pritchard described the division of labor in nonindustrial societies in terms of its relation to the home and, by implication, the spatial context in which women's and men's work occurs. Not only do women and men perform different tasks, they carry them out in different places. Whether based on herding, hunting and gathering, horticulture, or agriculture, nonindustrial societies are characterized by a clear gender division of labor. Men hunt while women gather, men clear fields while women cultivate, and men plow fields while women prepare food (Boulding 1976; Friedl 1975; Murdock 1937; Sanday 1981; Rosaldo and Lamphere 1974; Schlegel 1977). To the extent that task differentiation is accompanied by spatial segregation that gives women and men differential access to knowledge, women should have lower status.

The Gender Division of Labor

Murdock and Provost's (1973) data on the division of labor in 185 societies suggest that persons performing different work also occupy separate spaces (see table 4.1). Among the twelve tasks recorded as 95 percent or more "masculine," at least five (42 percent) take place away from the house or village. Seafaring expeditions, lumbering, hunting large game, fowling, and trapping all occur at some distance from the dwelling. The separation may be less, for example, if a forest is nearby, or greater, in the case of hunting trips that last for days or weeks.

The nearly one-third of all tasks carried out by both women and men are difficult to classify by location. But among the seven tasks identified as 80 percent or more "feminine," the majority take place within the dwelling or compound. Preparing food and drinks, cooking, and spinning are all located in or near the dwelling. Thus, women's work and men's work occur in separate places in many nonindustrial societies. While fulfilling complementary economic needs, such separation reduces contact between women and men.

Table 4.1 Gender Allocation of 50 Technological Activities in 185 Societies

Task	Male	Mostly Male	Equal	Mostly Female	Female	Index
1. Hunting large aquatic fauna	48	0	0	0	0	100.0
2. Smelting of ores	37	0	0	0	0	100.0
3. Metalworking	85	1	0	0	0	99.8
4. Lumbering	135	4	0	0	0	99.4
5. Hunting large land fauna	139	5	0	0	0	99.3
6. Work in wood	159	3	1	1	0	98.8
7. Fowling	132	4	3	0	0	98.3
8. Manufacture of musical instruments	83	3	1	0	1	97.6
9. Trapping of small land fauna	136	12	1	1	0	97.5
10. Boatbuilding	84	3	3	0	1	96.6
11. Stoneworking	67	0	6	0	0	95.9
12. Work in bone, horn, and shell	71	7	2	0	2	94.6
13. Mining and quarrying	31	1	2	0	1	93.7
14. Bonesetting and other surgery	34	6	4	0	0	92.7
15. Butchering	122	9	4	4	4	92.3
16. Collection of wild honey	39	5	2	0	2	91.7
17. Land clearance	95	34	6	3	1	90.5
18. Fishing	83	45	8	5	2	86.7
19. Tending large animals	54	24	14	3	3	82.4
20. Housebuilding	105	30	14	9	20	77.4
21. Soil preparation	66	27	14	17	10	73.1
22. Netmaking	42	2	5	1	15	71.2
23. Making of rope or cordage	62	7	18	5	19	69.9
24. Generation of fire	40	6	16	4	20	62.3
25. Bodily mutilation	36	4	48	6	12	60.8
26. Preparation of skins	39	4	2	5	31	54.6
27. Gathering of small land fauna	27	3	9	13	15	54.5
28. Crop planting	27	35	33	26	20	54.4
29. Manufacture of leather products	35	3	2	5	29	53.2
30. Harvesting	10	37	34	34	26	45.0
31. Crop tending	22	23	24	30	32	44.6
32. Milking	15	2	8	2	21	43.8
33. Basketmaking	37	9	15	18	51	42.5
34. Burden carrying	18	12	46	34	36	39.3
35. Matmaking	30	4	9	5	55	37.6

Table 4.1 (*Continued*)

Task	Male	Mostly Male	Equal	Mostly Female	Female	Index
36. Care of small animals	19	8	14	12	44	35.9
37. Preservation of meat and fish	18	2	3	3	40	32.9
38. Loom weaving	24	0	6	8	50	32.5
39. Gathering small aquatic fauna	11	4	1	12	27	31.1
40. Fuel gathering	25	12	12	23	94	27.2
41. Manufacture of clothing	16	4	11	13	78	22.4
42. Preparation of drinks	15	3	4	4	65	22.2
43. Potterymaking	14	5	6	6	74	21.1
44. Gathering wild vegetal foods	6	4	18	42	65	19.7
45. Dairy production	4	0	0	0	24	14.3
46. Spinning	7	3	4	5	72	13.6
47. Laundering	5	0	4	8	49	13.0
48. Water fetching	4	4	8	13	131	8.6
49. Cooking	0	2	2	63	117	8.3
50. Preparation of vegetal foods	3	1	4	21	145	5.7

Source: Murdock and Provost 1973, 207

Note: The last column presents an index of the average percentage of male participation.

85

Murdock and Provost (1973) propose that the gender division of labor resulted initially from relative advantages in completing tasks. The advantages may have been biologically or culturally determined, but they are reinforced by spatial separation. Men's greater strength suited them best for hunting and lumbering, for example, while the limitations imposed by childrearing restricted women's strength and mobility (Murdock and Provost 1973, 211; Friedl 1975, 18). However, as long as the skills needed for hunting are learned in the context of the hunt, away from the dwelling, women are restricted further in their ability to gain hunting competence. The practice of protecting women from the dangers of hunting may have given some societies an evolutionary edge (Lerner 1986, 41), but it also helped reinforce men's higher status as the distributors of surplus meat (Friedl 1975, 21).

Other similarities exist in the gender division of labor among nonindustrial societies. Women tend to process "soft" materials (cloth, leather, reeds), while men process "hard" materials such as metal, wood, and stone; the gender that produces an item also tends to use it (men mine, smelt, and work metal, while women gather vegetables, prepare them, and cook them); and new technologies tend to be appropriated by men (Murdock and Provost 1973, 211–12). Sanday interprets these patterns as demonstration of the need to establish gender identities through dichotomies. Masculine activities are those that are not feminine. Thus, if women work with soft materials, men must work with hard materials. If women are associated with reproduction and nurturing, men are associated with death and warfare. Sanday identifies the gender division of labor characteristic of nonindustrial societies as "sex-role plans" shaping behavior within an environmental context (Sanday 1981, 76).

Sanday comes closer than most anthropologists to considering the spatial context of the division of labor. Her hypothesis is that hunting-gathering societies in which hunting is predominant will be more segregated in work and childrearing and will be more competitive than societies in which gathering is predominant. Hunting, competition, and segregation are associated with masculine origin symbolism, while gathering, cooperation, and integration are associated with feminine origin symbolism. Origin symbolism, moreover, is hypothesized to influence the cultural plans that shape patterns of behavior (Sanday 1981, 90). Whether the division of labor is explained by differences in physical strength, reproductive roles, cultural patterning, or evolutionary selection, however, work segregation in nonindustrial societies is often associated with spatial segregation by gender.

Societies with Spatially Segregated Labor

North American Eskimo. The inland Eskimo of northern Alaska rely on caribou hunting for their subsistence, while the maritime Eskimo depend on whaling and fishing for a living. Among both groups men do the majority of the hunting and fishing, which takes them away from camp for long periods of time. Women stay in the camp and are responsible for preserving and preparing food. Eskimo men's knowledge of the environment, gained from their forays, gives them the ability to determine necessary migrations for the tribes. Women have neither the knowledge nor the experience to participate in this decision-making process (Chance 1966, 36; Damas 1972a; Friedl 1975, 40).

Maritime Eskimo living in "pre-contact settlements" along the North Alaskan coast were studied in the 1950s by Spencer. He found the social organization characteristic of whaling to be similar to that of caribou hunting—both had changed very little over time despite the introduction of new technologies. Traditional aspects of whaling persist in the matter of crew recruitment and the division of labor by gender (Spencer 1972).   **87**

Whaling occurs from the end of April until mid-June, when the ice opens and spouting whales can be sighted. Actual preparation for the expeditions begins in late February, however, when men begin to work together as a crew to construct the boat, harpoons, and lances. All steps of the procedure are accompanied by rituals to guarantee safety and a good catch. Crews move to the edge of the ice with their boats in April, ready to launch them as soon as a whale is spotted; their wives remain at home to insure a successful hunt.

Although there are no formal positions of political leadership among the Eskimo, a successful whaling crew leader (the *umealiq*) has the highest status (Spencer 1972, 117). The whaling crew and its leader operate as a social group bound together by economic goals. The solidarity necessary for successful hunts is reinforced by the traditional men's house (the *karigi* or *galegi*). Eskimo men's houses differ from those described in the previous chapter by virtue of their prevalence and their association with specific crews. Whereas a single men's hut serves as an educational institution in many nonindustrial societies, in Eskimo society clubs are more like work guilds. The Eskimo *karigi* is the equivalent of a separate workplace, rather than a common school.

Crews and their leaders occupy their respective men's houses, which are constructed like the typical semisubterranean sod dwellings and differ only by having benches built around four or five sides. Members recline on these benches while ritual games and dances are carried out in the center. Men identify themselves in the community by their men's house membership, which reflects their crew membership, and spend most of their time there when not hunting or whaling. A typical village day for an Eskimo male is spent largely in the men's house: "Although he generally slept at home, he went to his men's house as soon as awake, *bringing whatever small tasks he had to work on during his stay there*. His wife, like the wives of other men, brought his food to him at the men's house. . . . Women were not barred from entry into the men's house . . . but it was clearly the domain of men" (Spencer 1972, 118; emphasis added).

Thus, the men's house among the maritime Eskimo is a place in which work and socializing takes place separately from women (Chance 1966, 53). It reinforces cohesion among members of a crew by providing a separate place in which they can eat, joke, and prepare for upcoming dangerous expeditions. Among the North Alaskan Eskimo, spatial segregation by gender occurs throughout the year and in a variety of ways: three months of men's absence for whaling is supplemented by their work in the men's house during the remaining months. To the extent that the tasks performed in the men's hut are those associated with whaling preparations (in which women do not take part), the gender division of labor is reinforced by spatial segregation as well.

The status of Eskimo women is arguably among the lowest in nonindustrial societies. By the turn of the century, female infanticide had been practiced long enough to cause a skewed sex ratio (Damas 1972a; Friedl 1975). The shortage of women (and a heavy reliance on kinship and alliance systems) contributes to child betrothal over which women have little say (Damas 1972a; Guemple 1972). The system of spousal exchange, whereby a man grants other men the sexual services of his wife in order to forge social alliances, is carried out with little regard for the wife's wishes (Damas 1972a, 1972b; Friedl 1975; Guemple 1972). Eskimo women have no authority within or outside the household; men make decisions and women obey their orders. No positions of formal political leadership exist in this loosely stratified society, yet whaling crew leaders gain status by their generosity in distributing meat. Since women do not hunt whales, they are excluded from this avenue to status (Friedl 1975, 41, 43).

The one exception to women's lack of power in Eskimo society is their ability to qualify as shamans. Friedl explains this inconsistency by identifying male shamans as those who are marginal in some way (e.g., they cannot

88

hunt). Since no females hunt, female shamans (especially those who are postmenopausal) do not pose a threat to the social order (Friedl 1975, 44).

Sexually segregated labor and women's status appear to be negatively associated in Eskimo society. A high degree of spatial segregation—through long whaling absences and work performed in men's houses—is associated with women's lower status. Another society in which a similar relationship exists is the pastoral Fulani of Africa.

89

Fulani Wodaabe of Nigeria. The Wodaabe are a small subpopulation of the diverse African Fulani population. The pastoral Wodaabe are concentrated in northeastern Nigeria, where they derive their livelihood from cattle herding and market trade for cereal products. The simple or compound family is the primary domestic and economic unit in Fulani life. The Fulani were converted to Islam before the eleventh century, and the Wodaabe are at least partially acculturated to the Islamic world of the western Sudan (Stenning 1965).

The gender division of labor among the Wodaabe is clear. Men herd the cattle (i.e., move them seasonally, water and pasture them daily, see to their veterinary needs, and make their ropes). Women market the milk, prepare food, and care for the children and the homestead. The Wodaabe family is a "herd-owning and milk-selling enterprise," with men and boys owning and managing the herds, while women and girls milk and sell the products (Stenning 1965, 374). The exception to this division of labor occurs when the herds are away from the village for half the year and men necessarily do their own milking and cooking.

The Wodaabe generally consider it beyond a woman's strength to engage in dangerous herding (e.g., to protect the cows from wild animals or thieves), and the long absences from camp are incompatible with childrearing. It is inconceivable among the Wodaabe that a woman could be master of the herd (*jomna'i*). Thus, women perform tasks compatible with being near the dwelling, such as making butter, cooking, and tending sheep and goats (Dupire 1963, 75).

The spatial division of labor that separates Wodaabe women and men for long periods of time is re-created in their huts as well, so that when men are not herding they are separated from women within the compound. Much of the work of both sexes is carried out within the homestead, and the design of the complex reflects the spatial division of labor by gender. The Wodaabe compound differs from the segregated dwellings described in chapter 2 because it is much larger than a single dwelling and encompasses outside space for animals. This expansion of the living space to include work areas qualifies the homestead as a hybrid workplace/dwelling. Although the household is the economic unit in nonindustrial societies, not every society incorporates the dwelling into its economic production.

90

The Wodaabe homestead is divided into two parts by a rope to which calves are tethered when the herd is in its corral. East of the rope is the female side, where wives' beds and property are arranged in order of seniority and where they perform household chores. The only males who sleep east of the calf rope are the household head and his infant sons; no other males may enter the eastern side. West of the calf rope is the male side, where cattle are kept. The householder and his sons sit on the western side to discuss and inspect the cattle. Men enter the homestead from the west, eat in the western part, and are buried on the western side of the corral; women enter from the east, eat there, and are buried east of the back fence (Dupire 1963, 51; Stenning 1965, 376). In the Wodaabe homestead, the western male side is associated with property (cattle) and decisions about control of that property; the eastern female side is associated with the work of women.

Wodaabe women do not own cattle in a society in which wealth and status are determined by the number of cattle owned. Although a woman may sell stock given to her as part of her marriage present (the *sadaaki*), she must first ask her husband's permission: "A woman will say of the pack ox that forms part of her *sadaaki*, 'my pack ox,' and it is true that she has exclusive use of it so long as she remains with her husband; but she can neither sell it without her husband's consent, nor take it with her should her marriage be dissolved" (Dupire 1963, 82).

When a husband dies, the children, rather than the wife, inherit the stock. The property of a widow with no children is controlled by relatives of her late husband. Sons receive the greatest share of the livestock, with daughters often receiving only one cow. Women never take precedence over men in inheritance, so that an only daughter has no more chance of inheritance than a girl with brothers; the brothers of the deceased inherit if there are no sons (Dupire 1963, 83, 84).

Wodaabe women do not control property, having no rights of ownership to the cattle which form capital, but they are able to control the fruits of their labor to the extent that they generate a surplus of goods from tending sheep and goats (Dupire 1963, 80). The kinship system is patrilineal, polygyny is practiced, and homesteads are named after male heads (Stenning 1965, 376), suggesting that women assert little kinship power.

The criteria for political leadership include masculine qualities. The leader **91** (*ardo*) of the agnatic descent group "must have established a herd and household in the usual way and must have wives and children. It is preferred that he be a prosperous man" (Stenning 1965, 394). Women hold various ceremonial positions but have no legal or political rights. In cases of dispute, women must go through a male intermediary to approach the chief for a resolution. Thus, public affairs for the Wodaabe are exclusively a masculine arena (Dupire 1963, 86).

The pastoral Wodaabe exhibit a spatially segregated division of labor by gender and a relatively low status for women: women cannot own property (cattle), and they do not participate in political decision making. The Wodaabe and the Eskimo both reflect a high degree of spatially segregated labor and a relatively high degree of gender stratification for nonindustrial societies.

A gendered division of labor does not always mean a spatial division of labor, however. As the following section demonstrates, nonindustrial societies in which the division of labor is associated with spatial proximity of the sexes tend to have lower levels of gender stratification and higher status for women.

Societies with Spatially Integrated Labor

Western Bontoc of the Philippines. The Tanulong and Fedilizan people constitute a subgroup of the Western Bontoc in the Philippines. The residential and economic unit is the nuclear family, and households subsist on rice and sweet potatoes. Although the Western Bontoc were once head-hunters, this activity ceased after the extension of American colonial admin-istration. The following analysis of the division of labor and women's status is based on fieldwork conducted in 1975 by Albert Bacdayan (1977).

All economic tasks performed by the Tanulong and Fedilizan are classified according to whether they are performed by one sex only, shared equally, or performed typically by one sex but sometimes by another. Of the eighty-seven tasks counted by Bacdayan, 44 percent are classified as performed equally by women and men, 16 percent are considered strictly male tasks, 3 percent strictly female, and 37 percent are typically performed by one sex or another. In sum, 81 percent of all tasks are open to both men and women and only 19 percent are restricted by sex, a rate of interchangeability consid-erably higher than that reported by Murdock and Provost (Bacdayan 1977, 284).

A breakdown of tasks by their area of production shows that shared tasks account for 93 percent of domestic work, 87 percent of subsistence produc-tion, 50 percent of religious functions, 50 percent of the food gathering, and 50 percent of house building. In other words, no types of tasks are predomi-nantly masculine or feminine. Bacdayan attributes this mechanistic coopera-tion to the necessity for all members of the household to engage in produc-tion.

Most important from a spatial perspective is that these tasks are also carried out in close proximity: men, women, and children all prepare the soil for planting, bundle seedlings, plant the crops, and harvest. If performing different tasks, they still work together: while men repair broken terraces, plow, or haul rice to the village, women are close by smoothing the soil, cutting the grass, or harvesting rice. Domestic work also occurs within the same shared spatial context. The entire family sorts beans, spreads rice to dry, and cooks together in front of the dwelling (Bacdayan 1977, 286).

The Western Bontoc are more egalitarian than societies with a strict spatial division of labor. Both girls and boys have equal rights of inheritance among the Western Bontoc, the discriminating criterion being age rather than sex. The firstborn (male or female) inherits the best rice fields. The emphasis on sharing means that married women must consult their husbands before acquiring or disposing of property, but men are bound by the same necessity to consult with their wives (Bacdayan 1977, 276–77).

Women participate equally with men in the political life of the village by attending meetings, speaking openly in public, and running for office. Both women and men raise the children, stressing the importance of mutuality and equality. Further, women freely visit outside the home, joining social and work groups independently of their husbands (Bacdayan 1977, 278–80). Thus, in matters of control of property and political participation, Western Bontoc women enjoy relatively high status, compared with women in spatially segregated societies.

93

The Western Bontoc had a ceremonial men's hut at one time. But even three decades ago, when they were theoretically the political and religious centers of village life, Western Bontoc men's huts differed from those in other nonindustrial societies by allowing women's participation. Although men discussed important decisions in the men's hut, they interrupted proceedings to go from home to home drinking rice wine. They continued deliberations in the homes, and women were free to participate in issues of importance to them (Bacdayan 1977, 290).

Bacdayan interprets women's high status among the Western Bontoc as a result of the mechanistic division of labor by gender, a pattern of work that brings women and men together in the same working environment (Bacdayan 1977, 270). Although Bacdayan stresses the importance of the interchangeability of tasks, equally important is the fact that those tasks are performed in close proximity to one another. Thus, fewer restrictions exist on access to knowledge, as Bacdayan proposes: "This crosscutting pattern [of tasks] signifies that the Tanulong and Fedilizan worlds are not partitioned into strict domains controlled by one or the other sex. Rather, males and females interpenetrate what may be strictly men's or women's domains in other societies. In effect their worlds are so intertwined as to be one and the same. Thus, there exist no dark unknowns in the society that either sex would or does utilize to control or check the other" (Bacdayan 1977, 288).

The Bari of South America. The Bari are tropical horticulturists ranging over northeastern Colombia and northwestern Venezuela whose number was estimated at between 1,500 and 1,800 persons in the 1970s. They live in several autonomous groups and use certain areas for fishing, cultivation, hunting, and gathering, but they have no concept of landownership in the Western sense. Each group builds two or more communal dwellings that house forty to eighty persons (which are not, incidentally, symbolically or physically divided into separate areas by sex). The Bari practice of swidden (slash-and-burn) agriculture demands that groups move every several years in response to environmental changes. The information reported here comes from analysis of published data and fieldwork conducted in 1976 by Buenaventura-Posso and Brown (1980).

94   The division of labor among the Bari is spatially integrated. Assignment of tasks is flexible and no taboos limit men to some jobs and women to others. Tasks such as dwelling construction, fishing, and planting are carried out by women and men together, with each gender responsible for a particular phase of the project. The traditional double-dam fishing technique, for example, requires cooperation between men and women. Likewise, neither gender can build a house alone: women collect and prepare the palm branches for thatching, while men gather and place the frame poles (Buenaventura-Posso and Brown 1980, 128).

Cooking, gathering foods, carrying items, and child care are performed sometimes by men, sometimes by women, and sometimes by both together. While women construct looms, spin, and weave, men set up the looms on the ground. Men hunt with bows and arrows made by women, and men weave hammocks from sisal collected by women. In sum, women's and men's work among the Bari is communal and often brings women and men into close proximity: "At no moment of life do men affirm themselves as a group in opposition to women. On the rare occasions in which men get together without women (collecting the reeds for making arrow shafts, an important hunting trip), their getting together never appears as a collective activity, but rather is only a momentary association of independent individuals, all of whom are working for themselves and their families" (Buenaventura-Posso and Brown 1980, 119).

Stratification of any kind among the Bari is almost nonexistent. Their language has no word for the concept of "chief." There are nominal heads of household groups, but these people have no control over others' actions. In general, the Bari neither issue nor take commands but operate autonomously. Decisions are made collectively by the women and men who are most directly affected by their outcomes. Both men and women have special social positions of responsibility when a new dwelling is constructed, but these positions are not permanent. If a person is away, he or she may be replaced, and when the group moves periodically to another dwelling the positions rotate (Buenaventura-Posso and Brown 1980, 116–18).

The Cantos, important traditional singing rituals, include both men and women. Singing—sometimes lasting for days or weeks—is done in pairs by a visitor and the host or hostess sitting together in a hammock. Members of each sex sing songs about the items they make, so that women sing of the thread they spin and the clothing they weave, and men sing of their bows and arrows. Women and men are thus equally incorporated into the ritual of welcome to visitors and the exchange of labor information between the sexes (Buenaventura-Posso and Brown 1980, 119).

Bari women also play an important role in traditional healing practices. Female *curandas* collect, prepare, store, and administer leaves to make the *potencias* that are the principal element of Bari medicine. Although men might also act as *curandos* to administer the poultices, only women can collect and prepare the medicinal plants by drying them, grinding them to a powder, and storing them in a gourd. Ethnographers also report that women make and play reed flutes, the only musical instruments known to the Bari (Buenaventura-Posso and Brown 1980, 126, 130).

In sum, in a society with little spatially segregated labor, Bari women occupy positions of relatively high status, compared with women in societies with more segregated labor. Much of the egalitarian social structure of the Bari has been attributed to the fact that "no individual or group has more access to strategic resources, including authority or knowledge, than another" (Buenaventura-Posso and Brown 1980, 118).

Exceptions to the Pattern

The Bontoc and Bari are examples of societies in which spatially integrated labor is associated with higher status for women. The Eskimo and Fulani Wodaabe represent societies in which spatially segregated labor is associated with lower status for women. Between these two extremes are an entire

95

range of societies with greater and lesser degrees of both spatial division of labor and gender stratification. The Iroquois, for example, are a hunting-gathering society with spatial segregation of labor but relatively high status for women (they were identified in chapter 3 as an example of a society without men's huts) (Bonvillain 1980; Brown 1970; Rothenberg 1980). The Mundurucu of the Amazon River basin share tasks such as fishing and gardening, but women have relatively low status (Murphy and Murphy 1985, 91, 130, 153). The !Kung have a traditional division of labor, but with some spatial differences that are associated with higher status for women.

!Kung of Southern Africa. The !Kung are a hunting and gathering society living on the western edge of the Kalahari Desert in Angola, Botswana, and South-West Africa (now Namibia). Information about the !Kung comes primarily from fieldwork conducted by the Marshall family in the 1950s in the Nyae Nyae region of South-West Africa (Marshall 1965); from Lee's fieldwork in Botswana in 1964 (Lee 1972); and from the Harvard !Kung Bushmen Study Project in Botswana and South-West Africa in the late 1960s (Draper 1975). Although the majority of !Kung-speaking people have now abandoned their nomadic lifestyle for more sedentary communities, emphasis in this section is on the spatial division of labor characteristic of their earlier traditions.

As in other hunting-gathering societies, men do the hunting and women do the gathering. The !Kung are also similar to other subsistence societies in that women supply the majority of daily food by foraging, though meat killed in a hunt is the more highly valued food. Hunters typically range far afield and are absent from home for long periods, as with other hunter-gatherer societies. Yet there are several spatial differences in the gender division of labor among the !Kung that suggest a higher status for women.

First, while men are hunting, women are not tied to the settlement but forage for food and firewood. Although this pattern does not bring women and men into spatial proximity, it allows them equal mobility and comparable absences from camp. Women use their mobility to observe the environment for signs of game and watering holes, and they share this information with men on their return to camp (Draper 1975, 83, 85). Botswana !Kung men range more widely than women, but in a nightly debriefing around the campfire all members of the band are informed of the environmental conditions critical to survival. Thus, there is no knowledge of environmental or food resources that is available only to men by virtue of their travels. Women's travels expose them to the same information (Lee 1972).

Anthropologists disagree about whether women help in the hunt. The Botswana !Kung include women among those recruited to carry game back to camp (Lee 1972, 346), although the !Kung of South-West Africa rely solely on males for this work (Draper 1975, 88). Anthropologists further disagree about how long a hunt lasts. The !Kung of the inland Nyae Nyae region may be gone for several days in pursuit of antelope (Marshall 1965, 252), but those in Botswana typically return to camp each night (Lee 1972, 346). The length of absence from camp has important implications for the amount of time men and women spend together.

Greater agreement exists among anthropologists on other types of tasks shared by !Kung women and men. Men often help women gather mangetti nuts and tsi seeds during the day and collect firewood toward nightfall (Marshall 1965, 250, 256). Work typically considered women's, such as child care, carrying water, and building huts, is often performed by men (Draper 1975, 87, 92). Small animals, such as the leopard tortoise, are collected by both women and men for food (Lee 1972, 345).

More important than the division of labor among the !Kung, however, is the fact that relatively little labor had to be performed in traditional society. Among the Botswana !Kung, women work only two to three days per week, while men might hunt three days in a row and then not go out again for several weeks. In some camps, men of hunting age do not go out at all, and others are out only a few days a week (Lee 1972, 347). The net result of this variation in work schedules is that on any given day one-third to one-half of the adults are in camp instead of in a separate workplace (Draper 1975, 90). When in camp, men and women group together for talk. According to Lee, "The buzz of conversation is a constant background to the camp's activities: there is an endless flow of talk about gathering, hunting, the weather, food distribution, gift-giving, and scandal" (Lee 1972, 359).

Draper reports that men, women, and children sit together in small groups talking, joking, eating, and sharing tobacco, with no spatial or symbolic barriers to divide them. The primitive nature of the campsite has some influence on this intermingling, since the !Kung often do not construct grass huts (*scherms*) but sleep outdoors together (Draper 1975, 93, 83). There is no men's ceremonial hut among the !Kung, nor are there dwellings divided by gender, because often there are no dwellings of any type.

To the extent that status distinctions are possible in a society with so little surplus and almost no stratification system, !Kung women fare relatively well. Women retain control over the food they gather; it is up to them to distribute and cook food when they return to camp, with no interference from their husbands (Draper 1975, 84; Lee 1972, 348; Marshall 1965, 250, 254). This control of food is the equivalent of both control of property and control of labor, since the !Kung do not believe in private ownership of land (Lee 1972, 361; Marshall 1965, 267).

The few material items made and owned by each adult are the only source of inheritance in traditional nomadic society. If there is no eldest son, the goods are passed to a spouse or daughter. One form of ownership enjoyed by women is that of arrows. A woman can give or lend her arrow to a hunter, and if game is killed with that arrow, she has first rights to the meat (Marshall 1965, 253, 260).

Although headmen of territories are exclusively male among the !Kung, these chiefs have little power over the bands they head. There is no formal leadership, and the position rotates as groups move around. Neither are there councils or decision-making groups; individuals determine their own activities (Marshall 1965, 267). Domestic authority is thus a more meaningful measure of status among the !Kung than political participation. The autonomy required for nomadic survival is demonstrated within the household as in all aspects of !Kung life. Women discipline children without reference to the father's authority, and in fact children show fathers little of the deference associated with men as authority figures in other cultures (Draper 1975, 91–92). Fathers are not entitled to tell sons and daughters what to do (Lee 1972, 347). Wives have equal rights to divorce, and children always remain with their mothers when a marriage dissolves. In general, men do not expect obedience or subservience from women (Lee 1972, 359; Marshall 1965, 255).

The !Kung represent one of the least stratified of nonindustrial societies due to their lack of surplus, so one might expect a low degree of gender stratification. Yet, in contrast to hunters such as the Eskimo (also a society with little surplus), distinct spatial differences exist in the gender division of labor. Eskimo men are gone for protracted periods on whaling trips while women stay at home; the men have knowledge of the environment and women do not. By comparison, !Kung men and women range freely and share their common knowledge of the environment through frequent contact with one another in camp. This greater access to common knowledge through spatial proximity is associated with higher status for !Kung women.   **99**

Empirical Analysis

The HRAF data described earlier contain two variables that address the issue of the spatial segregation of labor: the presence of exclusively male work groups and the presence of exclusively female work groups. These two measures are at best proxy indicators of the spatial dimension of the division of labor since they reflect different tasks but only *imply* different settings for those tasks. The assumption underlying the use of these variables is that single-sex work groups involve the isolation of one group from another, and hence of one gender from another.

Approximately three-quarters of all nonindustrial societies sampled by Whyte (1978a) have exclusively male work groups, and approximately one-third report exclusively female work groups. The relationship between the presence of male and female groups is very strong (Gamma = .84). In other words, societies without male work groups also lack female work groups, and those with male work groups also have female work groups. The four-point index created by combining these two variables has been collapsed into a dichotomous variable indicating lesser and greater degrees of gender-segregated work.

Societies are approximately evenly divided by degree of segregated labor. Women's kinship power and control of labor and property are greater in societies with less segregated labor, while inheritance of property shows almost no association with segregated work. Nearly one-third (32 percent) of societies with less segregated labor are also those with the greatest kinship

Table 4.2 Distribution of Nonindustrial Societies by Presence of Spatially Segregated Labor and Women's Status

Measures of Women's Status		Percent of Societies with Segregated Labor	
		Lesser	Greater
TOTAL (N=66)		56%	44%
Power in kinship networks (N=66; Gamma = −.58)			
Least female power		11%	34%
Moderate female power		57	55
Greatest female power		32	10
		100%	99%
	X̄ value	2.22	1.76
Inheritance of property (N=50; Gamma = .08)			
Male predominance		26%	22%
Male preference		41	39
Equal treatment		26	35
Female preference		7	4
		100%	100%
	X̄ value	2.15	2.22
Control of labor and property (N=66; Gamma = −.17)			
Least female control		5%	7%
Less female control		19	21
More female control		65	69
Greatest female control		11	3
		100%	100%
	X̄ value	2.81	2.69

Source: Whyte's (1978a) Human Relations Area File data.

power for women, compared with one-tenth of societies with more segregated labor. Women are slightly more likely to control labor and property in societies with less segregated work (11 percent) than in those with greater segregation (3 percent). Average scores for kinship power and control of labor are higher in societies with less segregation.

Once again, power in kinship networks emerges as the type of status most strongly associated with spatial segregation. The ability to work together with men enhances women's status with members of a group external to the household unit. Contrary to theories proposed by Chafetz (1984) and Whyte (1978a, 101), the existence of separate work groups does not create collective solidarity conducive to economic power. Rather, greater integration of males and females in work groups is associated with women's greater control over the fruits of their own (and men's) labor. The lack of the anticipated relationship between inheritance and segregated work groups **101** suggests that transmission of durable goods may be insensitive to workplace segregation. These results indicate that knowledge about the typically most highly valued work in a society—that performed by men—is associated with greater kinship and economic power for women.

Conclusion

The gender division of labor in nonindustrial societies is accompanied by spatial separation of the sexes to varying degrees. In some societies, women and men perform completely different tasks in completely different places, such as when Eskimo men embark on long whaling expeditions and women stay near the hearth. Other societies are characterized by a mechanistic division of labor in which women and men share the same tasks in the same place, as when Bontoc men and women garden together. Between these two extremes fall a wide range of spatial work arrangements for men and women.

Examining the spatial division of labor in the context of gender stratification suggests that the greater the separation of men and women in subsistence tasks, the lower the status of women. Qualitative descriptions of five nonindustrial societies and quantitative analysis of cultures from the Human Relations Area Files support the hypothesized negative association between spatially segregated work and two measures of women's status. The exception is for the relationship between segregated work and inheritance of property.

It is now possible to summarize the analyses of all three measures of segregation and all three measures of women's status. Table 4.3 reports the

Table 4.3. Gamma Values for Relationships between Segregation and Women's Status

Measures of Women's Status	Measures of Segregation (Gamma Values)		
	Dwelling	Men's Hut	Labor
Women's kinship power	−.59	−.24	−.58
Female inheritance rights	−.24	−.29	.08
Female control of labor and property	.20	−.23	−.17

Source: Tables 2.1, 3.1, and 4.2.

Gamma values for each of the bivariate relationships reported in chapters 2 through 4.

Seven of a possible nine associations are in the predicted negative direction. The strongest relationships exist between women's kinship power and segregated dwellings and work groups. The most consistent associations exist for presence of a men's hut and all forms of women's status.

To discover whether the incorporation of other factors might affect the bivariate associations, adjusted means were computed for each measure of women's status taking the following independent variables into account: male contribution to domestic tasks, proportionate female contribution to subsistence, postmarital residence location, and economic base (i.e., horticultural vs. hunting-gathering dominance). Each of these variables represents an explanation for gender stratification reviewed in chapter 1. Table 4.4 presents the results of these calculations (see appendix A for an explanation of the method).

Controlling for other variables produces the predicted negative association between segregation and women's status in all but one of the relationships. In every instance except that between segregated dwellings and women's control of labor, the adjusted means in the absence of segregation are higher than the adjusted means in the presence of segregation. In other words, women's status is higher in the absence of segregation.

The positive association between segregated dwellings and women's control of labor is not reversed by additional explanatory factors. Its persistence

Table 4.4. Comparison of Unadjusted and Adjusted Means of Women's Status Scores by Type of Segregation

Type of Segregation	Measures of Women's Status					
	Mean Kinship Power		Mean Inheritance Rights		Mean Control of Labor	
	Unadjusted	Adjusted	Unadjusted	Adjusted	Unadjusted	Adjusted
Segregated dwelling						
Absent	2.08	2.09	2.30	2.20	2.82	2.82
Present	1.65	1.64	2.06	2.16	2.94	2.93
Ceremonial men's hut						
Absent	2.03	2.05	2.29	2.22	2.88	2.86
Present	1.86	1.88	1.94	1.96	2.68	2.69
Division of labor						
Less segregation	2.22	2.21	2.15	2.36	2.81	2.88
Greater segregation	1.76	1.79	2.22	1.88	2.69	2.58

Source: Whyte's (1978a) Human Relations Area File data for measures of women's status and segregated labor; sources cited in appendix B for data on dwellings and men's huts.

suggests that segregated dwellings do not remove women from knowledge of economic issues to the same extent as other types of segregation. In fact, separate spheres within dwellings in nonindustrial societies allow women slightly greater control of their labor.

The consistency of these relationships is notable since there are varying degrees of association among the three types of segregation and among the three measures of women's status (see table A.2). The ability of the majority of relationships to emerge as predicted, in spite of the diversity in both independent and dependent variables, suggests the merits of pursuing spatial arrangements as an avenue for insight into gender stratification.

PART TWO

Spatial Institutions in the United States

While the last three chapters have been devoted to comparative analyses of nonindustrial societies, the emphasis shifts now to an examination of spatial institutions in the United States. The family, education, and the labor force are analyzed for changes in their association with gender stratification since the nineteenth century.

The history of gendered spaces and women's status in the United States is shaped by this country's development as a capitalist economy. As Marxist feminists point out, a combination of economic structure (capitalism) and ideology (patriarchy) shape gender relations in advanced industrial societies today. Although gender segregation and inequalities exist outside capitalism, as the previous chapters have demonstrated, the organization of labor characteristic of capitalism contributes to separate spheres for women and men which interact with separate spheres of class.

The primary form of gender segregation created by capitalism is the separation of home from workplace. Removing production from the home, and simultaneously identifying paid work as something only men did for a "family wage," guaranteed the creation of predominantly masculine work spaces and predominantly feminine domestic spaces during the nineteenth century. The masculine production of labor was thus removed spatially from the feminine reproduction of labor. The "Cult of True Womanhood" (Welter 1966) encouraged women to aspire to the home-based virtues of a patriarchal ideology. With their energies focused on home and family, women had little reason to question their exclusion from the public spheres of formal education and the labor force.

Capitalism also contributes to gendered spaces *within* the workplace. By separating tasks into different places for greatest efficiency, and by defining those tasks by gender, the production of labor reproduces spatial separation by gender. When industries place women in some rooms doing poorly paid "women's work" and men in other rooms doing more highly paid "men's work," the transmission of technical skills from men to women (necessary for women's promotion and higher pay) is not possible. At the turn of the twentieth century, the telephone company created operators' jobs for women and repair and technical jobs for men. Female operators sat together in a central room, while male repairmen worked outside the building. Operators were paid less than repairmen (J. W. Scott 1982). When AT&T finally began to desegregate its workplace in the 1970s, women were assigned jobs that eventually were lost to automation (Hacker 1989). Thus, the female spaces soon became nongendered, automated spaces.

Minority and working-class status typically exacerbate the consequences of gender in dwellings, schools, and the workplace. Slavery took a particularly heavy toll on black women, who often spent more time in their masters' domestic space than in their own (Fox-Genovese 1988). Schools were segregated by race and social class throughout the nineteenth and well into the twentieth century. Workplaces often are segregated by both race and gender in ways that penalize black women most severely (Kessler-Harris 1982; Milkman 1987).

The remaining chapters document the relationship between gendered spaces in homes, schools, and the workplace and women's status; distinctions by race and class are variations to the central theme of gender segregation. Chapter 5 examines declining architectural segregation in homes, and chapter 6 looks at the largely successful reduction in both geographic and architectural segregation of American schools. Chapters 7 and 8 review segregation in the American workplace, starting with women's entry into the labor force in the nineteenth century and ending with observations about contemporary work spaces. Chapter 9 ends the book with suggestions about "degendering" spaces.

108

5

From Parlor to Great Room

Domestic architecture . . . illuminates norms concerning family life, sex roles, community relations, and social equality. Of course, architecture itself does not directly determine how people act or how they see themselves and others. Yet the associations a culture establishes at any particular time between a "model" or typical house and a notion of the model family do encourage certain roles and assumptions.

—Gwendolyn Wright, *Moralism and the Model Home*

Architectural historian Gwendolyn Wright (1980, 1) proposes that homes serve as metaphors, "suggesting and justifying social categories, values, and relations." Spatial and social relations mutually reinforce one another, and if status differences are engendered within the home, they are likely to be expressed outside it also.

Dwellings reflect the cultural values as well as the technological and geographic characteristics of the societies in which they are built. While the external form may be dictated by availability and cost of materials, climate, or topographical limitations, the internal form is dictated by a combination of religious, cultural, social, and political traditions (Hillier and Hanson 1984; Lawrence 1982, 1984; Rapoport 1969). Houses are shaped not just by materials and tools, but by ideas, values, and norms. They should not be regarded simply as utilitarian structures, but as "designs for living" (Corlin 1982, 173).

An ancient Hindu building manual, for example, listed rules governing the placement of courtyards, guest rooms, male and female quarters, and kitchens based on an anthropomorphic analogy of the dwelling and the human body. This manual, the *Manasara*, is followed today in Andhra Pradesh by craftsmen constructing bamboo housing (P. Oliver 1987, 166). In Victorian British country houses, separate wings for the servants were created to enable the gentry to minimize family contact with the lower classes. The larger the estate, the greater the specialization of rooms and the more telling of social customs of the day: in 1870 the grand mansion Kinmel had a room devoted exclusively to the ironing of newspapers (so the ink would not come off on the reader's hands) (Franklin 1981, 89).

This chapter examines the changing nature of American housing design and its relationship to gender stratification. Because early American history is intertwined with its British origins, I begin with an account of ideal elite British housing of the nineteenth century.

British Precedents

At the height of industrialization in Great Britain, when English workers were living in "cruel habitations" in urban slums (Gauldie 1974), the gentry were living on country estates in dwellings more closely resembling hotels than homes. These mansions were not typical British housing but represented the ideal to which both poor and wealthy aspired. The ideal reflected the class hierarchy that dictated separation between master and servants, parents and children, and men and women. Just as wealthy traditional Islamic families are more able to enforce purdah than poorer families who cannot afford many rooms, wealthy Victorian families were able to "control intimacy" in the home more easily than their less affluent neighbors.

112

The "gentleman's country house" was an architecturally nostalgic attempt to recapture an agrarian social order. The large estate presented the image of an upper class whose wealth came from landholdings rather than business investments (Franklin 1981; Girouard 1979). As such, the country house represents the embodiment of eighteenth-century ideals made possible through nineteenth-century industrialized technology. It also represents a case study of the relationship between spatially segregated housing and gender stratification.

The Gentleman's Country House. The typical country estate employed numerous servants (anywhere from eight to forty) and provided housing, schooling, and a chapel on the grounds for those servants. The house itself was organized into distinct quarters for the husband and wife, guests, children, and servants. The most essential of these divisions was that between servants and everyone else. The servants' wing was architecturally separated from the main block of the house in ways that reinforced social distinctions: it was positioned to be as unobtrusive as possible from the main block and was built lower so that "anyone could see at a glance the one part of the edifice as superior and the other inferior" (Franklin 1981, 86). Messages of social inferiority were conveyed by the interior design as well. None of the five bathrooms in John Walter's Bearwood estate was for the servants (Franklin 1981, 114).

Each room in the country house was designed for a single purpose, and each territory (except the nursery) was divided into male and female areas

(Franklin 1981; Girouard 1979). Architectural historians of the Victorian era draw analogies between industrial society and the ideal country house: "In an age when government was organized into departments, the middle class into professionals, science into different disciplines, and convicts into separate cells, country house life was neatly divided up into separate parcels" (Girouard 1979, 28). "The essence of Victorian planning was segregation and specialization. . . . The image of a great household was . . . of a giant, well-oiled machine running on so many cogs and the highest possible praise was to say 'It all ran like clockwork'" (Franklin 1981, 39). The need for **113** careful orchestration resulted in part from the large numbers of family, guests, and servants. Fifty people in residence was not unusual, and at its busiest a country house might contain three times that number (Girouard 1979, 28).

One way to manage all these people smoothly was to assign them to certain rooms at certain times of the day. When architect Robert Kerr published *The Gentleman's House; or How to Plan English Residences* in 1871, he included no fewer than twenty-seven necessary rooms, not counting main halls or galleries (Kerr [1871] 1972). Each of the rooms was described by the sex for whom it was intended as well as by its appropriate siting (kitchens on the northeast; morning rooms to the southeast) and the appropriate furniture arrangement (the bed with its left side to the bedroom window and its foot toward the fireplace). The drawing room was a "Lady's Apartment" to which the women "withdrew" after dinner, while the men had cigars in the smoking room or played a game in the billiards room. Among Kerr's recommendations for the appearance of different rooms were these instructions for the drawing room: "The *character* to be always aimed at in a Drawing-room is especial cheerfulness, refinement of elegance, and what is called lightness as opposed to massiveness. Decoration and furniture ought therefore to be comparatively delicate; in short, the rule in everything is this . . . to be entirely *ladylike*" (Kerr [1871] 1972, 107; emphasis in original).

Only two other rooms in addition to the drawing room were identified as feminine: the boudoir, a private room adjoining the bedroom that men never entered without special invitation, and the breakfast or morning room. The morning room was open to guests and family of both sexes. The drawing room was open to men at certain times: it was the staging area for the promenade into the dining room, and gentlemen eventually joined the ladies there after dinner. Thus, only one room out of the twenty-seven described by Kerr was intended strictly for women: the boudoir. By contrast, six rooms were identified as men's rooms by Kerr: the library, billiard room, gentleman's room (for business transactions), study, smoking room, and gentleman's odd room (where young gentlemen could "do as they like") (Kerr [1871] 1972, 130). These rooms were less likely to be open to women than women's rooms were to be open to men. Women hesitated before entering the library and would never be expected in the smoking room since ladies did not smoke.

114

In some houses a billiard room, smoking room, gun room, and study would have their own bathrooms and cloakrooms, functioning as a "gentlemen's suite" effectively removed from the women's end of the house (Franklin 1981, 56, 59). Ostensibly the billiard room was distanced from the rest of the house because of the noise, and the smoking room because of the smell of cigars, but Girouard acknowledged that the placement of such rooms probably resulted "as much because the men liked a sanctum to retire to . . . a comfortable little male territory" (Girouard 1979, 35). Instances of women playing billiards and invading the smoking and gun rooms were reported toward the end of the century (Franklin 1981, 61), but attitudes and behavior that might vary from house to house did not erase the ideology behind the original design of the rooms.

Concern about limiting contact between the sexes extended beyond the main block of the house. Servants' quarters were strictly segregated by gender. Often the maids slept in the attic and the butlers in the basement. To insure that male and female servants would not tarry over chance meetings, separate men's and women's staircases were built. The butler's room was placed strategically for monitoring the men servants, and the housekeeper's room was centrally located in order to supervise female servants. The servant's hall was the only place male and female servants could spend time together and entertain family and friends (Franklin 1981, 95–101).

Diagrams of the three floors of the Bearwood estate (built between 1865 and 1874 for John Walter III, owner of *The Times*) illustrate the epitome of Victorian country-house planning for segregation by class and gender. "Men's stairs" and "Women's stairs" were used by servants, while "Gentlemen's stairs," "Bachelors' stairs," and "Young ladies' stairs" were used by family and guests. Hallways and rooms also were identified by type of occupant. Bearwood was variously cited as "a showpiece of Victorian specialization and segregation" (Franklin 1981, 146) and "a sociological freak rather than an architectural triumph," representing the zenith of High Victorian domestic planning (Crook 1972, xv).

The design of the country estate was tailored to reinforce appropriate gender role behavior (Girouard 1979, 16). The "increasingly large and sacrosanct male domain" in Victorian estate houses was one result of Victorian chivalry; women had to be protected from "scandalous" talk of business or politics. "Male preserves were the natural result of this 'remember-there-are-ladies-present-sir' attitude" (Girouard 1979, 34). Proper manners, buttressed by spatial segregation, prevented both upper- and lower-class women from hearing discussions that might have been useful to them in acquiring public status. Just as traditional Mongolians kept sacred books on the male side of the tent, the Victorian gentry kept economic and political talk in the smoking rooms and libraries of the gentleman's house.

British Women's Status in the Nineteenth Century. The clearest statement of women's status in Great Britain in the nineteenth century was made by John Stuart Mill ([1869] 1970) in *The Subjection of Women.* Likening a married woman's status to that of a slave, Mill chronicled her legal lack of rights to children, earnings, or property. Although divorce was legally possible, the expense involved in obtaining a court decree made it prohibitive for the majority of women. Without divorce, a woman had few options: "If she leaves her husband, she can take nothing with her, neither her children nor anything which is rightfully her own. If he chooses, he can compel her to return, by law, or by physical force; or he may content himself with seizing for his own use anything which she may earn, or which may be given to her by her relatives" (Mill [1869] 1970, 32). Mill acknowledged that women's legal status was more grim than their actual treatment, and that if married life were all that laws alone predicted, "society would be a hell upon earth" (Mill [1869] 1970, 33).

English women gained economic rights before political rights. The Married Women's Property Act of 1870 made a woman's earnings her own, and the Married Women's Property Act of 1882 granted control of property. These two laws overturned the concept of coverture, by which husband and

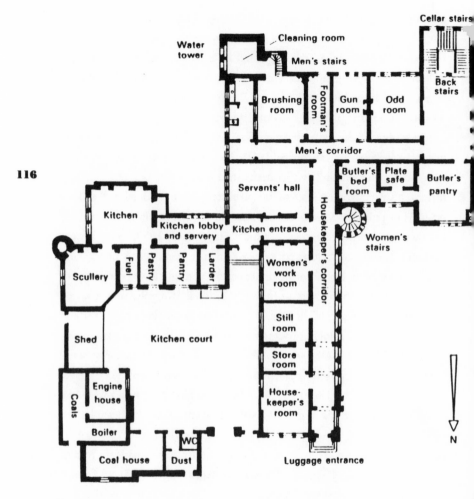

Fig. 5.1. The ground floor of Bearwood has a "gentlemen's suite" of gun and deed rooms, odd room, billiard room, and libraries; the "men's corridor" and "butler's

wife legally were identified as one person and the wife's property was controlled by the husband. Coverture had been used to deny women the vote and prevent them from holding public office, because the assumption was that wives would be represented by their husbands. Although the Victorian era ended without the vote for women, earlier economic legislative reforms laid the groundwork for passage of female suffrage in 1918 (Shanley 1986, 64, 72, 74).

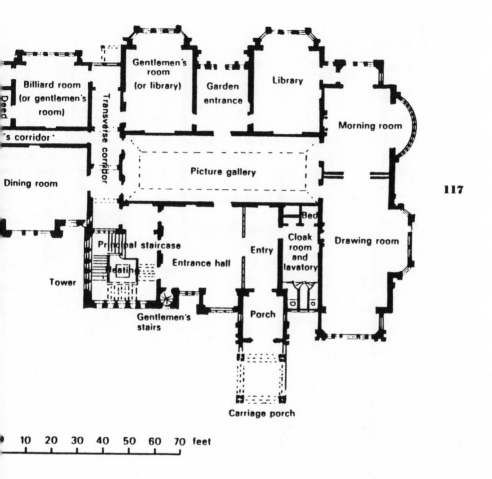

corridor" connect these rooms. Reproduced from Franklin (1981, 143) by permission of Norman Franklin.

American Housing Design

Housing for the urban elite in nineteenth-century America was modeled after that of the British gentry. Plantations of the rural elite in the South approximated as closely as possible, given the region's agricultural economic base, housing of the British gentry. The history of housing from the beginning of the century until its end reflects an increasing tendency toward

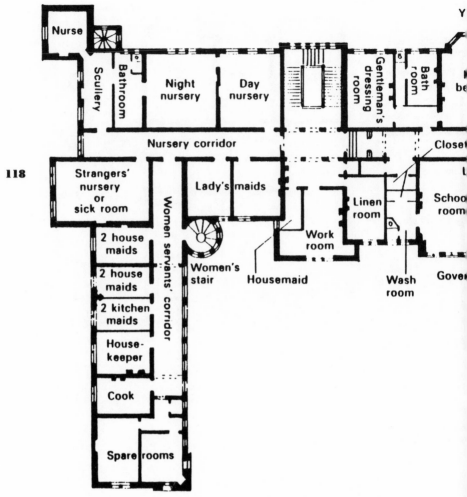

Fig. 5.2. The first floor of Bearwood was a feminine space consisting of boudoir, nur-series, and maids' rooms; the ground and first floors were connected by separate

gender integration and greater emphasis on egalitarianism rather than hier-archy. Contemporary pattern books at the turn of the century identified masculine and feminine rooms; by the end of the nineteenth century, these distinctions had largely disappeared.

The Southern Plantation. The institution of slavery provides a notable instance in which racial distinctions *within the dwelling* are relevant. Slave-holding women often used the phrase "my family, white and black" to

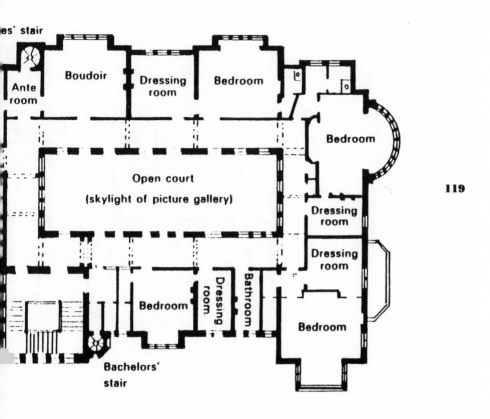

es' stair

Ante room

Boudoir

Dressing room

Bedroom

Bedroom

Open court
(skylight of picture gallery)

Dressing room

Dressing room

Bedroom

Dressing room

Bathroom

Bedroom

Bachelors' stair

119

women's and men's staircases. Reproduced from Franklin (1981, 144) by permission of Norman Franklin.

represent all members of the plantation household (Fox-Genovese 1988, 100). Thus, the antebellum South contained dwellings in which race intersected with gender to reflect and reproduce the gender stratification system.

Although the Southern rural elite shared the British ideology of women's proper place, they had neither the wealth nor the technology to create gendered spaces within their homes. But in its emphasis on distinctions between masters and servants, the antebellum Southern plantation closely

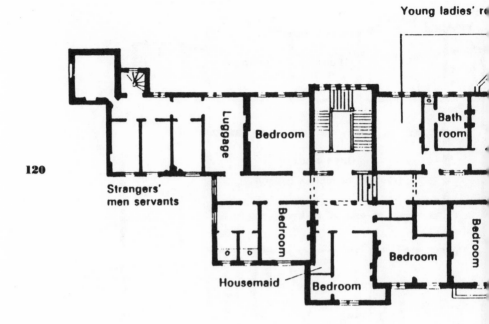

Fig. 5.3. The second floor of bedrooms at Bearwood was accessible by a "young ladies' stair" and a "bachelors' stair." Reproduced from Franklin (1981, 145) by permission of Norman Franklin.

resembled the British country gentleman's house. There are other similarities between the British and southern gentry's experience in the nineteenth century. First, plantations did not represent the "typical" housing of the era, but an idealized form available only to the slaveholding wealthy. Second, southern planters often housed large numbers of people and entertained even more. Mr. King, of Liberty Hall plantation in the Cumberland Mountains, regularly fed thirty to forty people (not including slaves); the number was larger when travelers stopped by (Fox-Genovese 1988, 105). Finally, rural southern gentry faced the dilemma of housing servants in ways that kept them under supervision (Fox-Genovese 1988, 151).

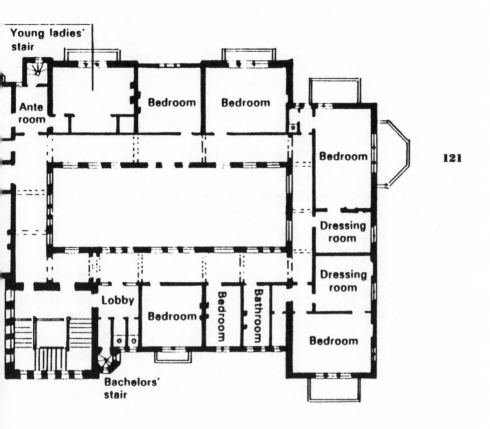

Southern planters solved the housing problem by placing slaves in cabins separate from the main house. A typical plantation consisted of "nearly as many roofs as rooms," with the master's house in the center surrounded by slave quarters and such outbuildings as the kitchen and smokehouse. Many of the "big houses" of the masters were modest, having few rooms and fewer luxuries. But the slave quarters were even cruder: Slave cabins typically consisted of a single room about sixteen by eighteen feet. Under the best of circumstances, they would have real floors, fireplaces, and windows; in the worst case, slaves might sleep in a kitchen or shed (Fox-Genovese 1988, 106, 149–50).

Women's status in the antebellum South was heavily dependent on their race and class. The prevailing ideology for wealthy white women included the graciousness, fragility, deference to men, and dedication to idle pursuits portrayed by the character of Scarlett O'Hara in *Gone with the Wind*. Black women had status only as the property of white slaveholders. Far from being protected from harsh realities, slave women were expected to work inside the big house and often in the fields. When Sojourner Truth proclaimed that she had "ploughed and planted, and gathered into barns. . . . And ain't I a **122** woman?" (Schneir 1972, 94), she identified one of the distinctions dividing women in the antebellum South.

Class divisions were added to racial differences as a means of distinguishing among southern women. A southern "lady" was not just a woman who happened to be more wealthy than others; she was white and had a privileged social position. The language of the day reinforced these distinctions: black females were called "women," while white females were called "ladies" (Fox-Genovese 1988, 202).

Cottage Residences. The widely read book *Cottage Residences*, published by popular landscaper/architect Andrew Jackson Downing in 1842, reproduced small-scale adaptations of Victorian, Gothic, Italianate, rustic, and bracketed styles of housing for middle-class Americans. *Cottage Residences*, along with *Treatise on the Theory and Practice of Landscape Gardening* (1841) and *The Architecture of Country Houses* (1850) went through dozens of printings in the next twenty years and established Downing as a codifier of the "aesthetic theory of the new movement" in American housing design (Clark 1986, 16).

Prosperity and industrialization had begun to create a middle class that could afford larger homes than the two-room frame structures occupied by colonial and eighteenth-century American households. At the same time, since the household was no longer the major economic unit of production, Americans felt that family life was threatened by the transfer of its traditional functions outside the home. A proliferation of books published in the first half of the nineteenth century championed the cult of domesticity as a stabilizer of the social order: William Alcott's *The Young Wife* (1838) and *The Young Husband* ([1839] 1972) were soon followed by Catharine Beecher's *Treatise on Domestic Economy* (1842).

Each of these books glorified the wife's role in creating a calm and peaceful retreat for her family. Downing's *Victorian Cottage Residences* helped her do that by carefully stipulating the proper placement of rooms and furnishings. His design for "A Cottage in the Pointed, or Tudor Style" specified that the parlor should "afford some scope for the 'faire ladye' to exercise her taste in a simple, elegant, and harmonious style of fitting and furnishing," while "there is no portion of the house which, to a man fond of . . . good books, is more peculiarly the sanctum or own room than the library" (Downing [1873] 1981, 51, 53). The library might also double as an office for the **123** "master of the house."

The strong American belief in the power of architecture to shape lives cannot be underestimated. Order within the household was expected to create order in society. Other plan books such as Gervase Wheeler's *Homes for the People in Suburb and Country* (1855) and Orson Squire Fowler's *A Home for All* (1856) stressed that each room in the house should have a clearly defined role and function. Libraries should be at the back of the house with a separate entrance so gentlemen with a "professional occupation or literary taste" could come and go without disturbing the family. The parlor, on the other hand, was a woman's space also open to outsiders. It should be "accessible to visitors" and display "elegance and the appearance of lady habitancy." The dining room was specifically designed for gender contact, but the upstairs was generally a private space for women and children (Clark 1986, 40). Ideal family life at mid-century was promoted by reformers, feminists, architects, and plan book authors as "a benevolent hierarchy, united by ties of obedience and responsibility . . . the instrument of reform for the nation" (Clark 1986, 37).

Plan books published toward the end of the century (the Palliser brothers' *Model Homes* and *American Cottage Homes* in 1878 and Robert Shoppell's *Modern Houses* in 1887) reflected the last vestiges of interior gender segregation. Designs by Shoppell and the Pallisers included libraries and parlors, although the physical barriers between rooms were diminishing in importance.

In trying to achieve social order through architecture, nineteenth-century Americans built into their homes a certain amount of gender segregation that both reflected and perpetuated men's higher status. At mid-century,

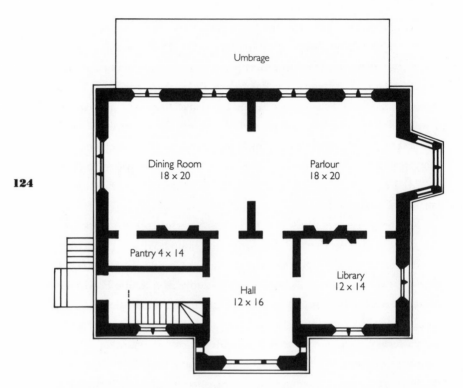

Fig. 5.4. The simple Downing cottage distinguished between the parlor for ladies and the library for gentlemen. Reproduced from Downing ([1873] 1981, 51) by permission of Dover Publications, Inc.

American women did not have property or voting rights, and very few had college educations. Segregation in the home, specifically in terms of a male domain of office and library with a separate entrance, removed women from the interaction with men that might have exposed them to information related to their public status.

By the end of the nineteenth century, population and urban growth following the Civil War opened up the housing market. Architects, plan book writers, builders, and social reformers became engaged in a struggle to define the middle-class family and the middle-class home (Wright 1980). The new ideal included less commitment to family hierarchy and greater emphasis on personal taste: "Although the mid-century ideal of the family had stressed the separation of public and private, the protective role of the household, and the importance of order and hierarchy in domestic life, the

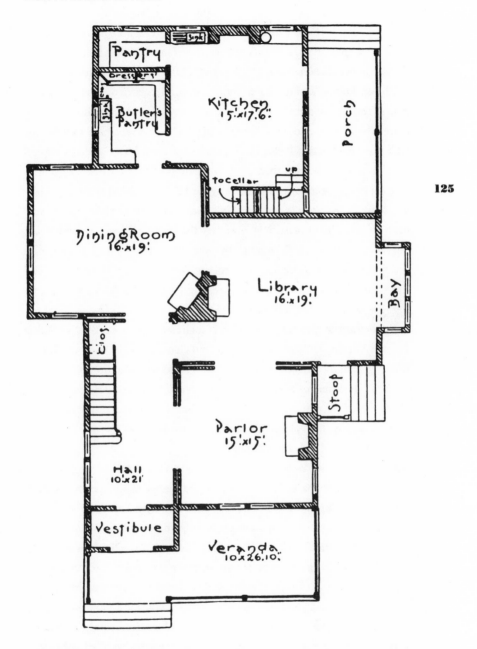

Fig. 5.5. Shoppell considered this a good house for a doctor, since the separate entrance to the library allowed it to double as an office. Reproduced from Shoppell ([1887] 1978, 31) by permission of Antiquity Reprints.

emphasis in the 1870s and 1880s on creativity and self-expression placed a new stress on individual talents, the display of material possessions, and the *equality of household members*" (Clark 1986, 108; emphasis added).

The egalitarian family created more independence for women. A clergyman's treatise toward the end of the century advocated the home as one place where "man and woman may meet and each freely, fully exercise the rights of each" (Clark 1986, 110). Even home furnishings reflected a trend toward more egalitarian themes, as an analysis of Sears, Roebuck catalogs reveals: fashionable parlor furniture in the 1870s consisted of a sofa, a large gentleman's armchair, a smaller lady's chair, and four straight-backed visitor's chairs. The armchairs symbolized the implicit hierarchy within the family. The Sears 1897 catalog, by contrast, offered parlor furniture in groups of a sofa, three chairs, and a rocker. Both the man's "Easy Chair" and the woman's rocker were the same size, implying that the family was becoming less hierarchical (Clark 1986, 125).

By the turn of the century, architects such as Frank Lloyd Wright, Walter Burnley Griffin, William Gray Purcell, and George Elmslie had transformed housing design by rejecting the complexity and specialization of Victorian models. The interiors as well as the exteriors of houses underwent a radical change. Designs eliminated the elaborate entrance halls and front and back parlors and in their place substituted the living room for more informal lifestyles (Clark 1986, 88, 132).

The Bungalow Years. The years between 1890 and the beginning of World War I were marked by extremely rapid change in popular architectural taste. In less than two decades, middle-class Victorian homes and family life were transformed from the ideal to "architectural atrocities" based on the "craze of imitation and deceit" (Clark 1986, 132). The intersection of numerous events and changes set the stage for Americans' receptiveness to rapid architectural change: fertility had declined so there were fewer children per household; labor-saving devices had altered the amount and type of housekeeping work; the country was becoming increasingly urbanized; national communications and transportation systems reduced provincialism; and consumerism was burgeoning. When all these changes coincided with the depression of 1893—the worst of the century—the stage was set for radical change (Clark 1986, 143).

The internal layout of Victorian homes, as well as their size and exterior appearance, came under attack. Parlors and libraries became superfluous. Contemporary issues of the *Ladies' Home Journal* and Gustav Stickley's *The Craftsman* began to display model floorplans in which "a pleasant living room with a cozy fireplace, bookcases, and a cupboard or two would serve the combined functions of library, parlor, and sitting room" (Clark 1986, 144–45).

As architects were simplifying housing design in line with aesthetic and technological principles, they were also reducing gender segregation. By bringing books into shared women's and men's space, they were setting the stage for (and reflecting) women's changing status. By the beginning of the twentieth century, American women could attend coeducational colleges, own property, and vote. Concomitantly, the middle-class ideal home was minimizing the segregation of women and men by combining previously single-purpose, gender-typed rooms into multipurpose, sexually integrated rooms.

Much of the new spatial integration was necessitated by rising construction costs. The "simple, honest" lines advocated by Gustav Stickley for the popular turn-of-the-century bungalow dovetailed with the need to keep building prices down. The expenses of materials, new plumbing, heating, and wiring, and increased land values meant that single-family homes had to be smaller than their Victorian predecessors. For example, a $3,000 house in 1905 had approximately 1,000 to 1,500 square feet of space, whereas a comparably priced house in the 1880s had 2,000 to 2,500 square feet. Insistence on the bungalow as "a distinctively American architecture" with "natural and organic" characteristics coalesced into a "minimalist aesthetic" that cost less to build than the earlier Victorian style (Clark 1986, 162).

The classic bungalow was a one-story structure with a front porch whose roof formed an integral line with the house; models with one-and-a-half or two stories were called semi-bungalows. It was advertised as a "democratic" building that renounced Victorian formalities. Thus, the interior became a "miracle of simplicity and efficiency": "The living-room and dining-room are practically one, so that you may see the cheery fire crackling in the hearth at meals" (Clark 1986, 173). The bungalow came to be associated with an informal lifestyle linked to the outdoors and conducive to good health. The small size of the home also encouraged family members' participation in outside activities. The appeal and affordability of the bungalow were insured when Sears and Montgomery Ward began to manufacture prefabricated models. By 1910 the bungalow had become the all-American family house (Clark 1986, 183).

Usonian Homes. By the time soldiers returned from World War II, the ranch house had replaced the bungalow as the most popular American model home. Just as the bungalow was cheaper to build than the Victorian, **128** the ranch cost less than the bungalow. Levitt was able to sell an 800-square-foot ranch to returning veterans for the sale price of $7,900 ($56 per month); he sold nearly 11,000 such houses between 1946 and 1950 (Clark 1986, 221–22).

The one-story rectangular box with a picture window carried the interior informality of the bungalow one step further. Most rooms in the modern ranch could serve multiple purposes: a study-guest room, living-dining room, kitchen-laundry. This was also the era of the "family room"—a new place that *Parents* magazine defined as the "don't-say-no" room for children and teenagers (Clark 1986, 215). Popular magazines stressed the joys of consumerism and suburban family life.

These newer styles were influenced by Frank Lloyd Wright, whose career began in the early 1890s in Chicago. In 1936 Wright designed his first "Usonian" home, representing his ideal for American society. The name "Usonian" was attributed by Wright to Samuel Butler's novel *Erewhon*, but the word did not in fact appear there. The term was used by Wright in conjunction with "organic" to describe his vision of social reform and the way it would occur naturally through architectural practice (Sergeant 1975, 16). The Usonian home, twenty-five of which were eventually built, was characterized by the blending of multiple purposes into flowing rooms: "If [the Prairie house] had weakened the identification of particular rooms with particular purposes, the Usonian house did away with certain rooms altogether, uniting more family activities in one place. The 'living room' in a Wright house was apt to be used for eating, relaxation, cooking, play, entertainment, cultural enrichment, and, with patio appended, for virtually all other family functions" (Twombly 1979, 258).

By the 1950s Wright's designs epitomized the ideal American home. The

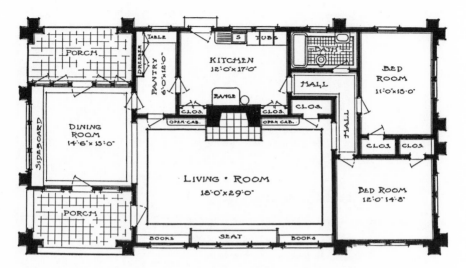

Fig. 5.6. By the early twentieth century, simple bungalows like this one designed by Gustav Stickley had eliminated separate parlors and libraries. Reproduced from Stickley ([1909] 1979, 37) by permission of Gibbs Smith Publisher.

November 1955 issue of *House Beautiful* was devoted entirely to Wright's work. One of the feature articles, titled "Wright's Contribution: A Life of Beauty Equal to the Great Concept of America," noted that the architect had "shown Americans how to match the new sense of man's [*sic*] inner spaciousness, of the inner grandeur and nobility which mark the people of a democracy, with buildings and ways of life that are worthy of it and strongly encourage it" (*House Beautiful* 1955, 236).

One of the designs that inspired this prose (strongly reminiscent of nineteenth-century reformer Catharine Beecher's belief in the ability of architecture to shape lives) was the Exhibition House displayed at New York City's Guggenheim Museum. Its caption applauded it as a "new kind of house in which back and front disappear, all rooms are equally handsome, equally comfortable, and with a new sense of flowing spaciousness" (*House Beautiful* 1955, 266).

Contemporary Floorplans. American women today do not spend as much time in the home as their grandmothers did. Their entry into colleges and the labor force has placed more than half of all women in the public sphere with men. Whereas nonindustrial societies are characterized by the eco-

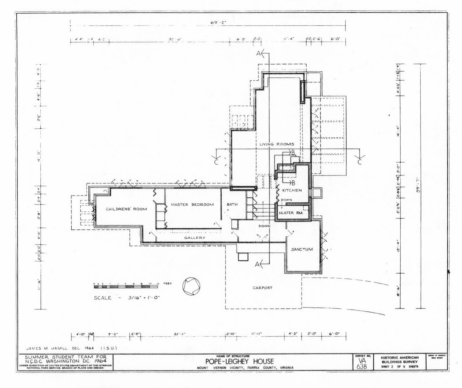

Fig. 5.7. Frank Lloyd Wright's Usonian design minimized the use of interior walls and maximized access to exterior space, as in the Pope-Leighey house built in Fairfax County, Virginia, in 1940. Library of Congress.

nomic activity of both sexes within the household, industrial society is increasingly characterized by the economic activity of both sexes *outside* the household. The shift from a household to a market-based economy has meant a shift out of the dwelling and into the public space of factories and offices. There are now a substantial number of hours in the day when neither men, women, nor children occupy the dwelling. Perhaps at no other time in history have as many dwellings remained as empty for as many hours.

What is the interior layout of these largely unoccupied dwellings? The trend toward multipurpose open areas has continued, so that new model homes now boast great rooms that replace traditional distinctions between living rooms and eating areas. The master bedroom now flows into a doorless bathroom, and recreation rooms open to outdoor decks and patios.

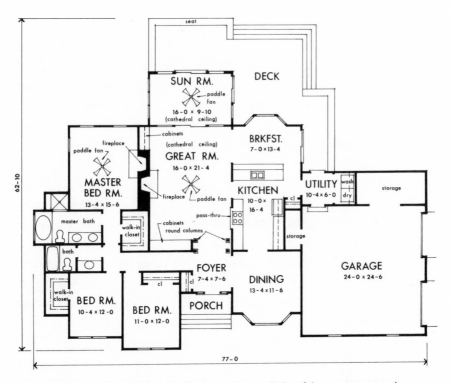

Fig. 5.8. This contemporary floorplan illustrates the popularity of the great room and its connections to the kitchen, sunroom, and breakfast room. Courtesy of Donald A. Gardner, Architect, Inc., Greenville, S.C.

By the late 1970s wealthy Americans who could afford to hire an architect were encouraged to engage in a mutual "pattern language" of design to specify all the possible uses for interior (and exterior) space. This design language theoretically allows architect and client to communicate about patterns of spatial use rather than relying on traditional names to identify rooms. Thus, the living-dining room becomes "the common area contain[ing] those functions that the children and the adults share: eating together, sitting together, games . . . whatever captures their needs for shared territory" (Alexander, Ishakawa, and Silverstein 1977, 383). The pattern language still advocates separate places for parents and children (and even for men and women), but instead of being isolated from each other, the realms are perceived as integrally connected.

More emphasis is now placed on the evolution of design through use.

Alexander and colleagues advise the reader that the patterns described in *A Pattern Language* are "hypotheses . . . all tentative, all free to evolve under the impact of new experience and observation" (Alexander, Ishakawa, and Silverstein 1977, xv). Such guidelines diverge significantly from Robert Kerr's principles of a "Gentleman's House," with its "elements of accommodation and arrangement . . . always the same" and based on the "unvarying . . . domestic habits of refined persons" throughout England (Kerr [1871] 1972, 63).

132   Whereas Victorian housing reflected a concern that each function and member of the household have a designated place, housing designs of the late twentieth century reflect the concern that no function or family member be limited to a particular space. Popular magazines such as *Metropolitan Home* and *House Beautiful* encourage readers to design large kitchens so that everyone—family and guests—can participate in meal preparation. An advertisement for Armstrong floors in the March 1988 issue of *Metropolitan Home* displayed a "kitchen suite" combining cooking and dining areas opening onto two artists' studios, "offering guests a peek at work in progress." The new plan was touted as a "very creative transformation of what once was a conventional kitchen, unused breezeway, and extra garage space."

Even the most specialized and private of all rooms has been expanded beyond its original single purpose. The winner of the 1987 National Kitchen and Bath Association Design Contest was a remodeled bathroom that included a sauna, steam shower, whirlpool bath, exercise equipment, and stereo system. At 340 square feet, this award-winning suite equaled nearly half the total area of an entire Levittown home for World War II veterans. A content analysis of housing plans appearing in *Better Homes and Gardens* for the past forty years documents the significant increase in size and number of amenities in master bath "retreats," at the same time that kitchen spaces have become less enclosed (Hasell and Peatross 1990).

New housing forms reflect changing family ideals and with them new ideas of women's and men's proper places. Emphasis on family rooms and master bedroom suites in magazines illustrates the decreasing force of the older ideals of separate male and female spheres. Instead of the nineteenth-century

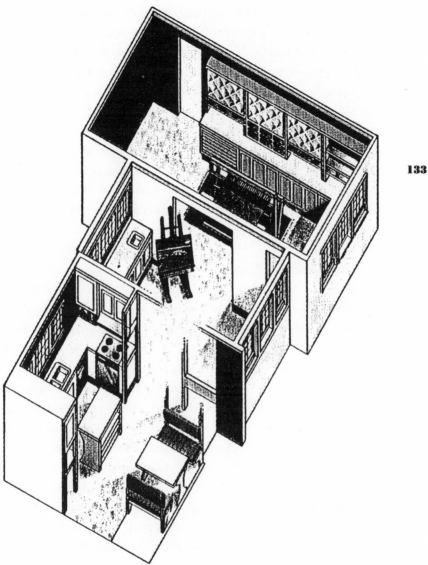

Fig. 5.9. "Think of it as three living spaces artfully united by an Armstrong floor" is the text that accompanied this illustration of a converted kitchen, breezeway, and partial garage that were made into a "kitchen suite." Reproduced from *Metropolitan Home* (March 1988) by permission of Armstrong World Industries, Inc.

view of specialized spaces for each family member, a new vision of companionate marriages and interactive families has emerged (Clark 1986, 216).

The history of middle-class housing in America is a microcosm of the social changes accompanying industrialization. Strict internal ordering of rooms and the separation of adults from children and of men from women were eventually replaced by open floorplans that encouraged family togetherness. Changes in design were affected by changes in aesthetic tastes, the search for a truly American housing style, and improved household technology. Architects did not set out to create more egalitarian environments specifically for women, yet the twentieth century was characterized by a gradual reduction in sexual spatial segregation and in gender stratification.

134

Women's Changing Status

Control of Labor. In the nineteenth century a woman owned her own labor and property only if she were single and over eighteen (sometimes if widowed). Approximately 90 percent of all women aged twenty-five and over were married at that time (U.S. Bureau of the Census 1975, 21), however, and working wives had no right to their earnings. Thus, the majority of women had no economic power. A wife was legally bound to give her wages to her husband even if he was a drunkard who had left her with no support for herself or her children (Flexner 1975, 63). Women's household goods produced for show or exchange were also subject to the same restrictions: prizes for needlework at the 1815 Oneida County Fair were given to men on the grounds that the work had been produced in the owner's household, and thus the proceeds were rightfully his (Ryan 1981, 33).

Women sometimes resorted to subversion to avoid legal responsibilities to their husbands. Harriet Robinson reported that it was not unusual to see mill hands hiding behind their looms when strangers approached: "Some of these [women] were known under assumed names, to prevent their husbands from trusteeing their wages. It was a very common thing for a male person of a certain kind to do this, depriving his wife of all her wages, perhaps, month after month. . . . Women's wages were also trusteed for the debts of their husbands, and children's for the debts of their parents" (Robinson [1898] 1976, 41).

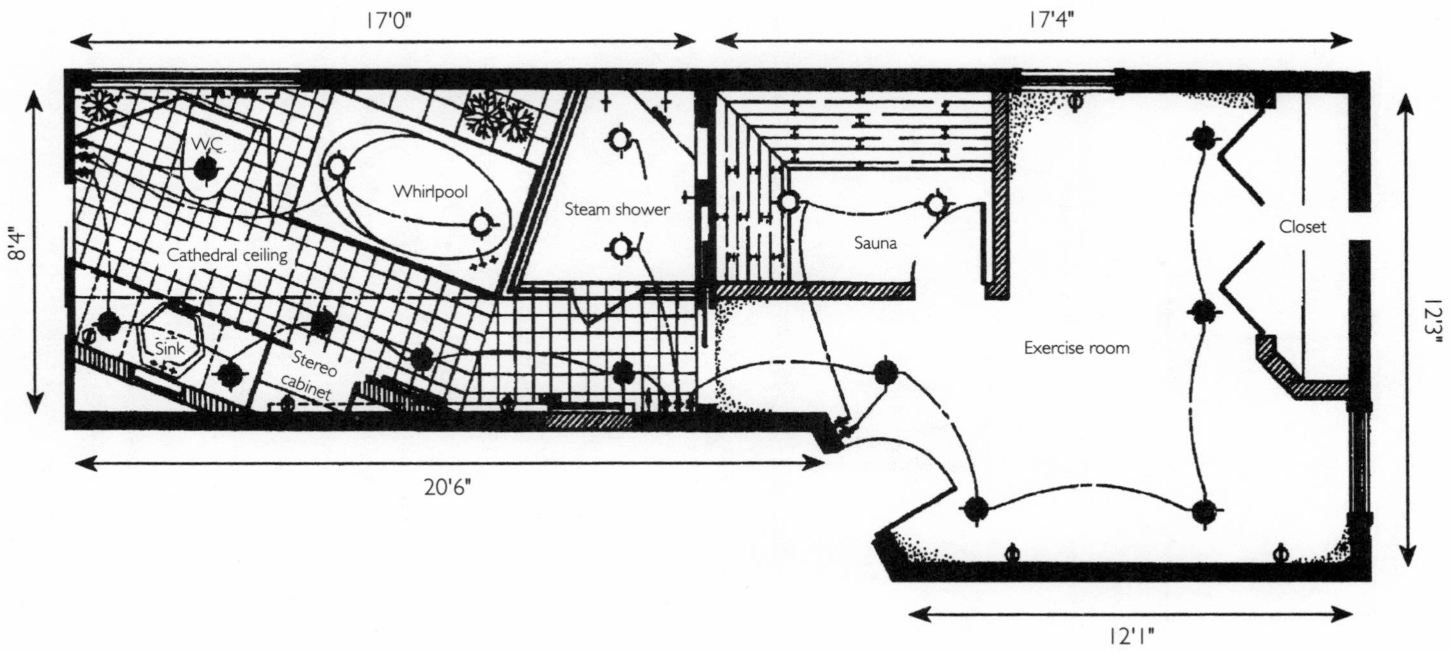

Fig. 5.10. This "bathroom suite" contains an exercise room, sauna, steam shower, whirlpool, and stereo system in addition to the usual amenities. Reproduced from *Kitchen and Bath Ideas* (Spring 1988) by permission of Classic Kitchen and Bath Center, Ltd., Roslyn, N.Y., and Don Boico, CKD, CR.

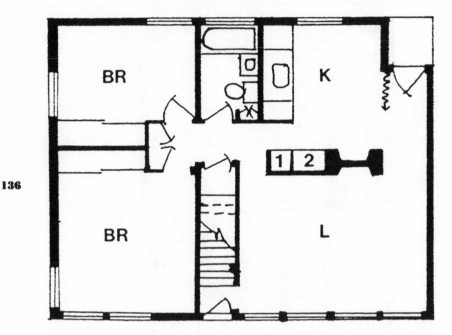

Fig. 5.11. This 1952 model of a 720-square-foot house in Levittown was only about twice the size of the contemporary award-winning bathroom suite. Reproduced from Hayden (1984, 9) by permission of the author and W. W. Norton and Company, Inc.

The injustice of this arrangement was acknowledged in the Seneca Falls Declaration of Sentiments of 1848. The right of women to control their own labor was not, however, included among the twelve resolutions for gender equality passed at the convention (Rossi 1973, 415–21). Nearly ten years after the Seneca Falls Convention, feminists Henry Blackwell and Lucy Stone professed in their radical marriage ceremony that they disavowed, among their protests of the legal system, a husband's "absolute right" to the product of his wife's "industry" (Kraditor 1968, 149).

The New York State Married Women's Property Act of 1860 addressed the issue of women's control of wages. The act was an advantage over previous legislation because it guaranteed that "the earnings of any married woman from her trade, business, labor, or services shall be her sole and separate property, and may be used or invested by her in her own name" (Schneir 1972, 123).

More than one hundred years would pass before the next significant legislation on wage parity was enacted. The Equal Pay Act of 1963 prohibits employers from discriminating on the basis of sex in paying wages for "equal work on jobs the performance of which requires skill, effort, and responsibility, and which are performed under similar working conditions" (Eastwood 1978, 109). Since the Equal Pay Act did not address occupational segregation, however, more recent demands have been for pay equity among jobs of "comparable worth." This latest call for federal intervention on behalf of women was relatively short-lived during the 1980s; the argument probably **137** will not emerge again until economic prosperity returns.

Control of Property. At the beginning of the nineteenth century, American women had few property rights. Henry Blackwell and Lucy Stone addressed this issue in their marriage contract of 1855. They renounced the laws by which husbands had "the sole ownership of [the wife's] personal property, and use of her real estate, unless previously settled upon her, or placed in the hands of trustees, as in the case of minors, lunatics, and idiots" (Kraditor 1968, 149).

Women did not have the right of custody to their own children in the rare instance of divorce, nor did the death of her husband insure a woman's access to the household's property. In Oneida County, New York, at the turn of the century, only one-half of all probated wills referred to the wife, and only 18 percent left the entire estate to her. In the majority of cases the widow faced restrictions that prevented her from disposing of the property (Ryan 1981, 251). In 1840 a widow could be left without any share in her husband's property and could actually become a legal incumbrance to the estate (Robinson [1898] 1976, 41).

Daughters did not fare much better, since fathers could make out wills without reference to their daughters' share of the inheritance in 1840 (Robinson [1898] 1976, 41). Ryan estimates that approximately one-third of bequests to daughters in Oneida County around that time were of lesser value than those to sons. She cites the extreme example of a farmer whose will divided his estate into thirteen equal parts, leaving two-thirteenths to each of five sons and one-thirteenth to each of three daughters. More typical was the distribution of movable property (household goods and livestock) to women and more valuable land to men (Ryan 1981, 29).

The first petition for women's property rights was introduced in the New York legislature in 1836. The Married Women's Property Act of 1848 insured that "the real and personal property of any female who may hereafter marry . . . and the rents, issues, and profits thereof, shall not be subject to the disposal of her husband" (Schneir 1972, 73). New York eventually expanded its law further to protect women's wages and rights to their children in its Married Women's Property Act of 1860 (Schneir 1972, 122). Other states followed New York's lead, and most states had some form of property protection for married women by the end of the nineteenth century (Flexner 1975, 64).

Over one hundred years passed between the time women first were granted control of their own property and the next significant legislation affecting women's property rights. In the early 1970s Congress enacted the Equal Credit Opportunity Act (ECOA) and amended the Fair Housing Act of 1968 to prohibit discrimination on the basis of sex. These laws evolved in response to mortgage lenders' practices of discounting women's income based on their age, occupation, and childbearing status. The income of married women often was disregarded completely in a couple's mortgage application, and single, divorced, or widowed women were defined as serious credit risks (Card 1981; Shalala and McGeorge 1981). Passage of the ECOA and the Fair Housing amendment opened the housing and mortgage markets to women for the first time in American history. The acquisition of assets through homeownership thus became an additional avenue of property control for women.

Public Participation. Part of the reason women had no control over their own labor or property in the nineteenth century was that they could not vote. Women's disenfranchisement contributed to their relegation to the private sphere and perpetuated the cycle that prevented them from entering public life.

The inability to vote was both symptom and cause of women's lower status. Women were admonished from speaking in public; the only women allowed to do so were missionaries. Mary Walker Ostrom of Utica, New York, for example, was eulogized at her death in 1859 for her evangelical zeal in preaching to the community (Ryan 1981, 186). Although women organized politically in trade unions and abolitionist societies (Flexner 1975;

138

Kessler-Harris 1982), these cases were short-lived exceptions to the general exhortation against women participating in public events.

Neither was holding office within all-female organizations necessarily an avenue to political power. In Massachusetts in 1840, a woman could not legally be treasurer of her own sewing circle unless a man took responsibility for her (Robinson [1898] 1976, 42). The proscription against political participation had become particularly onerous by the end of the century, when women seeking civil-service appointments lacked the connections that helped men obtain jobs (Aron 1987, 99).

139

Demanding the vote was a point of contention at the Seneca Falls Convention. It was the only resolution that failed to pass unanimously, because opponents thought its inclusion would jeopardize the rest of the platform. (Their fears were confirmed when the press ridiculed their proceedings and ministers denounced them from the pulpit [Rossi 1973, 420].) Such dissension within the ranks of the staunchest feminists, and the public outcry that accompanied the Seneca Falls Declaration, underscored the power that voting had in reinforcing the separate spheres of men and women.

Women began and ended the "Century of Struggle" without the vote. Exceptions existed in the frontier states of Wyoming and Utah, where women first voted in 1870. Yet the Nineteenth Amendment enfranchising all American women was not ratified until 1920 (Flexner 1975). Women did not immediately rush to the polls, nor did they vote differently from men, but enfranchisement would eventually become their avenue into the public sphere.

Three other trends in addition to voting mark women's increased role in the public sphere. The first, women's entry into the world of higher education, is documented in chapter 6. The second path to public participation for women has been entry into the labor force. In 1900 one out of five women worked outside the home; by 1980 more than one out of two were employed outside the home (Bianchi and Spain 1986, 141).

Neither two world wars, the Depression, nor the "baby boom" have affected significantly the trend of women's steadily greater rates of labor force participation. Protective labor legislation of the early part of the century was replaced in 1964 by the equal employment opportunity provisions (Title 7) of the Civil Rights Act (Eastwood 1978), which prohibits discrimination by gender in all aspects of employment, thereby increasing (at least theoretically) women's access to all areas of the workplace.

The third arena in which women's public participation has been improved is that of biological reproduction. The constitutional right to birth control was established in 1965 for married women and in 1972 for unmarried women. Women's rights to choose abortions were established in 1973 by the Supreme Court's *Roe vs. Wade* decision (Andersen 1988, 201). The ability to control the timing and occurrence of childbearing allows women options outside the home they did not previously possess. It is not surprising, therefore, that reproductive rights have become the topic of contentious political debate (Luker 1984).

140

Conclusion

This chapter began with the idea that domestic architecture mediates social relations, specifically those between women and men. Houses are the spatial context within which the social order is reproduced. Hillier and Hanson (1984, 147) define a dwelling as a set of social categories crosscut by a system of controls, which together define reality for both inhabitants and visitors. The history of American housing design indicates a gradual reduction in the gendered spaces creating, and created by, gender stratification.

Nineteenth-century housing for wealthy Americans mirrored the British gentry model of sexually segregated interiors. Like British women, American women of that era could not vote, keep their own wages, or own property. The twentieth century was ushered in by Frank Lloyd Wright's Usonian home, which reduced interior divisions and stressed the democracy of the new American family. No longer were certain rooms identified by gender or function; everyone belonged everywhere inside a house with few spatial boundaries. The loosening bonds of architecture reflected the changing society. Women in post–World War II America vote, own property, attend college, and control wages from labor performed outside the home. The home is now indicative of more egalitarian gender relations.

Education

Gate after gate seemed to close with gentle finality behind me. Innumerable beadles were fitting innumerable keys into well-oiled locks; the treasure-house was being made secure for another night.

—Virginia Woolf, *A Room of One's Own*

When Virginia Woolf penned those words about Oxbridge College, she was expressing outrage at her inability to enter its library. Women were admitted only when accompanied by a fellow or if furnished with a letter of introduction. Lacking either, Woolf retreated to the grounds to ponder women's status. These reflections form the core of her essay *A Room of One's Own*. She concluded that for a woman, "it is necessary to have five hundred a year and a room with a lock on the door if you are to write fiction or poetry" (Woolf 1929, 109). Woolf was lucky enough to have such an option; she recognized that most women of her era did not share her good fortune.

The institution of education was characterized until relatively recently by the spatial segregation of women and men. Just as ceremonial huts were places in which men shared knowledge and excluded women in nonindustrial societies, American schools historically were masculine places of learning that excluded women. Both are examples of spatial segregation reinforcing gender stratification by limiting women's access to resources important for the acquisition of status. Racially segregated schools have also contributed to stratification in American society and have placed black women at a double disadvantage. Black women were denied admission to both male and white schools for many years, thus restricting the space and content of their education in relation to white men's.

Both geographic and architectural separation have played a role in segregating women and men in formal education. Initially, women were denied admission to schools, creating geographic distance between them and sources of knowledge. When schools eventually opened their doors to women, many placed them in separate classrooms that substituted architectural for geographic segregation. Both types of segregation were justified by the prevailing ideology of separate spheres for women and men.

Private vs. Public Spheres

The roles of nineteenth-century American women and men were clearly demarcated between private and public spheres corresponding to home and workplace. Magazines and books for the white middle class lauded the cults of "true womanhood" and "domesticity" to which women should aspire (Welter 1966). "Woman's separate sphere" was understood to include religious piety, sexual purity, submissiveness, and domesticity. Hundreds of articles extolling these virtues were published in such magazines and books as *Ladies' Companion*, *Godey's Lady's Book*, *Sphere and Duties of Woman*, *Woman, in Her Social and Domestic Character*, and *Woman as She Was, Is, and Should Be*. They all explained the principles of gender role behavior by which women could achieve true happiness (Welter 1966). Catharine Beecher built an entire career by encouraging domesticity in her books *Treatise on Domestic Economy* (1842) and *The American Woman's Home* (written with her sister, Harriet Beecher Stowe, in 1869) (Sklar 1973). A clergyman's tract published in 1837 titled "Female Influence and the True Christian Mode of Its Exercise" summed up popular religious sentiment: "It is the province of woman to make home, whatever it is. If she makes that delightful and salutary—the abode of order and purity, though she may never herself step beyond the threshold, she may yet send forth from her humble dwelling, a power that will be felt round the globe" (Kraditor 1968, 47).

To be womanly in the urban white middle class of nineteenth-century America meant to provide a calm retreat where husbands and children were protected from the outside world. *A Voice to the Married*, published in Utica, New York, in 1841, told the husband to regard his home as "an elysium to which he can flee and find rest from the stormy strife of the selfish world." In the language of the early nineteenth century, "home" became synonymous with "retirement" or "retreat." In 1802 it was stated that a "woman's noblest station is retreat," and a single woman was said to have "passed her days in the shade of retirement" before her marriage (Cott 1977, 57). Home was an oasis in the desert, a sanctuary where a man "seeks refuge from the vexations . . . of business" (Cott 1977, 64). *Mother's Magazine* warned women to protect their children from "contamination of the streets" (Ryan 1981, 147).

The effect of the cult of domesticity was to remove women from competition with men in the public sphere of an industrializing society. Since status was beginning to be defined by characteristics achieved outside the home, women were at a disadvantage as long as their roles were defined primarily within the home. Historian Alice Kessler-Harris summarized the consequences of separate spheres for nineteenth-century women: "In return for an ideology that glorified their roles and perhaps offered some power within the family, women were denied a broad range of social and economic options. Whereas for men . . . the industrialization process included such potential benefits as economic mobility, freedom from some social restrictions, and occupational choice, women continued to be bound by the household and its ideological and economic constraints" (Kessler-Harris 1982, 50).

145

This belief in separate spheres set the general context for sexually segregated schools. Women did not need a formal education if their lives were to be spent entirely in the home. Higher education for women initially was endorsed as a way to produce better mothers: Mt. Holyoke opened in 1837 to prepare "Daughters of the Land to be good mothers" (Watson 1977, 134). Eventually women received educations for the same reasons as men. The following history of formal education in the United States briefly reviews seventeenth- and eighteenth-century precedents to the spatially segregated educational system of the nineteenth century.

The History of Formal Education

The history of formal education in America is a history of declining spatial segregation. From the earliest days when girls sat outside the one-room schoolhouse to the days when women finally sat in the same college classrooms as men, geographic and architectural separation between women and men gradually has been reduced. The eventual gender integration of professional programs paved the way for women's increasing public status in the twentieth century. Nineteenth- and twentieth-century experiences, however, were built on the foundations of public education in earlier centuries.

Seventeenth-Century Dame Schools. Formal education for colonial Americans was a luxury consisting of very rudimentary instruction in reading, writing, and mathematics. Pioneers could not spare their children from work long enough for much schooling, nor were there many people qualified to teach. "Dame schools" of the day were little more than child-care centers run by impoverished women who had little education themselves. One of the first was established by Goodwife Mirick in Springfield, Massachusetts, in 1682. Dame schools continued as the only form of female education for over a century, but "while the dame school was open to girls, its most important function was to give little boys the rudiments of English that they might enter the town schools" (Woody [1929] 1974, 1:138).

Colonial America's public schools typically did not admit girls. In Dedham, Massachusetts, for example, the seventeenth-century school assessment for households was based on the number of *boys* in the family aged four to fourteen (Cott 1977, 102). If towns neglected to specify the exclusion of girls when they established a school, the oversight was soon corrected. In the interim, girls would sit outside the school building or on its steps, eavesdropping on the boys' recitations; sometimes girls "were tolerated in the rear of the schoolhouse behind a curtain" (Kendall 1975, 12). Not surprisingly, girls who sat outside were decidedly more sickly than the boys inside, and the dangers education posed to their health were used to prevent girls from coming to school. At about the same time, Dutch settlers in New York allowed girls in church-sponsored primary schools as long as strict segregation was enforced. Small towns with only one schoolhouse had clear guidelines stipulating the separation of boys and girls (Kendall 1975, 14).

Such segregation had the effect of reducing the status of women as a group: the gap between male and female literacy rates actually widened during the colonial period. Whereas one-half of the men and one-third of the women who arrived in New England could sign their names, by 1700 the proportion of literate men had advanced to approximately 80 percent, but female literacy had reached only 40 percent—where it was to remain for the next century (Cott 1977, 103; Kendall 1975, 14).

The education of slaves during the seventeenth century was left largely to the discretion of the master. Slaves working in the main house were sometimes taught to read and write and acquired some knowledge through observation. Since house slaves were most likely to be women, black women had an educational advantage over black field hands simply by virtue of proximity to the white family. By 1740, however, teaching slaves to read and write was declared illegal by the Act of [South] Carolina in response to slave insurrections (Noble 1956, 15, 17, 154).

Eighteenth-Century Master's Schools. By the revolutionary era girls were more likely to be attending school than during colonial times; the first time girls went to a "master's school" with boys was in Ipswich, Massachusetts, in 1769 (Woody [1929] 1974, 1:142). But school attendance for girls was often at a different time of the day from boys. In Medford, Massachusetts, in 1766 the schoolmaster instructed girls for two hours per day after the boys were dismissed, and in 1787 it was arranged that girls attend "one hour in the forenoon and one in the afternoon for four months" (Woody [1929] 1974, 1:144). This practice was typical of other New England towns: a New London school taught girls between 5:00 and 7:00 A.M. during the summer of 1774; at Newburyport in 1792, girls were admitted to the master's school "in summer when boys were few" for one or two hours after school; in 1790 Haverhill provided two hours of school a day for girls between May and September; in Boston in 1785, Caleb Bingham's school for girls was open from April to October from 6:00 to 7:30 A.M. and from 5:00 to 6:00 P.M.; by 1789 Boston had opened reading and writing schools to girls, but only during the summer and after boys had left (Benson 1935, 149; Cott 1977, 112–13; Woody [1929] 1974, 1:144–46). The custom of teaching girls in the same building *but at separate hours* from the boys introduced temporal segregation as a proxy for spatial segregation.

Not only did girls attend school at different times than boys, they often learned different curricula. Girls were generally taught to read and write but received no instruction in arithmetic as boys did. Boys' courses included Latin, Greek, and English composition, while girls' courses included music, handwriting, and sewing (Woody [1929] 1974, 1:144–47). At the time, it was considered somewhat dangerous to teach women even to read and write, because they might forge their husband's signatures or neglect their household duties by reading cheap novels (Newcomer 1959, 7). Schooling for girls became acceptable when it was used to reinforce their domestic roles as wives and mothers. By the end of the eighteenth century, education for women was identified by progressive thinkers as the handmaiden of patriotism. In 1793 the Reverend John Ogden made the following case for educating women in *The Female Guide*: "Every man, by the Constitution, is born with an equal right to be elected to the highest office. . . . And every woman is born with an equal right to be the wife of the most eminent man" (quoted in Cott 1977, 109).

Nineteenth-Century Academies and Seminaries. If seventeenth-century dame schools were analogous to contemporary kindergartens and eighteenth-century master's schools to elementary schools, the academies and seminaries of the nineteenth century were the equivalent of modern public high schools in their curricula. "The age of the academies" spanned the years between the American Revolution and the Civil War and reflected the increasing educational demands of a growing democracy. The number of academies multiplied dramatically and equaled approximately 6,000 nationally by 1850 (Sizer 1964, 1–4). These schools were predominantly white. By 1860 the formal education of blacks in the slave states was virtually nonexistent, although white missionaries taught blacks in the free territories (Noble 1956, 154).

Academies prepared white upper-class boys for college. Since the purpose of college was preparation for the ministry or other professions, and women could not hold such occupations, there was no need for higher education for girls. Americans at the turn of the nineteenth century subscribed to Rousseau's dictum: "The whole education of women ought to be relative to men. To please them, to be useful to them, to make themselves loved and honored by them, to educate them when young, to care for them when grown, to counsel them, to console them and to make life sweet and agreeable to them—these are the duties of women at all times, and what should be taught them from infancy" (quoted in Flexner 1975, 23).

When girls were admitted to academies the segregated arrangements of earlier centuries persisted. Accounts of the Atkinson Academy in New Hampshire reported that in 1805 there were approximately "sixty youth, about an equal number of males and females," the academy being "in a spacious room" with females on one side and males on the other. The Franklin Academy in North Andover, Massachusetts, was built in 1799 with two rooms of equal size, "the north room for the male department and the south for the female department" (Pond 1930, 43).

When the Bradford Academy was opened in 1803 near Haverhill, New

Hampshire, it was a coeducational school modeled after Franklin rather than Atkinson. The rationale for segregation at Bradford was that the "male apartment" would have both summer and winter sessions, while the "female apartment" would have only summer sessions and could use a smaller room in the winter. The first advertisement for the Bradford Academy listed the boys' curriculum as "English, Latin and Greek languages; Reading, Writing, Geography, Arithmetic, and all other necessary branches of School Education." Girls were to be taught "Reading, Writing, English Grammar, Arithmetic, Embroidery, and all other forms of needlework together with Drawing and Painting" (Pond 1930, 54). Separation of boys and girls into different rooms reinforced the different curricula by which girls failed to acquire the Greek and Latin required for college admission. Despite such discrepancies, however, girls at Bradford had a curriculum closer to the boys' than did girls at other female academies (Sizer 1964, 32).

149

When the first term started at Bradford on June 1, 1803, there were fourteen boys in the male section and thirty-seven girls in the female section. Girls continued to outnumber boys throughout Bradford's early years, especially in the summer when boys worked in the fields. During the winter when the female department was closed, "increasing numbers of [girls] braved the rigors of the season, and the supposedly sterner atmosphere of the preceptor's room to keep up their studies with the boys" (Pond 1930, 59). In 1817 another room for girls had to be added to the original structure (see figure 6.1).

By 1830 the Bradford Academy had been converted from a coeducational institution to a school for girls. Bradford's historian, Jean Sarah Pond, saw the seeds of the eventual split in the original design of the building. Pond would have preferred the single-room approach of Atkinson to the separate rooms modeled after Franklin Academy: "To us, looking backward, it is evident that the segregation made possible the development of an independent school for girls" (Pond 1930, 53). Although Pond applauded any opportunity for higher education for girls, she perceived definite advantages to coeducation for women. In her account of the school's transition from mixed- to single-sex, she cited the 1795 boyhood experience of Joseph Story, U.S. Supreme Court justice, from his autobiography: "It was not necessary to separate the sexes in their studies. Generally we studied the same books

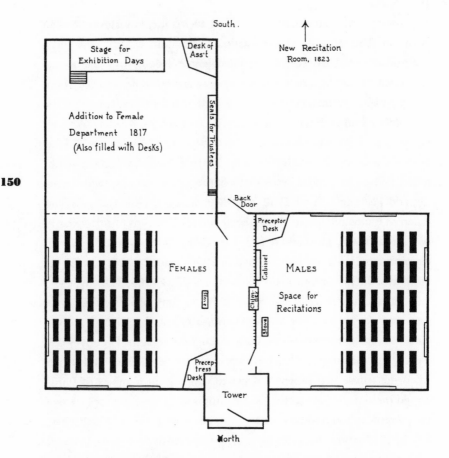

Fig. 6.1. The Bradford Academy began as a coeducational institution in 1803, but by 1830 it had become a school for girls only. Reproduced from Pond (1930, 56), by permission of Bradford College.

and recited our lessons in the presence of each other. . . . I was early struck with the flexibility, activity, and power of the female mind. Girls of the same age were . . . quite equal in their studies and acquirements . . . [to] the boys" (Pond 1930, 53). Pond's narration conveys a certain wistfulness regarding the enlightening effects of coeducation for both boys and girls: girls are given the opportunity to learn a stricter "male curriculum," and boys are exposed to girls who can handle the same subjects as themselves. Had Pond designed the original academy building, she likely would have chosen spatial integration.

Bradford's conversion to an all-female school placed it among the growing ranks of female academies (or seminaries, as they were called toward the end of the nineteenth century). Their chief distinction from "real" academies was their omission of Greek and Latin and the inclusion of domestic skills. Although educational historian Thomas Woody cites the New Orleans convent of the Ursuline sisters established in 1727 as the first school for girls in the United States, he gives "the honor of establishing the first exclusively female seminary in the nineteenth century" to the female academy at Salem, North Carolina, founded by the Moravians in 1802 (Woody [1929] 1974, **151** 1:329, 341). He acknowledged Bradford as the first northern academy open to girls (Woody [1929] 1974, 1:342). The first seminary for black girls was established by Mytilla Minor in Washington, D.C., in 1857 and eventually became Minor Teachers College (Noble 1956, 18).

The Troy Female Seminary, established by Emma Willard in upstate New York in 1821, was the "beginning of higher education for women in the United States" (Woody [1929] 1974, 1:344). Willard tried to provide the same courses as boys' academies, but it was difficult since neither she nor other women who taught at Troy were allowed the training they needed for "male subjects." When Willard was denied admission to the University of Middlebury (Vermont), she studied alone, spending long hours teaching herself algebra, geometry, trigonometry, geography, and history. Her herculean efforts to provide girls with an education comparable to boys' were not always appreciated by the public. The general feeling about female seminaries at the time was that they should confer the title of "Mrs." rather than diplomas for "literary attainments" (Sizer 1964, 32).

Catharine Beecher's Hartford Female Seminary, established in 1828, was another school that tried to set rigorous academic standards. Beecher's memoirs reflect the difficulty of the task and the "painful contrast" between her own school and those for boys: "I began teaching and employing teachers without the previous preparation given to boys in preparatory school, for no such had ever been offered to girls. . . . Then no library or apparatus was provided . . . I was obliged to take the expenses and cares of housekeeping for several years, while all the instruction and government of the institution and finances rested on me alone. . . . Thus I had the responsibilities which in colleges are divided among the faculty, treasurer and boarding housekeeper, and at the same time taught four and five hours a day" (Woody [1929] 1974, 1:355).

Beecher's energies were divided intellectually as well as administratively. Her life represented the paradox of nineteenth-century female reformers: she advocated strict professional training for women but believed strongly in women's separate sphere. She is acknowledged as both a founder of teacher training and a proponent of domestic science. Her numerous editions of *The American Woman's Home* were best-selling guides to cooking, cleaning, and **152** marital happiness (Flexner 1975, 31).

Women's Colleges and Curricula

Female academies and seminaries eventually evolved into female colleges. (The overlap between "academies" and "colleges" was still so great in the 1800s that some states grouped them together for statistical purposes [Sizer 1964, 18ff.].) The rising educational standards of the nation and the ability to hire female teachers for half the salary of male teachers created a need for more highly educated women. Between 1860 and 1880 the proportion of all elementary and secondary teachers who were female rose from 25 to 60 percent; by 1910 women equaled 80 percent of all schoolteachers (Lerner 1971, 110). Such demand for teachers insured the development of college courses for women that would prepare them for caretaking both inside and outside the family.

Mary Lyon's Mt. Holyoke Seminary, opened in 1837, is generally credited with being the first women's college, although it did not become recognized as a college until 1893 (Woody [1929] 1974, 1:359, 362). Mt. Holyoke was established to train teachers, a task at which it was enormously successful: 70 percent of the graduates in the first forty years went on to teach school (Newcomer 1959, 11). The colleges that would come to be known collectively as the "Seven Sisters" (Mt. Holyoke, Vassar, Wellesley, Smith, Radcliffe, Bryn Mawr, and Barnard) had all been established by 1889. Created predominantly by and for white Protestants, the Seven Sisters colleges did not knowingly admit black students; Wellesley was the only exception (Horowitz 1984, 155). The black corollary to Mt. Holyoke was

Spelman Seminary in Atlanta. Begun in 1881 as the first institution of higher education for black women, Spelman became a college in 1925. Its founders, Sophia Packard and Harriet Giles, shared Mary Lyon's emphasis on training women to become teachers (Noble 1956, 22; Solomon 1985, 145).

Mary Lyon had definite ideas about the appropriate curriculum for future teachers: "It is no part of our design to teach young ladies domestic work. This branch of education is important, but a literary institution is not the place to gain it" (quoted in Woody [1929] 1974, 1:360). Mt. Holyoke's **153** requirement that all students perform housekeeping chores was an economic move designed to reduce the costs of tuition, rather than give women practical experience for married life (Woody [1929] 1974, 1:361).

Separate colleges for women were a natural outgrowth of the female academies. They also served to perpetuate women's segregation from men and from "male knowledge." As the Seven Sisters colleges opened between 1865 and 1890, their curricula reflected Dr. Edward Clarke's medical theory that higher education harmed women's health. Women's colleges emphasized physical education and personal hygiene more than men's colleges because they needed to disprove Dr. Clarke's theory. One of Vassar's three original buildings was the gymnasium, and the school required physical education, physiology, and hygiene in the freshman year. By contrast, no such courses were required at Harvard, Yale, or Columbia at the time (Newcomer 1959, 28; Rothman and Rothman 1987).

Dr. Clarke had been considered an advocate of higher education for women before the 1873 publication of *Sex in Education, or a Fair Chance for the Girls*, in which he stated that women's unique physiology limited their educational capacity. He based his conclusions on five college women, whom he labeled hysterical, and proposed that exposing women to the rigors of a Harvard education would seriously threaten their reproductive capacities (Rosenberg 1982, 5). Since Dr. Clarke's advice was "for women's own good," it was difficult for them to challenge his popular theory. Although the first woman had already graduated from medical school (Elizabeth Blackwell in 1848), there were not yet enough college-educated or professionally trained women to refute Clarke's statements (Lerner 1971, 46).

Women's colleges attempted to replicate men's curricula as closely as possible, and with greater success than their academy predecessors. Smith had the most rigorous standards of admission in 1875, closely followed by Wellesley: their criteria equaled those of the men's colleges of the day (Woody [1929] 1974, 2:182). Once again, however, the public did not share the priorities of the founders of women's colleges. An article in *Godey's Lady's Book* in 1853 lamented that "our girls have no *home* education. They are educated in schools where 'no feminine employments, no domestic habits, can be learned'" (Woody [1929] 1974, 2:216).

154

Perhaps because most of the girls who attended college in the nineteenth century were from elite homes with servants (Mt. Holyoke's students were an exception), few of the original women's colleges offered courses in "domestic economy." With the exception of Vassar, the Seven Sisters and their southern counterparts (Judson, Salem, Sophie Newcomb, and Agnes Scott), the majority of women's colleges did not introduce home economics until the early 1900s (Newcomer 1959, 72–103).

As higher education became more affordable and industrialization created a shortage of domestic servants, colleges began to prepare middle-class women for the new field of home economics. Once schools became coeducational, "home ec" would become an effective agent of segregation. Marion Talbot, who joined the University of Chicago as a dean in 1892, vigorously opposed President Harper's attempts to separate men and women in classrooms. Yet by 1902 Talbot had been removed—at her own request—from her social science post and put in charge of a department of "household administration"; she became a "victim to the very process of academic sexual segregation that she was trying to fight" (Rosenberg 1982, 49).

The Coeducation Movement

When the U.S. Commissioner of Education first published statistics in 1870, approximately 3,000 women were attending colleges that offered a bachelor's degree. About 2,200 of them (73 percent) were enrolled in women's colleges. The Morrill Act of 1862 legislated coeducation in land-grant colleges, but only 200 women were attending the eight state univer-

Fig. 6.2. The patrons of this "Free Reading Room" in New York City in 1891 were all men. Library of Congress.

sities open to them in 1870 (Newcomer 1959, 19). The first "undisputed instance" of women receiving bachelor's degrees equal to those of men occurred in 1841 when three women graduated from Oberlin (in Ohio) (Newcomer 1959, 5). Not until 1858, however, would an Oberlin woman be permitted to speak publicly at commencement (Solomon 1985, 29).

Founded in 1833, Oberlin was the first college to open its doors to students regardless of race or sex. By 1835 the first black students had arrived and soon constituted nearly 5 percent of the student body. This figure rose to 8 percent following the Civil War, then declined, and averaged 4 percent after 1900 (Bigglestone 1971, 198). Among Oberlin's early alumna were Mary Jane Patterson in 1862, Fanny Jackson (Coppin) in 1865, and Mary Church (Terrell) and Anna Julia Cooper in 1884, the first black women to earn college degrees. Oberlin accounted for a large proportion of black college women in the late nineteenth century: all-black Fisk enrolled only twelve women in 1892 and Howard University none; only thirty black women were estimated to be attending college in 1891 (Solomon 1985, 76).

156

Feminist Lucy Stone was one of Oberlin's first graduates and referred to the school as "the gray dawn of . . . morning" for women's education (Flexner 1975, 29). Coeducation in the nineteenth century, however, was different from today's version. Oberlin's policy was that women should remain in their special sphere, for if a woman became any sort of "public character" such as a doctor or lawyer, she would neglect her home. The girls' experiences at Oberlin were meant to remind them of the ultimate purpose of their educations: "Washing the men's clothes, caring for their rooms, serving them at table, listening to their orations, but themselves remaining respectfully silent in public assemblages, the Oberlin 'co-eds' were being prepared for intelligent motherhood and a properly subservient wifehood" (quoted in Flexner 1975, 30).

This division of labor was patterned after family relationships in which the man was the head of the household. At Oberlin men were often referred to as "the leading sex" (Fletcher 1943, 1:382). But despite its traditionally prescribed gender roles, Oberlin provided the first opportunity for men and women to receive the same curriculum in the same space. Some of the introductory courses were segregated, but the advanced classes were offered to both men and women (Fletcher 1943, 1:379). The dilemma inherent in this experimental approach to education was that women had been taught modesty and public silence for so long that they hesitated to speak in the presence of men. An early Oberlin coeducational course in rhetoric ended when the women requested a return to separate classes (Solomon 1985, 28).

Most of the women seemed unaware of the potential for enhanced status accompanying this radical departure from earlier segregated days, for "there was no tendency to feminism. The only right demanded for women by the

Oberlin leaders was 'the right to be educated'" (Fletcher 1943, 1:382). They seem to have failed entirely to realize that education would open to women the way to all the other privileges hitherto the exclusive property of the male. The potential did not escape Antoinette Brown Blackwell, who became the first woman to graduate from a theological school when she received her Oberlin degree in 1851 (Woody [1929] 1974, 2:368).

Other schools followed Oberlin's example. Most notable in their efforts at early coeducation were the University of Chicago, the University of Michigan, the University of Wisconsin, Antioch College, and Cornell. The Civil War proved to be a boon to women's enrollment, due to the shortage of men and the universities' needs for tuition. Rising demand for schoolteachers also made higher education for women more acceptable (Woody [1929] 1974, 2:240). Women in coeducational colleges increased from approximately 3,000 in 1875 to almost 20,000 in 1900, a faster rate than the men's increase (Woody [1929] 1974, 2:252). The proportion of all colleges that were coeducational increased from 29 percent in 1870 to 43 percent in 1890 and 58 percent in 1910 (Newcomer 1959, 37). Most black colleges had been coeducational since their foundation in the 1860s and 1870s because their communities could not afford "the luxury of single-sex schools" (Solomon 1985, 145).

As women's attendance at coeducational institutions grew, so did resistance to the practice. The battle at the University of Virginia was particularly bitter. The issue of higher education for Virginia women was first introduced in the state legislature in 1879. Between then and 1920, when women finally were admitted at the postgraduate level, controversy over coeducation at the University of Virginia characterized each legislative session. Opponents believed that "women would encroach on the rights of men; there would be new problems of government, perhaps scandal; the old honor system would have to be changed; standards would be lowered to those of other coeducational schools; and the glorious reputation of the university, as a school for men, would be trailed in the dust" (Woody [1929] 1974, 2:255). The University of Virginia became fully coeducational at the undergraduate level in 1972, the last major state university to do so. As Mabel Newcomer had observed eleven years earlier, "most of the opposition was less concerned with whether education was good for women than

157

whether educated women were acceptable to men" (Newcomer 1959, 31). The opposition to coeducation was so intense partially because it represented a breakdown in men's control of knowledge.

Instances of backsliding into segregated arrangements occurred at some colleges. Most notable of these was the University of Chicago. When it opened in 1892, women comprised 40 percent of all undergraduates. In the next decade the enrollment of women surpassed that of men, and women earned more than half of the Phi Beta Kappa awards. The administration feared that Chicago would soon become a women's school if something were not done to reverse the trend (Rosenberg 1982, 43; Solomon 1985, 58).

At the turn of the century, the University of Chicago received the offer of an endowment stipulating that women should be segregated from men in the classroom. President Harper lobbied a hesitant faculty to promote such a change, and in 1902 the board of trustees passed a policy that included the following conditions: a separate junior college for women; separate sections of courses for upper-level men and women; sex segregation in chapel; and separate laboratories (Woody [1929] 1974, 2:285). The *School Journal*, reporting the board's actions, stated: "The work of segregation will be gradual, but when it has been completed men and women will never meet in class, at lectures, or in chapel" (Woody [1929] 1974, 2:281). Within five years the segregation policy lapsed due to student resistance and the expenses of duplicating classes.

Various other institutions attempted some form of "natural segregation" of the sexes. The first women entered the University of Wisconsin in 1863, were abruptly banned in 1867 when a female college was formed, and were readmitted (to segregated classes) in 1873. Although the original charter of the University of Michigan called for a female department, no women were actually admitted until 1870. In 1908 President Jordan of Stanford University proposed a junior college division for women similar to Chicago's, and shortly thereafter President Wheeler of the University of California tried to establish a statewide system of junior colleges for women. All of these colleges eventually reversed their segregationist policies after pressure from alumnae and students (Solomon 1985, 53–59).

Some universities solved the "coeducation problem" by establishing coordinate colleges for women. Often called "sister schools," their distance from the sponsoring institution was seemingly a function of the controversy surrounding coeducation. Sophie Newcomb College, for example, was established on the same campus as Tulane, where there was already a long tradition of education for women. By comparison, the University of Virginia's coordinate college (Mary Washington) was placed ninety miles away in Fredericksburg after years of bitter opposition to incorporating women on "the grounds" of the main university in Charlottesville. Coordinate colleges constituted a compromise between women's colleges and coeducation. These colleges suffered from a lack of the recognition and resources that accrued to their male counterparts (Newcomer 1959, 40), just as "separate but equal" public institutions for blacks suffered by comparison with white public institutions (Jencks and Riesman 1968, 422, 433).

159

The very fear that men expressed about coeducation was its ability to open traditionally male doors of knowledge to women. Psychologist G. Stanley Hall stated at the beginning of the twentieth century that Dr. Clarke had been right about the dangers of higher education for women. Coeducation, in particular, was the most threatening of all because "coeducation harms girls by assimilating them to boys' ways and work, robbing them of their sense of feminine character" (Rosenberg 1982, 42). Assimilating women into "boys' ways and work" was easier to accomplish when higher education was spatially integrated by gender. Coeducation thus became the first institutionalized avenue by which women as a group gained the potential for higher public status. The form "public status" took at the time was teaching, but continued exposure to men and traditionally male curricula would eventually open other professions to women as well. Coeducation established "the right of every woman to the highest educational facilities" and explained the "freedom that women enjoy in this country with respect to the pursuit of careers" (Woody [1929] 1974, 2:302–3).

Martha Carey Thomas, herself a product of coeducation, was one of its strongest advocates despite her long presidency of Bryn Mawr. Thomas graduated Phi Beta Kappa from Cornell in 1877 and received her Ph.D. in Zurich in 1882. She fought hard to establish rigorous academic standards at Bryn Mawr and insisted on well-trained male faculty as one way of achieving her goal. In a 1907 address to the Association of Collegiate Alumnae, she warned her colleagues against "insertion of so-called practical courses which are falsely supposed to prepare for life" into the curricula of women's colleges. She believed that "nothing more disastrous for women, or for men, can be conceived than this specialized education for women as a sex" (Kraditor 1968, 94–95). At the time she made those comments, Thomas saw women's colleges as the primary source of higher education for women. Two decades later she was outspokenly promoting coeducation. In a speech to the International Federation of University Women delivered in 1920, Thomas stated: "The very first next step seems to me to be the demand for unqualified, true, out and out coeducation. Only by having the schools and universities coeducational can we ensure the girls of the world receiving a thoroughly good education" (Kraditor 1968, 264).

160

A lifetime of "endless vigilance" for resources and academic credibility for Bryn Mawr had convinced Thomas that there would never be enough money to support segregated institutions, nor could women's colleges maintain the standards of men's colleges without comparable resources. Women's colleges were also beginning to lose students as coeducational opportunities increased. In 1870 approximately 60 percent of all women enrolled in institutions of higher learning were attending women's colleges; by 1900 only 29 percent of women in school were in women's colleges (Newcomer 1959, 49). The actual number of students in women's colleges had risen from 10,000 to only 16,000 between 1875 and 1900 (Woody [1929] 1974, 2:252).

One of the major accomplishments of coeducation was to expose women to a curriculum that would prepare them for professional training other than teaching. Medicine, law, and the ministry were institutions that had long defined women's proper place as the home. The exclusion of women from these fields of knowledge guaranteed that status inequalities would remain unchallenged. Once undergraduate coeducation became a reality, however, professional and graduate education soon followed.

Coeducation in Graduate and Professional Schools

Just as undergraduate coeducation proceeded sporadically from segregated to integrated arrangements, the early days of professional coeducation were

Fig. 6.3. Women students had joined men in the chemistry labs at the Massachusetts Institute of Technology by 1869. Reproduced from *Frank Leslie's Illustrated Newspaper*, courtesy of Princeton University Library.

characterized by spatial separation of the sexes. The University of Michigan's medical school admitted women in 1871, but they were put in separate classes (Lerner 1971, 111). When Anna Howard Shaw entered Boston University as a theology student in 1875, she shared the same classroom with her male colleagues, but little else: "The young men of my class . . . were given free accommodations in the dormitory, and their board, at a club formed for their assistance, cost each of them only $1.25 a week. For me no such kindly provision was made. I was not allowed a place in the dormitory, but instead was given $2 a week to pay the rent of a room outside. Neither was I admitted to the economical comforts of the club" (Flexner 1975, 122).

Professional women were rare in the nineteenth century. College education for women was still suspect, and additional training was almost scandalous. M. Carey Thomas reported that when she went to Europe for her Ph.D., "my mother used to write me that my name was never mentioned to her by women of her acquaintance. I was thought by them to be as much of a disgrace to my family as if I had eloped with the coachman" (Kraditor 1968, 92).

A college or graduate degree was not the only path to professional status in the nineteenth century. The few women who entered these occupations without formal training typically relied on help from a family member and a great deal of personal determination. College training, and specifically coeducational graduate training, allowed a larger number of women access to a wider range of professional occupations.

By 1900, 9 percent of the 343 Ph.D.'s granted and 21 percent of the 1,401 master's degrees went to women. In that same year women made up 29 percent of the 6,865 graduate students enrolled in public and private institutions (Woody [1929] 1974, 2:337–38). Also in 1900, 1,456 women were enrolled in medical schools (6 percent of all students), 181 (2 percent) in theological schools, and 151 (1 percent) in law schools (Woody [1929] 1974, 2:360, 369, 375). In 1921 doctorates were awarded for the first time to three black women (Noble 1956, 30). The census of 1900 listed 3,373 women "clergymen," 1,010 female lawyers and judges, and 7,387 female physicians and surgeons (Woody [1929] 1974, 2:381). Although not all of these practicing professionals were college-educated, the admission of women to professional programs enhanced the probability that they would later become practitioners in large enough numbers to improve women's status as a group.

Contemporary Coeducation

The proportion of all colleges that were coeducational rose steadily from 29 percent in 1870 to 74 percent in 1957 and equaled 94 percent by 1985 (National Center for Education Statistics 1988, table 162; Solomon 1985, 44). Thus, most college men and women in the postwar years have attended sexually integrated institutions. Interestingly, fraternities and sororities began to emerge in the late nineteenth century at about the same time as coeducation. "The 'Greek' system may, indeed, have been as much a response to the problem of segregating and organizing relations between the sexes as to that of relations between classes and ethnic groups, though the two are obviously related" (Jencks and Riesman 1968, 296).

Table 6.1 documents the gradual transformation of institutions of higher education from predominantly male to sexually integrated environments. In 1870 approximately one in five students was female, a ratio that had reached just over one in three by 1900. Succeeding years saw an increase in female

Table 6.1. Women Enrolled in Institutions of Higher Education, 1870 to 1988

Year	Number of Women Enrolled (1,000s)	Women as a Percentage of All Students Enrolled	Percentage of Bachelor's Degrees Awarded to Women
1870	11	21.0%	14.7%
1880	40	33.4	19.3
1890	56	35.9	17.3
1900	85	36.8	19.1
1910	140	39.6	22.7
1920	283	47.3	34.2
1930	481	43.7	39.9
1940	601	40.2	41.3
1950	806	30.2	23.9
1960	1,223	37.9	35.0
1970	3,537	41.2	41.5
1980	6,222	51.4	47.3
1985	6,429	52.5	50.8
1987	6,834	53.5	51.5
1988	7,045	54.0	52.0

Source: Solomon 1985, 63; U.S. Bureau of the Census 1975, 385–86; U.S. Department of Education 1991, 167–232.

proportions until women accounted for one in two students by 1980. For the first time in history, the 1980s recorded more female than male students enrolled in institutions of higher learning.

Similar enrollment rates are just beginning to translate into comparable graduation rates. The third column of table 6.1 reveals the historical discrepancy between the proportion of students who are female and the proportion of bachelor's degrees granted to women. In 1870, for example, when 21 percent of all students were women, only 15 percent of degrees were awarded to women. In 1950, when approximately one-third of students were female, less than one-quarter of degrees went to women.

In 1940 the proportion of degrees granted to women slightly exceeded their representation among the student body. This temporary aberration from the historical trend was the result of male mobilization for World War II. The postwar years were marked by a dramatic decline in both enrollment rates and degrees granted to women: in 1950 women accounted for a smaller proportion of all students than in 1880. In the early 1940s women dropped out of college for defense jobs; by the mid-1940s they were competing with the vast influx of veterans attending school on the GI bill; and by the late 1940s they were dropping out of school to marry those veterans and start families (Solomon 1985, 189–90). By 1970 enrollments and degrees granted had reestablished their prewar levels. In 1980 the proportion of degrees granted to women was only slightly lower than women's representation among all students, and by 1988 the gap had nearly closed.

164   Women are now as likely as men to be occupying the public sphere of colleges and universities. When proportions of all adults with college degrees are examined, however, women's educational attainment is still lower than men's. Table 6.2 demonstrates the increase in proportions of adult women with a college degree, compared to proportions of men with a college degree.

Beginning with 1940 as the baseline against which to measure postwar changes, approximately 4 percent of women and 5 percent of men aged twenty-five and over were college graduates. By 1988, 17 percent of adult women, compared with 24 percent of adult men, had completed college. College completion rates are consistently higher for whites than for blacks of both sexes (Bianchi and Spain 1986, 114). There are two ways in which to interpret these data. The positive interpretation is that one in six women is now a college graduate, compared with only one in twenty-five before World War II. The proportion of women earning college degrees has quadrupled in forty-five years.

On the other hand, the gap between the proportion of women and men with a college degree has risen steadily over time, from 1.7 percentage points in 1940 to 7.5 percentage points in 1980; it began to decline slightly in 1985, to 7.1 percentage points (where it remains). Thus, men as a group are still educationally advantaged, compared with women as a group. This discrepancy influences entry into the labor force and occupational opportunities. The higher the educational attainment, the more likely women are to be in the labor force and the more likely they will hold more prestigious positions relative to men. Educational differences can thus affect the degree of occupational segregation, which in turn can affect women's wages relative to men's.

Table 6.2. Percentage of Women and Men* with a College Degree, 1940 to 1988

Year	Percentage with a College Degree		Percentage Point Difference
	Women	Men	
1940	3.7	5.4	1.7
1950	5.0	7.1	2.1
1960	5.8	9.6	3.8
1970	7.9	13.5	5.6
1980	12.9	20.4	7.5
1985	16.0	23.1	7.1
1987	16.5	23.6	7.1
1988	17.0	24.0	7.0

Source: Bianchi and Spain 1986, 115; U.S. Bureau of the Census 1975, 380; 1986, 122; 1990a, 134; 1990b, 131.
*All persons aged 25 and over.

The Case for Women's Colleges. In early May 1990 trustees of the all-female Mills College in California announced that the school would begin admitting men in 1991. By the end of the same month the trustees had reversed their decision and President Mary Metz had resigned in response to vehement student protests organized around the theme of "Better Dead than Coed" (Goodman 1990; Gordon 1990). There is a general perception that women's colleges produce more successful women than coeducational colleges—that is, that gender segregation may work to women's advantage (Jencks and Riesman 1968, 306–10). Research conducted during the 1960s and 1970s comparing the achievements of women from single-sex colleges with those from coeducational colleges suggests that assumption is debatable.

Using the *Who's Who of American Women 1966–1971*, Tidball found that graduates of women's colleges were approximately twice as likely to be included in the directory as female graduates of coeducational colleges. She attributed this higher rate of achievement to the greater presence of female faculty at women's colleges, the smaller size of women's colleges, their selectivity, and higher levels of faculty compensation (Tidball 1973, 1980).

Another measure of achievement that varies by type of college is the proportion of undergraduates who earn Ph.D.'s. Data from the National

Research Council's Doctorate Record Files from 1920 to 1973 showed that women's colleges were the major contributors of female doctorates (Tidball and Kistiakowsky 1976). In both studies conducted by Tidball, the presence of men students was interpreted as a deterrent to women's success (Kaplan 1978).

Astin's study of the effects of single-sex colleges on undergraduates supported Tidball's conclusions. He found female students in women's colleges to be more involved in positions of political leadership, more likely to express high achievement aspirations, and more likely to graduate than women in coeducational institutions. While Astin acknowledged that "men seem to deter women's assertiveness during the undergraduate years," he also noted that women at single-sex colleges were less likely to get good grades than women at coeducational colleges; competition with men spurred women to higher academic achievements (Astin 1977, 232–33).

Other researchers disagree with Tidball and Astin. Oates and Williamson (1978) used the *Who's Who in America 1974–1975* (rather than the *Who's Who of American Women*) to test Tidball's assertion regarding the positive effects of single-sex colleges. They agree with Tidball that women's colleges have graduated notable women at a higher rate than coeducational colleges but point out that a large proportion of those women had attended Seven Sisters colleges. They propose that the average socioeconomic status of the student bodies of the Seven Sisters may account more for these women's achievements than any effect of the school itself. Had the comparable Ivy League schools been accepting women, high achievers may have chosen to go there instead. There are not yet enough female graduates of Ivy League schools to test their lifetime accomplishments against graduates of women's colleges. Oates and Williamson further criticize Tidball's study for omitting Catholic women's colleges—schools with high proportions of female faculty but relatively few prominent achievers (Oates and Williamson 1980).

Barbara Solomon agrees with Oates and Williamson's assessment of the relative socioeconomic status of women in the Seven Sisters colleges and proposes that students gain certain advantages by attending elite schools regardless of their backgrounds. She also questions the mentoring role played by female faculty. She found relatively few professors of either sex who played a significant role in a student's development (Solomon 1985, 208).

166

The effects of women's colleges on women's achievements are tangential to an argument about space and status. First, when single-sex colleges were the only schools open to women, no comparisons existed of the relative benefits of one type of school over another. When gender segregation was pervasive, as it was until the turn of the century, any woman who attended college attended a single-sex college. The *enforced* segregation that existed until relatively recently created different conditions than the *choice* of segregation in contemporary higher education.

Second, so few women now attend single sex colleges that their experiences are less important for gender stratification than are the experiences of the vast majority of American women who attend coeducational colleges or no college at all. In 1990 approximately 125,000 women were enrolled in women's colleges (Goodman 1990), compared with 6.7 million enrolled in coeducational colleges.

167

Third, women who attend single-sex colleges tend to be from wealthier families—and have more life options—than women who attend coeducational institutions. Tuition and fees at the all-female Mills College, for example, are close to $13,000, compared with less than $2,000 for a state resident attending the University of California (Gordon 1990). Such small numbers of elite women—regardless of their own personal accomplishments—do not reflect the status of women as a group in American society.

Conclusion

The treasure-houses of knowledge so coveted by Virginia Woolf eventually unlocked their doors to women. That event began the process toward greater gender equality by granting women access to knowledge necessary for higher public status. As documented in the preceding chapter, American women won the right to vote, were granted equal property rights with men, and gained control of their own labor during the same era in which schools were becoming sexually integrated.

The beginning of the nineteenth century was characterized by the exclusion of women from access to formal education, much as women were excluded from men's huts in nonindustrial societies. Both men's huts and schools were institutions of knowledge that enhanced men's status only as long as their secrets were not revealed to women. As the century progressed, women gradually gained access to higher education, first in completely segregated colleges and then in coeducational institutions. By the beginning of the twentieth century, women had a foothold on professional training as well. At every point in the process of coeducation, women's entry was denied because masculine knowledge supposedly would harm them in some way. When a few pioneers successfully challenged contemporary practices, the rationale for excluding women from higher education weakened. As spatial barriers to equal education fell away, so too did barriers to greater public status for women.

168

The spatial arrangements of formal education are hypothesized to have a stronger association with women's status than the design of dwellings. As the United States industrialized, education became increasingly important as an avenue to public status. The educational system was organized originally around the ideology of separate spheres for women and men. Women did not need to be educated for their roles in the home, but men required an education for their roles outside the home. Schools were places in which men prepared for their positions in society, and their higher status was reinforced by their control of school admissions policies. Thus, the school is a more powerful agent of change than the dwelling. Status differences produced by differential access to education are reproduced in and reflected by dwelling design. When schools excluded women, houses had distinctly gendered room designations. As geographic and architectural segregation declined in schools, house interiors became more integrated as well.

Such structural changes in the family and in education were partially a result of industrialization. As the economy changed, so did the tasks demanded of women and men. Tracing parallel developments in the spatial segregation of home and school underscores the interdependence of institutions in reinforcing gender stratification. Education also is related to the economy, since "divisions of knowledge . . . correspond . . . to divisions of labour" (Shaw 1976, 134). Education is the critical link between private and public status for women, and thus the spatial arrangements of schools form an important connection between the home and workplace. The demise of separate spheres for women and men was hastened by the gender integration of education, which in turn contributed to gender integration of the labor force.

The Nineteenth-Century Workplace

When I was a girl, I seemed to be shut out of everything I wanted to do. I might teach school . . . I might go out dress-making or tailoring, or trim bonnets, or I might work in a factory or go out to domestic service; there the mights ended and the might nots began.—Feminist Lucy Stone, quoted in Sheila Rothman, *Woman's Proper Place*

When Lucy Stone uttered her lament in the early nineteenth century, there were only eight paid occupations an American woman might hold: teaching, needlework, keeping boarders, working in cotton mills, typesetting, bookbinding, shoe binding, or domestic service (Abbott [1910] 1969, 354). By the time the first occupational data for women were published from the census of 1870, when 15 percent of all women were employed outside the home, just four occupations (servant, clerk, teacher, factory worker) employed 93 percent of all women working in nonagricultural jobs. Four categories still accounted for nearly 80 percent of all female wage earners by 1900, when one in five women worked outside the home (Hill 1929, 3, 19, 45). These statistics are probably an undercount of women's paid labor force participation since enumerators in the nineteenth century were likely to forget to ask women about their employment, as "those so engaged constitute the exception" (Abbott 1906, 615).

Among those who constituted the exception were "women adrift," who not only entered the labor force but lived apart from family. Estimates are that 20 percent of urban wage-earning women lived outside of families in 1900. When those women mingled freely with men at work and in rooming houses, they undermined the separation of male and female spheres. These single women bridged the female domestic world of predominantly rural nineteenth-century America and the sexually integrated urban-industrial twentieth century (Meyerowitz 1988, xvii–xxiii).

The experience of black women also deviated from the norms defining separate spheres. As slaves, black women had worked inside the master's house and in the fields. Emancipated slave women who withdrew from field labor during Reconstruction had returned to it by the 1870s to contribute to the family's income under the sharecropping system (Foner 1988, 85–86). The legacy of slavery and economic necessity contributed to labor force participation rates for black women approximately double those of white women throughout the late nineteenth and well into the twentieth century (Goldin 1977). Racial discrimination in nearly every occupation open to women in the nineteenth century limited black women's options to domestic and laundry work (Goldin 1977; Katzman 1978; Pleck 1978). Thus, black women were disproportionately relegated to feminine workspaces.

Examined from the perspective of spatial segregation, there were only two types of occupations for American women in the nineteenth century: those keeping them inside the home and those taking them outside the home. Household production and domestic service kept women safely within the private sphere and raised little public disapproval, but more controversial factory and clerical jobs took women outside the home and into contact with men in the public sphere. Teaching took women outside the home but restricted their contacts primarily to other women and children and thus came closer to the acceptable domestic model than either factory or office work.* Appropriate jobs for women kept them spatially segregated from men, while controversial jobs created gender integration—and the potential for improved status for women.

It is possible that labor force participation, per se, rather than exposure to men in integrated settings, could affect women's status. Yet the occupations that limited women's contact with men in the nineteenth century were invariably ill paid and did little to enhance women's status inside or outside the home. The integrated jobs—factory and clerical work—paid better wages and led to transferable skills in an industrializing society. For example, knowledge of the machinery in textile mills and in government offices gave women a glimpse of technology typically controlled by men (see Cockburn 1983).

Sexually Segregated Occupations

Household Production. Colonial families were capable of almost total economic independence because of the large number of goods produced within

---

*Nursing, like teaching, was a predominantly female occupation that placed women in contact with other women and powerless (i.e., sick) people. Nursing was not considered a profession in the nineteenth century, however, and was classified by the census under "nurses and midwives" in the domestic and personal service category (Hill 1929, 41).

the home. The success of the Revolutionary War has been traced to the self-sufficiency of the colonists in the face of English blockades (Tryon [1917] 1966, 5). The ability to sell household goods such as cloth, butter, and produce thus was an economic option long available to American women.

Textiles became a major home industry by the late eighteenth century, with surplus bartered or sold. The introduction of cotton and woolen mills in the nineteenth century reduced the profits possible from this endeavor, and by the end of the Civil War few women did any spinning or weaving at home. Butter production took the place of cloth production as an added source of income for farm women. Records of a country store in Louisiana in 1850 reported that women from 285 farms produced 24,000 pounds of butter for sale, while 256 farms in Delaware produced an average of 602 pounds of butter per farm in the same year. Women in urban areas often took in boarders to supplement family income. An 1892 U.S. Labor Statistics report on cotton-worker families in seventeen states found that over one-quarter of all wives took in boarders, ranging from a low of 1 percent of families in Rhode Island to a high of 44 percent in Virginia (Jensen 1980).

As the nineteenth century progressed, work at home was transformed from the production of household goods to participation in the "putting-out" system, by which contractors hired women to complete piecework. Compared with the number of women who worked outside their homes, the number who worked within them was large. National estimates placed the number of women working in cotton mills in 1831 at about 39,000; estimates for Massachusetts alone placed the number of women braiding hats and binding shoes at home at 33,000 (Abbott [1910] 1969). The nation's four largest cities were estimated to have 12,000 to 13,000 women who worked at home that same year, and New York City counted more than 10,000 seamstresses working at home in 1845 (Kessler-Harris 1982, 48).

When factory looms replaced home looms, shoe binding became women's most important home occupation. By 1837 in Massachusetts, shoe binding employed more women than the cotton mills. The wages in shoe binding were neither as good nor as reliable as in the mills. Compared with women's factory wages ranging from $2 to $10 per week, shoe binding paid $1 to $4 per week and was subject to constant household interruptions. Hat making at home was next in numerical importance but had the same economic limitations as shoe binding (Abbott 1906, 621).

173

The clothing industry relied heavily on home workers. "Ready-made" garments before the invention of the sewing machine in 1850 were entirely hand sewn. Large quantities of material cut by dealers in New York City, Boston, and Philadelphia were sent to neighboring villages where the wives of farmers and sailors sewed the clothes and returned them for sale. The Massachusetts Tables of Industry reported 2,500 female seamstresses in Boston in 1837, and the number in the surrounding countryside was estimated to have been much greater (Abbott [1910] 1969, 220).

174   Technological innovations did not improve the wages of women working at home. Introduction of the sewing machine after the Civil War, though enabling women to sew more garments, also created new opportunities for exploitation by contractors. Women who sewed at home had previously had to pay for their own thread, heat, and light; now they had to buy or rent their machines as well. Seamstresses were paid four cents per pair of underwear in 1869 and could produce five pairs a day; rooms cost about $1 a week, leaving almost nothing for food or clothing. Because women worked in isolation, they were not able to fight for higher wages through unionization as men had (Kessler-Harris 1982, 78, 86).

The inability of some seamstresses to buy or rent their own sewing machines meant the women had to join shops where the machines were provided. This trend typified the shift from women's home production to their entry into factories. The transition of household production to wage labor in a central location occurred slowly but steadily, as the case of the boot and shoe industry demonstrates.

During the eighteenth century women sewed leather provided from their own livestock into shoe uppers as time permitted. By the end of the century merchants distributed cut leather to them at home, and instead of working part-time they began to work full-time. As shoe manufacturing became centralized, women were required to pick up and return the leather at a set time and place. By the 1840s women were leaving their homes to make shoes in factories. The hat making industry followed the same path from handicraft produced in a woman's spare time, to "put-out" work, to factory centralization. Even some of the cotton mills initially relied on women to spin the fabric at home before the process became routinized (Kessler-Harris 1982, 24, 28).

Women who worked in their own homes were able to stay within the appropriately prescribed domestic sphere while still contributing to family income. Since women had always been an integral part of the household economy, there was little public objection to women who earned money at home. Equally unobjectionable, because it was carried out in the private sphere, was domestic service.

Domestic Service. At the turn of the nineteenth century, many girls as young as ten or twelve years of age entered domestic service out of economic necessity and stayed with it their entire lives. Some young women saw it as **175** preferable to factory work and "lived in" with families for several years before they married. Still others were blacks or new immigrants with few skills whose only choice was housekeeping (Katzman 1978, 231). Between 1800 and 1850, domestic service was almost the only paid occupation open to women other than home production. Domestic service employed the majority of all working women at mid-century and a significant proportion up until 1900. In 1870 two-thirds of all women in nonagricultural jobs worked as household laborers; by 1900 that figure had dropped to one-third (but still accounted for the single largest proportion of all working women) (Hill 1929, 45; Katzman 1978, 53).

Black women were disproportionately represented among domestic servants during the nineteenth century due to a lack of opportunities elsewhere. Textile mills in the North hired only native born whites before turning to immigrant labor, and shops, offices, and factories in the South refused to hire black women (Kessler-Harris 1982, 137–40). Thus, an increasingly urbanized free black female population turned to domestic and laundry work after the Civil War. In 1870 one-third of black working women were servants or laundresses, compared with 6 percent of white working women (Goldin 1977). Of all servants and laundresses working in the United States in 1890, one-third were black, although black women represented only about one-tenth of all women in nonagricultural occupations (Katzman 1978, 73). Access to industrializing, gender-integrated workplaces therefore was even slower for black women than for white women.

As immigration of Irish, Germans, and blacks to the Northeast increased, and as other employment opportunities opened to women, native born whites comprised a smaller and smaller proportion of domestic servants.

Three other structural changes affected the occupation during the nineteenth century. First, domestic service shifted from work performed by single women to that performed by married women. In the process it shifted from "live in" to "day" work. Second, child labor laws and compulsory education reduced the supply of young girls. Finally, household technology reduced the need for manual labor (Katzman 1978, 93; Salmon [1897] 1972). One historian of household technology claims that society "can have vacuum cleaners or live-in maids, but not both" (Cowan 1983, 127).

176   With the exception of Chinese male servants in California, household workers were predominantly female. Gardening and maintenance work was sometimes performed by men, but 90 to 95 percent of the cooking, cleaning, laundry, and child care was performed by women (Katzman 1978, 45). Those tasks were endless in the nineteenth century. Clothes were washed by hand in water boiled on a wood stove, then ironed with heavy flatirons that had to be heated repeatedly. The washing was sometimes done by an itinerate laundress, but seldom the more backbreaking ironing. Fires were tended, bread made from scratch, vegetables canned, and soap and candles produced. The technology that standardized the manufacture of textiles had yet to be applied to other home products. In 1850 less than 10 percent of all bread eaten in the United States was provided by commercial bakeries; by 1900 that figure had reached only 25 percent (Katzman 1978, 129).

A typical day in the life of a live-in servant could extend from 6:00 A.M. to 9:00 P.M., but she was on call to the family whenever she was in the house. The weekly schedule might include a Thursday afternoon or Sunday evening off. The number of hours worked on their *days off* averaged seven for a group of servants interviewed in Massachusetts in 1898, contrasting with the ten to twelve they worked on a regular day (Salmon [1897] 1972, 144).*

Whether servants were adequately compensated for their work was a matter of debate. Some girls reportedly received only old clothes and firewood from their mistresses, yet there were few documented cases of such abuse (Katzman 1978). In her defense of domestic service, progressive reformer Lucy Maynard Salmon argued that servants were able to save more

---

*By comparison, the typical mill operative in 1845 worked eleven to thirteen hours a day but always had a full day off on Sunday (Ware 1931, 249).

than teachers when room, board, clothing, and travel expenses were considered. Salmon's 1889 survey reported domestics' wages as $168 per year, to which she added $250 per year as the value of room and board. Public school teachers, by comparison, earned an average of $545 per year, from which Salmon subtracted $260 for room and board (with no explanation for the $10 discrepancy). This gave domestics an annual income equivalent to $418, compared with a teachers' salary of $295 (Salmon [1897] 1972, 98–101).

Salmon's zeal in promoting the rewards of domestic service as a solution **177** to the "servant problem" of the day may explain her creative bookkeeping, since few other accounts placed servants so well off. Factory girls in 1889 were averaging $5.24 per week in wages and paid $1.25 per week for board, netting about $4 per week (Abbott [1910] 1969, 290). Servants were paid $3.23 per week that year and had no expenses for room and board (Salmon [1897] 1972, 88). A comparison of wages in 1900 concluded that household workers earned a real wage of $3.99 per week, compared with $5.99 for textile workers and $6.45 per week for shoe factory workers. When one considers that servants worked an average of seventy-five hours per week, compared with fifty-three hours per week for factory girls, domestic service wage rates are reduced even further (Katzman 1978, 142).

The financial differences between occupations were not always clear to working women. Factory girls declared they went to the mills because they could not live on servants' wages, while servants said they worked as domestics because they could save more than factory girls. The decision regarding factory or household work may have had less to do with the actual wages— since they varied dramatically in both kinds of work—than with personal tolerance for type of work, skill level, and desire for independence. Many factory girls said they could not tolerate the lack of privacy inherent in domestic work, and many servants said they preferred living with a family in a nice house to living in a factory boardinghouse (Robinson [1898] 1976; Salmon [1897] 1972). By the end of the century these arguments had become moot since fewer and fewer women were choosing domestic work. Its irregular hours, isolation, social stigma, and lack of independence and promotability were cited by social workers in 1913 as reasons for the decline of domestic service once other jobs became open to women. Other jobs did not open to black women, however, and domestic service became identified increasingly as black women's work (Katzman 1978, 78–140).

The isolation of domestic work brings us to its relevance for understanding the relationship between spatial segregation and gender stratification. Domestic service formed an atypically gender-segregated niche in an industrializing, sexually integrating society. Katzman identified domestic service as a "nonindustrial" occupation structured on the relationship between women that had no counterpart in other nineteenth-century occupations: "What set domestic service apart from other occupations was the mistress/servant relationship, a highly personalized one in which the worker herself was hired rather than just her labor. . . . Moreover, the high degree of personalization of the work, the retention of the home as workplace, and the relatively little job specialization was maintained in a society moving toward impersonal economic and work relationships. Household work remained outside the trend in a modernizing society that was separating workplace and home" (Katzman 1978, 146).

178

Domestic work did not prepare women to join modern society. The home was not an adequate testing ground for skills needed during industrialization, either for the mistress or the servant. Women were not schooled in the hiring and supervision of staff, and there were few principles of household management by which women were trained, due to the isolation of the workplace. Servants' skills were not transferable outside the home, and sometimes not even between homes, since every mistress had her own method of housework.

If factories represented the paternalistic approach toward employees, domestic service represented the maternalistic system. Both employer and employee were women in the vast majority of cases, and the relationship between mistress and servant was often modeled after that between mother and daughter. Terms of employment were seldom codified, with mistresses granting and withholding privileges as they would with children. The result was that domestic servants continued to operate in a nonstandardized occupation subject to the idiosyncrasies of individual mistresses, while factory girls were exposed to the discipline, skills, and scheduling increasingly necessary for success in a hierarchical workplace. Not only did domestic servants work with other women, but they did so in isolated homes and within a system that did not prepare them for independence or status in the public sphere.

Some women who had performed different types of work recognized the implications of domestic service. A mill hand who had once been a servant responded to Lucy Salmon's 1889 questionnaire about why girls disliked household service with the following: "A shop or factory girl knows just what she has to do and can go ahead and do it. I also think going out [to domestic service] makes a girl stupid in time. She gets out of style, so to speak. She never reads and does not know what is going on in the world . . . **179** it makes gossips of girls that if they worked in shops or factories would be smart girls" (Salmon [1897] 1972, 149). Rose Cohen, whose family was in need of their daughter's income, tried being a servant instead of working in a shop because she was curious about how rich people lived. In her memoirs she recalls that she did not last long because she "realized that though in the shop too I had been driven, at least there I had not been alone. I had been a worker among other workers who looked upon me as an equal and a companion" (Katzman 1978, 12).

Cohen returned to the shop because she disliked the inferior social position experienced by servants and the lack of control over her own time. These were common complaints of the day and contributed to the constant undersupply of servants. When working women chose not to enter domestic service, in part they were rejecting isolated work with other women for centralized work, often with men. Women who worked outside the home— whether their own or another's—gained the greatest autonomy and potential for status in an increasingly industrial society.

Teaching. The occupation of teaching fell midway between the sexually segregated jobs of household production and domestic service and the sexually integrated jobs of factory and office. Because it so closely duplicated the domestic sphere, teaching was an acceptable occupation for women. In fact, one was considered training for the other.

Catharine Beecher, a prominent educator and writer, felt strongly that women were better suited than men for teaching. In *An Essay on the Education of Female Teachers*, published in 1835, Beecher wrote: "It is woman, fitted by disposition, and habits, and circumstances for such duties, who . . . must aid in educating the childhood and youth of this nation. . . . Most happily, the education necessary to fit a woman to be a teacher, is exactly the one that best fits her for that domestic relation she is primarily designed to fill" (Rothman 1978, 57).

Teachers acknowledged that it was "the nature of being of the mother-sex to gather together into her care and brood over and instruct creatures younger and feebler than herself" (Rothman 1978, 58). The instruction was often of a very general nature and on a casual schedule. Women were first hired to teach summer schools (which met only several weeks or months) for **180** girls not needed at home. "Girls' academies," which stressed accomplishments like needlework and printing, were another option for women at the time. Both the content and the hours of the school day were left to the discretion of schoolteachers in the early part of the nineteenth century (Cott 1977, 32).

Encouraged by the cult of true womanhood (and poor wages), an occupation that had begun as male had become almost totally female by the end of the nineteenth century. Between 1838 and 1847 the number of women teaching in Massachusetts increased by 1,647, while the number of men declined by sixty-seven (Abbott [1910] 1969, 140). In 1840, 50 percent of all teachers in Massachusetts were male, compared with only 14 percent by 1865 (Kessler-Harris 1982, 68). In Utica, New York, in 1855, public schoolteachers were all female (Ryan 1981, 163). The Civil War shortage of men and the postwar expansion of school systems accelerated women's entrance into the field. By 1870 national estimates were that about 60 percent of all teachers were women; that figure had risen to 70 percent by 1900 (Aron 1987, 27; Hill 1929, 42; Rothman 1978, 57). The men who stayed in public education were typically in administrative or supervisory posts, while women remained in the classrooms (Rothman 1978, 59; Ryan 1981, 209). Thus, the occupation was as safely sexually segregated as if women had stayed at home.

The feminization of the profession became both a result and cause of its lesser appeal to men. School boards hired women at lower salaries than men, thus driving men out and reinforcing the cycle of lower wages. In mid-century Utica, for example, female teachers were paid $5 to $7 per week, compared with the $12 to $14 paid to males (Ryan 1981, 224). Pay scales in Massachusetts were better, but the wage gap was wider: $14 per week for female and $35 per week for male teachers. The Massachusetts Board of

Fig. 7.1. Schoolteachers at the turn of the century, like domestic servants, worked primarily with children and other women. Library of Congress.

Education reported in 1893 that women's wages, compared with men's, were "so low as to make it humiliating to report the two in connection" (Rothman 1978, 59). They were apparently not too humiliated to continue hiring women for less, however, and school boards across the nation joined Massachusetts in hiring female teachers at about one-third to one-half what they paid men (Kessler-Harris 1982, 57; Lerner 1971, 44).

Wages for women in teaching, like those in other gender-segregated work, were lower than those in the sexually integrated occupations of office and factory. Indeed, many women in the eighteenth century had not even accepted wages for teaching because it was considered a form of community service (Cott 1977, 32). Estimates for 1840 are that female cotton-mill workers in Massachusetts earned approximately $3 per week (Abbott [1910] 1969, 290). By comparison, teachers at about that same time earned "little more than a dollar a week plus board—less than a skilled factory operative earned—[and] she could work an annual term of twelve to sixteen weeks and face idleness for the rest of the year" (Kessler-Harris 1982, 56). Because wages were so poor and the work seasonal, women often combined teaching with other occupations. Women moved back and forth between teaching and mill work (Kessler-Harris 1982, 57), teaching and domestic service (Katzman 1978, 10), and teaching and clerical work (Aron 1987, 45).

After the Civil War the combination of immigration and lower wages had taken most "middling" class women out of the mills, and clerical work became the benchmark to which teaching was compared. Schoolteachers in the District of Columbia in the 1870s earned $400 to $700 per year; those in Chicago earned $500 to $875 per year at the end of the century (Aron 1987, 205). Female clerical workers, by comparison, earned $900 per year. Most importantly, clerks were eligible for promotions that could eventually lead to much higher wages than teachers'—up to $1,800 in 1894 for a woman who had clerked for twenty-five years (Aron 1987, 58, 76).

Susan B. Anthony recognized the costs associated with the increasingly gender-segregated teaching occupation. In 1853 she attended a New York State teachers convention where her male colleagues were complaining of the low status and subsistence wages characteristic of teaching. Anthony addressed the floor with the following observation: "Do you not see that so long as society says woman is incompetent to be a lawyer, minister or doctor, but has ample ability to be a teacher, every man of you who chooses this profession tacitly acknowledges that he has no more brains than a woman? And this, too, is the reason that teaching is a less lucrative profession as here men must compete with the cheap labor of woman" (Lerner 1971, 44). Anthony went on to exhort the assembly to raise wages for women, but with little success. Teaching remained a predominantly female—and poorly paid—occupation up to and throughout the twentieth century.

These three occupations—home production, domestic service, and teaching—were characterized by their identification with women's separate sphere. They were performed in a home or homelike environment and con-

sisted of more contact with other women and children than with the technological innovations of the era. While men were moving out of the home and
into time-disciplined work habits connecting them with strangers in a team
effort, women pursued tasks more responsive to the human needs of family
members than to the clock (Cott 1977, 60). Only in the sexually integrated
jobs in offices and factories were women exposed to the technological
knowledge that would prepare them for public status similar to men's.
Although inventing and repairing machines was overwhelmingly men's
work in the nineteenth century, women who entered integrated occupations
were also entering the masculine world of technology. They gained knowledge of looms in textile mills (Dublin 1979), typewriters in offices (Aron
1987), and switchboards in the telephone company (J. W. Scott 1982).
(Interestingly, clerical and operators' work became increasingly feminized as
the technology was simplified, so that by the end of the century both
occupations were predominantly female.)

183

Sexually Integrated Occupations

Because mill work was one of the few occupations open to women that
brought them into contact with men outside the home, the textile industry
provides a particularly important case study in the discussion of the relationship between spatial segregation and gender stratification. The history of the
New England cotton industry has been called the history of industrialization
in America. In 1789 Messrs. Almy and Brown of Rhode Island invited
Samuel Slater to come to Providence to build their mill in the English
tradition. By 1791 the new machinery, tended by children, was turning out
yarn. This was the beginning of American cotton manufacturing, and it
marked the beginning of the industrial revolution in this country (Ware
1931, 21).

From 1791 until the depression of 1837–39, the industry experienced
major growth. Following the depression an immigrant labor force, reduced
wages, and factory speedups revived production and profits until the Civil
War, after which the industry slowly declined. This era of American history
finally came to an end with the closing of the world's largest textile factory in
Manchester, New Hampshire, in 1936 (Hareven 1982).

"The Lowell Girls." The New England textile mills provided one of the few opportunities for independence to women in early-nineteenth-century America. Of all occupations open to women at that time, factory work paid the closest to a living wage. Women's average pay in cotton mills in the 1830s ranged from $2 to $3 per week, compared with $1.50 to $2.00 per week for teachers. Board was typically included with both jobs (Kessler-Harris 1982, 37, 57). Domestic servants earned $1.25 to $1.50 per week plus board (Salmon [1897] 1972, 58). Thus, despite work days that lasted from 5:00 A.M. until 7:00 P.M., the mills initially had little difficulty recruiting a sufficient number of native born American girls (Kessler-Harris 1982; Ware 1931).

184

Factories were organized according to the "family" system or the "boardinghouse" system. The family system was modeled after the British textile industry and existed in Rhode Island, Connecticut, and southern Massachusetts. Whole families moved to mill villages and typically lived in tenements owned by the company. All members of the family, including children over age seven or eight, worked in the factory (Ware 1931, 199).

In contrast, Francis Cabot Lowell specifically wanted to avoid mill villages of permanently poor families. His model for the Merrimack Manufacturing Company (based on earlier experience in Waltham, Massachusetts) included boardinghouses for a veritable army of farmers' daughters. He planned to attract a rotating group of young women from rural middle-class families to staff his mills. To overcome the prejudice against factory work, he provided company-run boardinghouses supervised by matrons who enforced the company's paternalistic policies of strict curfews, mandatory church attendance, and abstinence from alcohol and sex. The boardinghouses formed small communities ranging in size from thirty to sixty members, who ate meals and spent their leisure time together (Dublin 1979; Robinson [1898] 1976; Ware 1931). The success of this scheme was reflected in the transformation of East Chelmsford from a small town of 200 persons in 1820 to the glorious "city of spindles" numbering nearly 30,000 which Lowell had become by 1845 (Coolidge 1942, 45). The Merrimack Company was to become the predominant factory in New England before the Civil War, and Lowell the new model for factory towns.

Some of the girls were attracted to Lowell by its circulating library and opportunities for informal education. In 1843 there were at least five "Improvement Circles" in Lowell in which women talked about current events and shared their original essays and poetry. The outgrowth of one of these circles was the *Lowell Offering*, the first literary magazine edited and written by women (Robinson [1898] 1976).*

Lowell was internationally renowned for the virtue of its girls. Rev. William Scoresby visited the mills in 1844 to learn the secrets of "the superior moral and intellectual condition of the Lowell factory girls" for the benefit of British factory workers (Scoresby [1845] 1968). Each Lowell girl **185** was required to have a paper attesting to her character, and those suspected of being disreputable were immediately dismissed. Harriet Robinson reported that the women prided themselves on attending the same church as, and sometimes marrying into, the "best families" in the community. Lowell girls, she assured her readers, had "high standards of behavior" and "pure surroundings" (Robinson [1898] 1976, 48).

The New England textile labor force was predominantly female at the beginning of the nineteenth century. Hence, the image of the "Lowell girls" came to epitomize the industry. The social experiment that took young women out of their homes and protected their virtue in boardinghouses while putting them to profitable work in factories was innovative in comparison with the familiar British family system. Yet boardinghouse mills were few in number, compared with the hundreds that used entire families, and boardinghouse mills' aggregate labor force at any point in time amounted to less than one-half the total number of mill workers employed in New England (Ware 1931, 202).

Even in the Lowell mills there were significant numbers of men. Although men had more employment options than women in the nineteenth century, they came to Lowell for the same reasons as the women: to support families or pay off the mortgage on the farm. Also like the women, single men lived in boardinghouses with other mill hands (Robinson [1898] 1976, 18, 38–

---

*The *Offering* painted a generally rosy picture of factory life and was supported by the management as a recruitment tool (Ware 1931, 220). It was a novelty that attracted attention from such personalities of the day as Charles Dickens, Harriet Martineau, and George Sand (Robinson [1898] 1976).

39). Statistics compiled for all the factories in Lowell in 1844 show that about 6,000 women and 2,000 men were employed (Scoresby [1845] 1968, 134). The one completely gender-segregated factory was the Locks and Canals Machine Shop, which employed only men. Some men worked as supervisors or overseers of women, and others were hired as blacksmiths, carpenters, and brick masons to build the factories. Those who worked in the factories with women were mule spinners, calico printers, and dyers (Ware 1931, 243).

186   Ninety percent female in 1828, the New England textile factories were only 69 percent female in 1848 and had declined to 41 percent female by the end of the century (Kessler-Harris 1982, 68). Lowell mirrored the change. The Hamilton Company, which had been 85 percent female in 1836, was only 70 percent female by 1860 (Dublin 1979, 198). Thus, the mill-girl system that relied on farmers' daughters was relatively short-lived in the longer history of the textile industry. Gender integration of the mills proceeded simultaneously with the influx of immigrants. When Irish men entered the factories at wages below those of native born men, the boundaries between women's and men's occupations began to blur. The first men to perform "women's work" (e.g., weaving) were immigrants whose wages were also comparable to women's wages. Hiring Irish men to do women's work reinforced the lower status of both the Irish and women. The rise in proportions of men in the mills was thus matched by a rise in the proportions of foreign born, the only men who would perform "women's work" (Dublin 1979, 142–43, 198).

When the Merrimack Company of Lowell began recruiting in the 1820s, virtually all their young women were native born. After the depression of 1837–39, when wages declined and layoffs were common, mill work became less attractive to Americans, and factories began to hire more immigrants. By 1840 Irish women and men were entering the mills, and by 1850 half of all Lowell workers were Irish (Ware 1931, 230). Replacement of the spinning jenny with the spinning mule in the 1850s required greater physical strength of the operatives, as did the introduction of high-speed horizontal warping mills. The trend toward speedups and the supervision of more machines, combined with the heavier equipment, led to replacing women with men (Dublin 1979, 142; Kessler-Harris 1982, 64, 144). As the labor

Fig. 7.2. This photograph from a stereopticon company shows women and men "sorting wool after cleaning and washing" at a factory in Lawrence, Massachusetts, ca. 1916. Library of Congress.

force changed from native born American to Irish immigrant and from female to male, the boardinghouse system gave way to the family employment system (Ware 1931, 230). Thus, the extreme gender segregation characteristic of Lowell work and living arrangements lasted less than three decades out of an entire century of production (Dublin 1979; J. W. Scott 1982).

The Amoskeag Mills in Manchester, New Hampshire, were patterned after Lowell and experienced a similar transition from reliance on single girls in boardinghouses to immigrant families in tenements. The cotton depart-

Table 7.1. Sex of Employees in Amoskeag Cotton Mills by Workroom, ca. 1900

Workroom	Males	Females	Percent Female
Carding	847	451	34.7%
Spinning	741	973	56.8
Dressing	354	652	64.8
Weaving	1,914	2,372	55.3
Clothrooms	613	164	21.1
Dyehouses	393	—	0.0
Yard	208	3	1.4
Mechanical power	766	7	0.9
Land, water power	334	—	0.0
Miscellaneous	312	29	8.5
Clerical	95	121	56.0
Overseers, officials	123	22	15.2
TOTAL	6,700	4,794	41.7

Source: Hareven 1982, table 2.1.

ment of Amoskeag employed men and women in every workroom except the dye house, which was men's work. By 1900 there were even several female overseers and officials (Hareven 1982; Scoresby [1845] 1968, 134).

Further evidence that workrooms were sexually integrated is provided by a picture of the "burling room" at Amoskeag that shows five women sitting at their machines and six men standing at the folding tables beside them (Hareven 1982, 34).

A description of the seventeen major textile occupations in the cotton industry at the turn of the century identified five as employing men and women, eight as suitable only for men, and two as solely women's work. Two occupations were not identified by sex, at least one of which (doffer) was typically performed by children (Hareven 1982, appendix F).

Factory work throughout the nineteenth century, even in the twenty years in which it was most sexually segregated, provided women their first opportunities to earn a living wage. In an era characterized by little power or status for women outside the home, a salary provided avenues to both power and status beyond the domestic sphere. Contributors to the *Lowell Offering* parlayed their talents into attracting better husbands than they might have

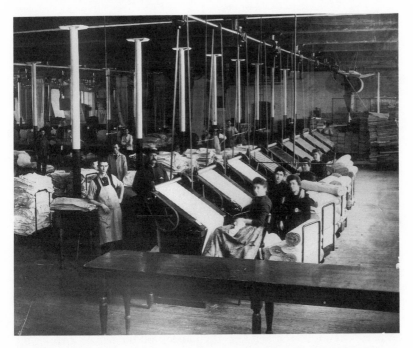

Fig. 7.3. The burling room of Amoskeag Mills in New Hampshire, 1910. Courtesy of Manchester, N.H., Historic Association, Amoskeag Manufacturing Co. Records

met back home on the farm, and many of them went on to public achievements in later life. Among the "graduates" from the Lowell factories were teachers, missionaries, a sculptor, an acting U.S. treasurer, and newspaper and magazine editors and writers (Robinson [1898] 1976, xii). These were remarkable accomplishments given the domestic role considered appropriate for women at the time.

A certain number of elite women always have received better education and training and achieved greater public status than their contemporaries in eras when women's status was lowest. What makes the experience of the factory girls so interesting is that thousands of them passed through the mills. They represented not the American elite but the emerging middle class. Joining a paid labor force, with men, could provide the experience and knowledge necessary to allow women as a group access to greater status outside the family. Harriet Robinson recognized that potential in her memoirs: "For the first time in this country woman's labor had a money value.

She had become not only an earner and producer, but also a spender of money, a recognized factor in the political economy of her time. And thus a long upward step in our material civilization was taken; woman had begun to earn and hold her own money, and through its aid had learned to think and act for herself" (Robinson [1898] 1976, 42).

After the original Lowell girls were replaced by immigrant successors, there were few socially acceptable employment outlets for middle-class women. Teaching continued to pay poorly, making it difficult for women to support themselves or others by that occupation. The acceptable alternative that emerged after the Civil War, which eventually outstripped the textile industry in providing jobs for women, was clerical work.

"*Ladies of the Civil Service.*" The federal government led the way in hiring female clerks. There were no women employed in executive offices in 1859, but by 1870 there were nearly 1,000 (16 percent of all clerks); by the end of the century approximately 6,000 women constituted one-third of all federal clerical workers (Aron 1987, 5). Private industry followed the government's example, and between 1870 and 1900 the female share of the clerical labor force increased from 2 to 30 percent (Rotella 1981, 62). Clerical work accounted for less than 1 percent of all working women in 1870 but had increased to 9 percent by 1900 (Hill 1929, table 33).

Clerks in the nineteenth century performed a wider variety of duties than clerical workers today. The work of civil-service offices varied from routinized copying to establishing federal regulations of eligibility for government benefits. The antebellum civil service employed men for legal and accounting tasks, and when women were hired after the Civil War, their work eventually became as varied as that of men. Although the bureaucracy was becoming more rationalized, a great deal of variation existed among offices in the types of jobs considered appropriate for women. Some supervisors relegated women to typing and stenography, but others promoted them to responsible positions requiring judicial decision making (Aron 1987, 72–76).

As offices became more mechanized, clerical work became more routinized and more feminized. Eighteenth- and early-nineteenth-century offices consisted of a bookkeeper, general clerk, and an executive (all male). Clerks were expected to take on managerial functions and to know some

Fig. 7.4. Women and men worked side by side in the printshops of the Bureau of Engraving and Printing at the turn of the century. Frances Benjamin Johnston Collection and Waldon Fawcett Collection, Library of Congress.

191

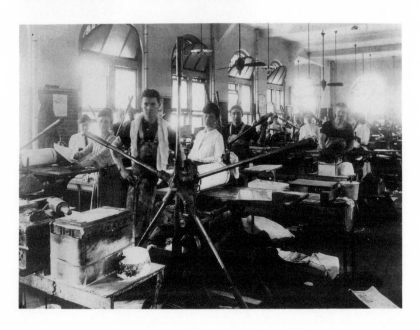

Latin, Greek, arithmetic, science, and geography. Their tools were the quill pen, ledger book, and letter press (for duplicating). After the typewriter was introduced in 1874, there was an explosion in growth of the clerical sector: by 1890—less than twenty years after the invention of the machine—over 33,000 people were employed as typists. Most of them were women. By the beginning of the twentieth century clerical work, which had been described in 1871 as requiring "knowledge of languages, skills in accounts, familiarity with even minute details of business, energy, promptitude, tact, and delicacy of perception," had become routine and mechanized (Rotella 1981, 70). This routinization and feminization would eventually lead to the female secretarial "pools" supervised by male managers.

It took more than fifty years for clerical work to become predominantly female, however, and Aron (1987) suggests that the white-collar workplace in which clerks operated was one of the interstices between the separate spheres of women and men in the nineteenth century. Clerical work thus became the testing ground for a society less segregated by gender. It may also have been, like factory work, one of the first times women were exposed to information and on-the-job training similar to that which men received.

Initially, women were recruited to civil-service work because they could be hired at lower salaries than men. The work was clean and appealed to native born, middle-class women as a respectable way to earn a living. Female clerks first worked in the Treasury Department clipping currency. Male clerks earning $1,200 per year had been performing the task, but after one woman was tested on a trial basis and excelled at the work, only women were subsequently hired for the job. The decision was purely economic: women were paid $600 per year, exactly one-half the male salary. Even when Congress raised women's salaries to $900 per year in 1865, female clerks were more cost-effective than males (Aron 1987, 70).

Women in the bureaucracy initially were segregated from men. The currency clippers generally worked only in rooms with other women, and female Patent Office employees were required to do their copying at home. This soon proved to be inefficient. In 1869, when the Patent Office employed sixty-five women at home, the commissioner changed office policy. He noted that "in order to secure proper discipline and efficient work," it was "obvious that this force must labor within the Office." He then hired

Fig. 7.5. The currency counting room at the Bureau of Engraving and Printing brought women into contact with male supervisors in a white-collar workplace. Frances Benjamin Johnston Collection, Library of Congress.

additional female employees and put them to work in six rooms in the Patent Office building (Aron 1987, 73).

Just as cloth and shoe manufacturers shifted women from household production to "put-out" work and then into the factory, the integration of women into the white-collar workplace proceeded in stages as well. Women first worked at home, then in gender-segregated rooms, and eventually in sexually integrated offices. The trip from home to office was often accompanied by an improvement in salaries. Whereas women who worked at home or in sexually segregated rooms averaged $700 to $900 per year, those who had been promoted to work in sexually integrated offices might be earning up to $1,800 per year (Aron 1987, 73–76).

Just as factory work paid more than other blue-collar work, office work paid more than other white-collar occupations open to women at the time. Federal female office workers earned an average salary of $900 per year, compared with teachers' salaries of $400 to $700 per year in the 1870s (Rotella 1981, 158). The office women shared another characteristic with New England farm girls: they often used their high earnings to buy brothers or sons the college educations for which they were not eligible. With the

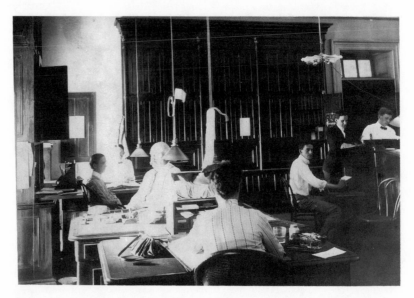

Fig. 7.6. The U.S. Secret Service had sexually integrated offices by 1906. Waldon Fawcett Collection, Library of Congress.

same goal as the "provident mill girl" of forty years earlier, Marion Porter went to work for the government in 1889 at the age of eighteen so that her seventeen-year-old brother might continue studying for the university (Aron 1987, 49). Harriet Robinson remembered that she had "known more than one [girl] to give every cent of her wages, month after month, to her brother, that he might get the education necessary to enter some profession." One estimate was that one-quarter of the men at Harvard were "being carried through by the special self-denial and sacrifices of women" working in the mills (Robinson [1898] 1976, 47).

It is not possible to conclude that women working with men earned more than women working with other women (or alone) solely because of the sexual integration of the workplace. The occupations and the factors that determined their wages were too complex. However, women gained advantages by entering an integrated work environment that set the stage for opportunities not possible in segregated work. Becoming a supervisor in the mills, for example, depends on being exposed to all types of workers and tasks. Promotions in an office are won by learning skills from colleagues. Wages are raised through collective action, not by working in isolation.

Aron was correct in assessing the federal bureaucracy as a crucible of change in gender relations in nineteenth-century America: "The women who sat down in government offices, picked up their pens, and successfully carried out duties identical to those of the man at the next desk, necessarily came into daily and direct contact with their male coworkers—something that raised a host of new situations for nineteenth-century, middle-class ladies and gentlemen" (Aron 1987, 91).

Not only did a sexually integrated workplace create a crisis of middle-class manners and morals, it created an economic crisis—the possibility that women could hold the same occupations and earn the same salaries as men. Although men continued to earn more than women throughout the century, male and female clerical wages more closely approximated each other as work was reorganized within the bureaucracy. As women took formerly "male" jobs and men took "female" jobs, women received raises and men took demotions that reduced the wage gap. By 1901 there were more women earning top salaries and more men earning the lowest salaries in the federal government than there had been in 1863 (Aron 1987, 84).

Another parallel between factory and office work was the public concern over the morality of men and women working in the same place. In 1855 the secretary of the interior was quoted as saying he had no objection to the employment of competent women as long as they worked at home, but "there is such an obvious impropriety in the mixing of the sexes within the walls of public office, that I determined to arrest the practice" (Aron 1987, 211). That same sentiment was expressed about the working conditions in factories. In 1885 a male representative from the Cleveland Cigar Makers' Union #17 stated: "There is one thing existing in our trade that I would like to have abolished, and that is . . . women and men working together in one shop. That, we claim, is improper and detrimental to morality under the present system" (Kessler-Harris 1982, 102).*

There may have been some cause for concern in an era when the boundaries of appropriate behavior were being redefined. Sexual improprieties

---

*In the British pottery industry, women who worked in same-sex departments were reportedly "a better class of girl" than those in departments where they "mixed with the lads" (Bradley 1989, 121).

within the Treasury Department were investigated within three years of women's arrival, and newspaper accounts of "treasury courtesans" threatened to tarnish the image of every woman working in an office. Passages from Mary Clemmer Ames's *Ten Years in Washington*, published in 1873, echoed Harriet Robinson's tone in defending the working girl's virtue: "The truth is, that there is not any other company of women workers in the land which number so many ladies of high character, intelligence, culture, and social position" (Aron 1987, 168).

196   Public distrust of sexually integrated offices persisted until the twentieth century. As long as women were engaged in household production, teaching, or domestic service, they were perceived as morally protected. In the home women were in contact primarily with relatives, and in the schools teachers were in contact primarily with children. The acceptability of domestic service was based on the (often erroneous) assumption that it provided a moral environment free from the vices of factory and office. (In fact, servants were often subject to sexual exploitation by masters [Katzman 1978, 216].)

When women entered the public (i.e., male) sphere, they ran the risk of being stigmatized as morally suspect—whether in the factory or in the office. Such informal mechanisms of control served to discourage women from pushing into a predominantly male labor force. Expressing fears of loose morals may have been more socially acceptable than expressing fears of economic competition. The sexual integration of the workplace was clearly perceived as a threat when it first occurred, but the threat was defined on moral grounds rather than on the economic grounds which seem, in retrospect, to be the more realistic fear.

Conclusion

In nineteenth-century America, women's separate sphere began to crumble when colleges opened their doors and an industrializing labor force demanded more workers. Public opposition to working women was least pronounced for jobs that kept women at home and most vociferous for jobs that took them outside the home.

Household production of butter, bonnets, or clothing was acceptable, as was domestic service. Teaching was also acceptable for women because it took place in a homelike environment in which women were in contact primarily with other women and children. These three sexually segregated occupations—home production, domestic service, and teaching—separated women from access to the newly emerging technology fueling industrialization. Whether isolated in separate homes or concentrated with other powerless individuals, women in sexually segregated occupations subscribed to a matriarchal model of work that ill suited them to success in the new economy.

197

Two sexually integrated jobs open to women in the nineteenth century were factory and clerical work. Not surprisingly, these were the most controversial occupations for women. Contact between the sexes in the workplace was highly suspect; misgivings were couched in terms of fears for women's virtue. Just as higher education initially threatened women's physical health, sexually integrated workplaces threatened women's moral well-being.

In retrospect, the real danger of having women and men in the same workplace was that it provided women access to the same technology as men. Like coeducation, the road from sexually separated to sexually integrated factories and offices was characterized by advances and retreats. Women gained access to occupations but often were denied apprenticeships necessary to master the new technology. Labor unions played a pivotal role in blocking women's access to the most technologically sophisticated jobs, thereby perpetuating gendered workspaces (Bradley 1989; Cockburn 1983).

In sum, women's low status in the nineteenth century was reinforced by their segregation from men in the domestic sphere, in higher education, and in acceptable "women's occupations." Lack of access to knowledge in school and the workplace limited women's ability to gain property rights and the vote. Exclusion from the political arena, in turn, reinforced public insistence on women's "proper place" in the home. The twentieth century would see more women in coeducational colleges and in the labor force, but relatively little change in workplace segregation.

The Contemporary Workplace

Job segregation by sex . . . is the primary mechanism in capitalist society that maintains the superiority of men over women, because it enforces lower wages for women in the labor market.—Heidi Hartmann, "Capitalism, Patriarchy, and Job Segregation by Sex"

While Hartmann may not have had spatial segregation in mind when she made this declaration, often it accompanies occupational segregation. Spatial arrangements at work help reinforce status differentials between women and men. Unlike segregation in dwellings and in schools, however, segregation in the workplace has remained fairly stable since the nineteenth century.

The twentieth century began with 18 percent of white women and 43 percent of black women in the labor force (Goldin 1977, 88). In 1900 one out of five workers was female (Bianchi and Spain 1986, 141). The twentieth century is ending with labor force participation rates of 58 percent for both white and black women (U.S. Department of Labor 1991, 165, 166). Black women began and are ending the century disproportionately concentrated in private household and service work (Katzman 1978, 74; Kessler-Harris 1982, 270; Rosenfeld 1984; U.S. Department of Labor 1990, 182). Thus, black women are more likely than white women to be working in a separate domestic sphere. Both white and black women are now more likely to be working in clerical and secretarial jobs than at the turn of the century, and these occupations are now more "feminine" than in 1900. The current distribution of women's jobs is not so different from that at the turn of the century when one considers the magnitude of changes in the occupational structure since 1900. Although women now constitute nearly half of the labor force, they do not necessarily constitute half of the workers in any given workplace.

Occupational Segregation

Extensive research has been conducted on the occupational segregation of women and men (Blaxall and Reagan 1976; Brinton 1989; Brown and Pechman 1987; Jacobs 1989; Reskin 1984; Reskin and Hartmann 1986; Roos 1985). Relatively high levels of gender occupational segregation have existed since the turn of the century and have only recently begun to decline.

In 1900 approximately two-thirds of working women would have had to change jobs to have the same occupational distribution as men (Gross 1968), a proportion that had declined to just over one-half by 1986 (Jacobs 1989) (see table 8.1). A 1910 survey of thirty-one American factories reported that 99 percent of employees worked only with their own sex; of nearly 4,000 workers interviewed, only ten women were in "male" jobs and seven men in "female" jobs (Bradley 1989, 155).

Occupational segregation by gender has declined for both whites and blacks. Occupations contributing most to the reduction among blacks are those of laborer and service worker. The dramatic decline in numbers of private household maids has had the most significant impact on occupational segregation among blacks, although black women are still more likely than white women to work in service occupations (Beller 1984; Rosenfeld 1984).

The labor force was 45 percent female in 1989. Three categories of occupations were disproportionately female: administrative support (80 percent), private household workers (96 percent), and service workers (65 percent). Just over one-quarter of all employed women worked in administrative support occupations in 1989. By comparison, the largest category for men (executive, administrative, and managerial) accounted for only 14 percent of all male workers (U.S. Department of Labor 1990, 182–85).

Explanations. The occupational choices made by women and men are influenced by the cultural, social, political, and structural contexts within which they occur. Stereotypes about appropriate or inappropriate occupations affect workers' choices by influencing their aspirations, identity, and commitment (Reskin and Hartmann 1986, 42), and family responsibilities may require part-time work of women but not of men.

Protective labor legislation, in effect from 1874 until 1964, prevented women from holding jobs requiring heavy lifting, long hours, or night work. Hiring preferences for veterans and the exclusion of women (but not men) of childbearing age from exposure to toxic chemicals further reduce women's access to certain jobs (Reskin and Hartmann 1986, 46). Once in the workplace, such factors as discrimination, nepotism rules, seniority preferences, the locations of job postings, and even the design of tools (e.g., for large, rather than small, hands) can present obstacles to job integration. Informal barriers, such as exclusion from social networks or clubs, can also

202

Table 8.1. Gender Segregation in Occupations in the United States, 1900–1986

Date	Index of Dissimilarity Score*
1900	66.9
1910	69.0
1920	65.7
1930	68.4
1940	69.0
1950	65.6
1960	68.4
1970	67.9
1980	59.4
1986	57.3

Source: 1900–1960 scores from Gross 1968; 1970 and 1980 scores from Bianchi and Rytina 1986; 1986 score from Jacobs 1989.
*The percentage of employees (male or female) who would have to change occupations to achieve gender integration.

operate to reduce women's mobility and thus their potential for integration. The sexually segregated structure of the labor market is further reinforced by the operation of same-sex information networks. Women are most likely to hear of job vacancies from other women in "female" occupations, while men are most likely to hear of "male" job vacancies (Holden and Hansen 1987, 235).

The opportunity structure of the labor market tends to influence occupational segregation as well. Demand for certain types of occupations can create a supply of workers. As clerical work expanded at the turn of the century, for example, the occupation became increasingly female. Clerical work and typewriting were eventually reclassified from "male" to "female" occupations due to the strong response of women to the demand for clerks and typists (and to employers' willingness to hire women for lower wages). By 1908 the Audit and Policy Division of the Metropolitan Life Insurance Company employed 287 bookkeepers, all of whom were men, and 752 clerks, all of whom were women. The earliest telephone operators were men, but women replaced them in the 1880s; one hundred years later, more than 90 percent of telephone operators are women (while telephone installers and repairers are predominantly male) (J. W. Scott 1982).

Racial discrimination also interacts with gender to create occupational segregation. Often the firms most likely to hire women are least likely to hire blacks. Before World War I, for example, department stores rarely hired black women (Kessler-Harris 1982, 139). Even during the labor shortages of World War II, electrical manufacturing firms relied heavily on female labor but resisted hiring black women (Milkman 1987, 55). Robert Weaver concluded in his authoritative 1946 publication titled *Negro Labor* that "those industries which delayed longest the employment of Negroes were usually light and clean manufacturing. They were the industries in which women (white) were used in the largest proportions" (Milkman 1987, 55).*

204

Consequences. Occupational segregation carries costs for all of society to the extent that allocation of human resources on the basis of gender may depress overall productivity. In more concrete terms, however, women pay the greater costs associated with segregation, since "women's occupations" are less economically rewarding than "men's occupations" (Roos 1985; Rosenfeld and Kalleberg 1990).

A substantial part of the discrepancy between women's and men's earnings has been attributed to segregation *between occupations*. The higher the percentage female in an occupation, the lower the wages. Employment in female occupations lowers incomes for both sexes, but since there are relatively more women than men in such jobs, the greatest effect is on women's earnings (England et al., 1988). The National Research Council's Committee on Occupational Classification and Analysis concluded that occupational segregation accounts for about 35 to 40 percent of the sex difference in average earnings (Treiman and Hartmann 1981).

Sex segregation *within occupations* also contributes to the wage gap. That is, women and men reporting the same *occupation* may work in different *jobs*. When expensive restaurants hire men to wait tables and coffee shops hire women, job segregation within the occupational category of waiter exists. Under these circumstances, male waiters will earn more in salaries and tips than female waiters.

---

*Parallels exist in Great Britain, where traditionally female jobs such as secretary, receptionist, and shop assistant are seldom held by black (West Indian) women (Bradley 1989, 15).

Segregation *between firms* also operates to reduce women's earnings if men are disproportionately employed in better-paying firms. In a sexually integrated occupation such as that of accounting clerk, men tend to earn more than women because they work in firms that pay more (Blau 1977). Similar discrepancies in the salary ranges of firms hiring predominantly one sex have been found for retail sales clerks (Talbert and Bose 1977) and for college faculty (Johnson and Stafford 1974).

Finally, segregation *within firms* plays a role in earnings differences. When men and women filling the same occupations in the same firm are assigned **205** different jobs, different wages typically result. Male retail clerks in a department store, for example, are likely to be assigned to "big ticket" departments, such as appliances and furniture, while female clerks are assigned departments with smaller commissions (Talbert and Bose 1977).

Female employees of Sears, Roebuck, and Company filed suit over such segregation in the 1980s. They argued that the company's practices reflected an outdated era in which "in a *normally* organized department store, there will be men in the sports-goods department, women to sell curtains and dishware, men to sell hardware . . . wedding silver and furniture" (Caplow 1964, 232; emphasis added). (Wedding silver, arguably a "feminine" item, seems to fall into the masculine domain by virtue of its price.)

Lower wages are only one of the negative consequences of occupational segregation for women. Others include fewer retirement benefits, higher susceptibility to unemployment, lower occupational prestige, and less domestic authority. Partly because they are concentrated in low-wage, less profitable firms, women are less likely than men to be covered by private pension plans. The retail and service industries—which employ one-quarter of all women—have the lowest pension coverage rates of any occupational category. Once retired, only one in ten women receives private pension income, compared with more than one in four men. Because women earn less than men throughout their lives, their social security and retirement benefits also are lower (Reskin and Hartmann 1986, 13–17).

The implications of occupational segregation for women's wages and status are clear. There are no conditions under which occupational segregation works to women's benefit. Rather, women's jobs pay less and offer fewer benefits than men's jobs. Indeed, the persuasiveness of the argument that occupational segregation contributes significantly to wage differences is buttressed by the fact that both occupational segregation scores and the ratio of women's to men's wages have remained relatively stable over time despite increases in women's educational attainment, labor force participation rates, and labor force attachment.

Spatial Segregation in the Workplace

206 To what extent do women and men who work in different occupations also work in different spaces? Baran and Teegarden (1987, 206) propose that occupational segregation in the insurance industry is "tantamount to spatial segregation by gender" since managers are overwhelmingly male and clerical staff are predominantly female. This section examines the spatial conditions of women's work and men's work and proposes that working women and men come into daily contact with one another very infrequently. Further, women's jobs can be classified as "open floor," but men's jobs are more likely to be "closed door." That is, women work in a more public environment with less control of their space than men. This lack of spatial control both reflects and contributes to women's lower occupational status by limiting opportunities for the transfer of knowledge from men to women.

It bears repeating that my argument concerning space and status deals with structural workplace arrangements of women as a group and men as a group, *not* with occupational mobility for individual men and women. Extraordinary people always escape the statistical norm and experience upward mobility under a variety of circumstances. The emphasis here is on the ways in which workplaces are structured to provide different spatial arrangements for the typical working woman and the typical working man and how those arrangements contribute to gender stratification.

Relatively little information exists on the spatial context in which people perform their jobs. Bielby and Baron's work on occupational segregation includes acknowledgment of "spatial desegregation" in which men and women occupy the same job but in different locations. Their research included over 400 California firms for a twenty-year period and found numerous instances of nominal job-title integration but de facto locational segregation. For example, some real estate firms employed male and female

Fig. 8.1. The "open floor" aspect of women's jobs is reflected in this clerical space at the Johnson Wax Corporation Building in Racine, Wisconsin, designed by Frank Lloyd Wright and built in the late 1930s. Frank Lloyd Wright Collection, Library of Congress.

managers and sales representatives (identical job descriptions), but female managers supervised only female clerks in some offices, while male managers supervised salespeople elsewhere (Baron and Bielby 1985, 240).

Another example was a real estate management business that employed 23 male and 126 female apartment managers, who worked and lived in 149 different buildings; male and female managers of the escrow service were dispersed across field offices throughout a large metropolitan area. In both cases women and men had the same rank and responsibilities, but each workplace had near-perfect spatial gender segregation. Residential children's camps and special educational institutions in which male counselors supervise boys and female counselors supervise girls provide similar instances of de facto spatial segregation despite ostensible occupational integration (Bielby and Baron 1984, 43).

The Bielby and Baron research shows that only one-half of the firms studied employed both men and women in mixed occupations. Of the 12,000 workers employed in mixed occupations, one-third were in organizations that did not hire members of the opposite sex in their line of work. This separation of women from men in the workplace suggests a spatial basis for gender differences in promotions and earnings potential (Bielby and Baron 1986, 779, 788). Spatial segregation may also work to the employers' advantage: if women lack information about the reward structure for men, they will not know they are working for less (Bielby and Bielby 1988, 1035). Walby (1986, 154) argues that employers deliberately create occupational segregation as a way to appease men's objections to competition with women and as justification for paying women less.*

*Great Britain's labor force is characterized by similar levels of occupational segregation (Crompton and Sanderson 1990). The 1946 Royal Commission on Equal Pay found only sixteen tasks in the entire manufacturing industry that had any overlap in men's and women's employment. "Factories had become strange segregated environments, in which men and women worked in separate spaces, at different tasks." Case studies of the formerly gender-integrated fishing and mining industries reveal both as now completely male. Pottery manufacturing is even more gender-segregated now than during the late nineteenth century. Hosiery plants still spatially separate male and female workers, often segregating white from black workers as well (Bradley 1989, 116, 129, 143).

Another data source with tangential information on spatial segregation is a survey conducted by Barbara Gutek to assess sexual harassment in the workplace (Gutek 1985). Gutek interviewed 1,232 randomly selected employed men and women in Los Angeles County in 1980 to determine the extent of their contact with members of the opposite sex. The initial sample consisted of 1,392 persons, 160 (11.5 percent) of whom were eliminated from further participation because they did not come into contact with the opposite sex at work in any capacity (as coworkers, supervisors, customers, or clients) (Gutek 1985, 187). Thus, more than one in ten workers was **209** completely segregated from the other sex on the job.

After those ineligible for the study had been eliminated, three questions were used to measure daily contact between male and female employees. Those items are reproduced in table 8.2.

The majority of workers (51.2 percent) reported having "a great deal" of opportunity for job-related talk with the opposite sex at work; approximately one-third reported a great deal of opportunity to talk socially with the opposite sex; and 44 percent reported a great deal of time spent working with the opposite sex. However, approximately one in ten workers reported no contact with the opposite sex on any of these three criteria: 8.6 percent did not engage in job-related talk, 12.1 percent did not talk socially with the opposite sex, and 12.5 percent spent no time working with the opposite sex.

This last measure shows the largest discrepancy between male and female responses. Women are more likely to work with men than men are to work with women (see also Bielby and Baron 1986, 793). These results suggest that women work in more sexually integrated environments than men, a finding contrary to what the high female proportions in "female" jobs would indicate. However, the occupational classification of respondents to the Gutek survey reflects a greater representation of men in blue-collar jobs (31 percent were in skilled, semi-skilled, or unskilled work, compared with 10 percent of women) and women in white-collar jobs (47 percent were clerical, compared with 18 percent of men) (Gutek 1985, 23). Thus, women's work is more likely to bring them into contact with male supervisors, clients, or customers, but men's work (in construction or trucking) is unlikely to expose them to women.

The inclusion of clients and customers in these measures of contact

Table 8.2. Measures of Contact between Female and Male Workers in Los Angeles County, 1980

Degree of Contact	Percent of Workers*		
	Total	Female	Male
Opportunity for job-related talk with opposite sex:			
A great deal	51.2%	53.8%	45.9%
Some	39.9	37.7	44.4
None	8.6	8.1	9.6
Opportunity to talk socially with opposite sex:			
A great deal	30.6	30.7	30.4
Some	57.1	56.3	58.8
None	12.1	12.8	10.6
Amount of time required to work with opposite sex:			
A great deal	44.2	49.4	33.3
Some	42.9	40.1	48.6
None	12.5	9.9	17.8
N	1,232	827	405

Source: Gutek, personal communication.
*May not equal 100.0% due to missing data.

210

strengthen the data because it assigns a very liberal definition to "contact." Given the breadth of possible interaction, 12 percent of all workers were eliminated from the survey because they worked entirely with the same sex, *and* another 9 to 12 percent reported no opportunity to talk or work with the opposite sex. Taken together, the data suggest that a conservative estimate is that one-fifth to one-quarter of employed persons have no contact of any kind with the opposite sex in the workplace.

Two other studies have mentioned the spatial context of work. Mennerick's (1975) analysis of the New York City travel industry revealed that female top executives most often manage female subordinates, while male top executives most often manage male subordinates. Further, male managers predominate in the more prestigious agencies, and female managers are more often found in the less prestigious. Talbert and Bose's (1977) study of retail clerks found what they called an "environmental context" of wage differences between women and men. Male clerks tend to be concentrated in higher-paying specialty shops, and female clerks are concentrated in lower-paying department or discount stores. Within stores, men are more likely than women to be working in high-status departments with larger sales volumes (Talbert and Bose 1977).

These limited examples of the existence of spatial segregation in the workplace point up the paucity of data on the topic. The remainder of this **211** chapter attempts to deal with this lack of data by concentrating on typical women's and men's occupations in terms of the spatial conditions of the work. Both secrecy and privacy are reinforced by the ability to control the space in which important knowledge is kept. As the next section demonstrates, women are much less likely than men to work in jobs in which they control space and information.

Typical Women's Work: "Open-Floor Jobs." A significant proportion of women are employed in just three occupations: teaching, nursing, and secretarial work. In 1990 these three categories alone accounted for 16.5 million women, or 31 percent of all women in the labor force (U.S. Department of Labor 1991, 163, 183). Aside from being concentrated in occupations that bring them primarily into contact with other women, women are also concentrated spatially in jobs that limit their access to knowledge. The work of elementary schoolteachers, for example, brings them into daily contact with children, but with few other adults. When not dealing with patients, nurses spend their time in a lounge separate from the doctors' lounge. Nursing and teaching share common spatial characteristics with the third major "women's job"—that of secretary.

Secretarial/clerical work is the single largest job category for American women. In 1990, 14.9 million women, or more than one of every four employed women, were classified as "administrative support, including clerical"; 98 percent of all secretaries are female (U.S. Department of Labor 1991, 163, 183). Secretarial and clerical occupations account for over three-quarters of this category and epitomize the typical "woman's job." It is similar to teaching and nursing in terms of the spatial context in which it occurs.

Two spatial aspects of secretarial work operate to reduce women's status. One is the concentration of many women together in one place (the secretarial "pool") that removes them from observation of and/or input into the decision-making processes of the organization. Those decisions occur behind the "closed doors" of the managers' offices. Second, paradoxically, is the very public nature of the space in which secretaries work. The lack of privacy, repeated interruptions, and potential for surveillance contribute to an inability to turn valuable knowledge into human capital that might advance careers or improve women's salaries relative to men's.

212

Like teachers and nurses, secretaries process knowledge, but seldom in a way beneficial to their own status. In fact, secretaries may wield considerable informal power in an organization, because they control the information flow. Management, however, has very clear expectations about how secretaries are to handle office information. Drawing from their successful experience with grid theory, business consultants Robert Blake, Jane Mouton, and Artie Stockton have outlined the ideal boss-secretary relationship for effective office teamwork. In the first chapter of *The Secretary Grid*, an American Management Association publication, the following advice is offered:

> The secretary's position at the center of the information network raises the issue of privileged communications and how best to handle it. Privileged communication is information the secretary is not free to divulge, no matter how helpful it might be to others. And the key to handling it is the answer to the question "Who owns the information?" The answer is, "The boss does." . . . The secretary's position with regard to this information is that of the hotel desk clerk to the contents of the safety deposit box that stores the guest's valuables. She doesn't own it, but she knows what it is and what is in it. The root of the word *secretary* is, after all, *secret*: something kept from the knowledge of others. (Blake, Mouton, and Stockton 1983, 4–5; emphasis in original)

In other words, secretaries are paid *not* to use their knowledge for personal gain, but only for their employers' gain. The workplace arrangements that separate secretaries from managers within the same office reinforce status differences by exposing the secretary mainly to other secretaries bound by the same rules of confidentiality. Lack of access to and interaction

Fig. 8.2. The secretarial space in the School of Architecture at the University of Virginia is visible from a window at the entrance of Campbell Hall (built in 1970). Photograph by Marsha Spain Fuller.

with managers inherently limits the status women can achieve within the organization.

The executive secretary is an exception to the rule of gendered spatial segregation in the workplace. The executive secretary may have her own office, and she has access to more aspects of the managerial process than other secretaries. According to another American Management Association publication titled *The Successful Secretary*: "Probably no person gets to observe and see management principles in operation on a more practical basis than an executive secretary. She is privy to nearly every decision the executive makes. She has the opportunity to witness the gathering of information and the elements that are considered before major decisions are made and implemented" (Belker 1981, 191).

Yet instructions to the successful executive secretary suggest that those

Fig. 8.3. The office of the dean's secretary in Campbell Hall has a door that shuts, although the wall is made of glass. Photograph by Marsha Spain Fuller.

with the closest access to power are subject to the strictest guidelines regarding confidentiality. When physical barriers are breached and secretaries spend a great deal of time with the managers, rules governing the secretary's use of information become more important. The executive secretary is cautioned to hide shorthand notes, remove partially typed letters from the typewriter, lock files, and personally deliver interoffice memos to prevent unauthorized persons from gaining confidential information from the boss's office (Belker 1981, 66).

The executive secretary has access to substantial information about the company, but the highest compliment that can be paid her is that she does not divulge it to anyone or use it for personal gain. Comparing the importance of confidentiality to the seal of the confessional, Belker counsels secretaries that "the importance of confidentiality can't be over-emphasized. Your company can be involved in some delicate business matters or negotiations, and the wrong thing leaked to the wrong person could have an adverse effect on the result. . . . Years ago, executive secretaries were sometimes referred to as confidential secretaries. It's a shame that title fell out of popular usage, because it's an accurate description of the job" (Belker 1981, 73–74).

Typical Men's Work: "Closed-Door Jobs." The largest occupational category for men is that of manager. In 1990, 8.9 million men were classified as "executive, administrative, and managerial." This group constituted 14 percent of all employed men (U.S. Department of Labor 1991, 163, 183). Thus, more than one in ten men works in a supervisory position.

Spatial arrangements in the workplace reinforce these status distinctions, partially by providing more "closed door" potential to managers than to those they supervise. Although sales and production supervisors may circulate among their employees, their higher status within the organization is reflected by the private offices to which they can withdraw. The expectation is that privacy is required for making decisions that affect the organization. Rather than sharing this privacy, the secretary is often in charge of "gatekeeping"—protecting the boss from interruptions.

Just as there are professional manuals for the successful secretary, there are also numerous guidelines for the aspiring manager. Harry Levinson's widely read *Executive* (1981) (a revision of his 1968 *The Exceptional Executive*) stresses the importance of managerial knowledge of the entire organization. A survey of large American companies asking presidents about suitable qualities in their successors revealed the following profile: "A desirable successor is a person with a general knowledge and an understanding of the whole organization, capable of fitting specialized contributions into profitable patterns. . . . The person needs a wide range of liberal arts knowledge together with a fundamental knowledge of business. . . . A leader will be able to view the business in global historical and technical perspective. Such a perspective is itself the basis for the most important requisite, what one might call 'feel'—a certain intuitive sensitivity for the right action and for handling relationships with people" (Levinson 1981, 136).

The importance of knowledge is stressed repeatedly in this description. The successful manager needs knowledge of the organization, of liberal arts, and of business in general. But equally important is the intuitive ability to carry out actions. This "feel" is not truly intuitive, of course, but is developed through observation and emulation of successful executives. Levinson iden-

215

Fig. 8.4. The dean's office in the School of Architecture has windows with closable blinds and a door. Photograph by Marsha Spain Fuller.

216

tifies managerial leadership as "an art to be cultivated and developed," which is why it cannot be learned by the book; rather, "it must be learned in a relationship, through identification with a teacher" (Levinson 1981, 145).

Because the transfer of knowledge and the ability to use it are so crucial to leadership, Levinson devotes a chapter to "The Executive as Teacher." He advises that there is no prescription an executive can follow in acting as a teacher. The best strategy is the "shine and show them" approach—the manager carries out the duties of office as effectively as possible and thereby demonstrates to subordinates how decisions are made. There are no formal conditions under which teaching takes place; it is incorporated as part of the routine of the business day. In Levinson's words, "The process of example-setting goes on all the time. Executives behave in certain ways, sizing up problems, considering the resources . . . that can be utilized to meet them, and making decisions about procedure. Subordinates, likewise, watch what they are doing and how they do it" (Levinson 1981, 154).

Just as in the ceremonial men's huts of nonindustrial societies, constant contact between elders and initiates is necessary for the transmission of knowledge. Levinson implies that it should be frequent contact to transfer most effectively formal and informal knowledge. Such frequent and significant contact is missing from the interaction between managers and secretaries. Given the spatial distance between the closed doors of managers and the open floors of secretaries, it is highly unlikely that sufficient contact between the two groups could occur for secretaries to alter their positions within the organization.

In addition to giving subordinates an opportunity to learn from the boss, spatial proximity provides opportunities for subordinates to be seen by the boss. This opportunity has been labeled "visiposure" by the author of *Routes* to the Executive Suite (Jennings 1971, 113). A combination of "visibility" and "exposure," visiposure refers to the opportunity to "see and be seen by the right people" (Jennings 1971, 113). Jennings counsels the rising executive that "the abilities to see and copy those who can influence his career and to keep himself in view of those who might promote him are all-important to success." The ultimate form of visiposure is for the subordinate's manager to be seen by the right managers as well. Such "serial visiposure" is the "sine qua non of fast upward mobility" and is facilitated by face-to-face interaction among several levels of managers and subordinates (Jennings 1971, 113–14).

Both Levinson and Jennings acknowledge the importance of physical proximity to achieving power within an organization, yet neither pursues the assumptions underlying the transactions they discuss—that is, the spatial context within which such interactions occur. To the extent women are segregated from men, the transfer of knowledge—with the potential for improving women's status—is limited.

Office Design and Gender Stratification

Contemporary office design clearly reflects the spatial segregation separating women and men. Secretaries (almost all of whom are women) and managers (nearly two-thirds of whom are men) have designated areas assigned within the organization. The following diagram prepared by an architectural firm for a business client demonstrates the open floorplan for secretaries and the closed doors behind which managers work. This diagram is typical of those in other books on office design (Black, Roark, and Schwartz 1986; Duffy, Cave, and Worthington 1976; Mogulescu 1970).

Although salesmen have been given an open floorplan similar to that for secretaries (room 2b), their space is beside the managers' offices. Thus, salesmen are subject to less scrutiny than secretaries, whose desks are placed directly in front of the managers' doors. Indeed, the secretaries in this "pool" are potentially observable by four managers (from rooms 3, 4, 5, and 6). In an ironic twist of the panoptic principle, members of the subordinate group (secretaries) have now been placed at the center to enhance supervision by managers at the periphery.

Privacy can be a scarce resource in the modern office. Empirical studies have shown that privacy in the office involves "the ability to control access to one's self or group, particularly the ability to *limit others' access to one's workspace*" (Sundstrom 1986, 178; emphasis added). Business executives commonly define privacy as the ability to control information and space. In other words, privacy is connected in people's minds with the spatial reinforcement of secrecy. Studies of executives, managers, technicians, and clerical employees have found a high correlation between enclosure of the work space (walls and doors) and perceptions of privacy; the greater the privacy, the greater the satisfaction with work. Employees perceive spatial control as a resource in the workplace that affects their job satisfaction and performance (Sundstrom, Burt, and Kemp 1980; Sundstrom 1986).

Not surprisingly, higher status within an organization is accompanied by greater control of space. In the Sundstrom study, most secretaries (75 percent) reported sharing an office; about one-half (55 percent) of bookkeepers and accountants shared an office; and only 18 percent of managers and administrators shared space. Secretaries had the least physical separation from other workers, while executives had the most (Sundstrom 1986, 184).

Two aspects of the work environment are striking when the spatial features of the workplaces for secretaries and executives are compared: the low number of walls or partitions surrounding secretaries (an average of 2.1), compared with executives (an average of 3.5), and the greater surveillance that accompanies the public space of secretaries. Three-quarters of all secretaries were visible to their supervisors, compared with only one-tenth of executives. As one would expect given the physical description of their

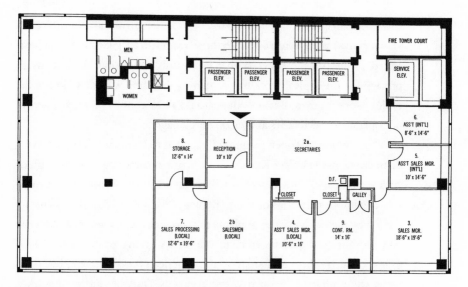

Fig. 8.5. The office architect is cautioned that the initial space study must illustrate the "relationships of the organization" clearly to the client. Reproduced from Saphier (1968, 76) by permission of McGraw-Hill, Inc.

respective offices, executives report the greatest sense of privacy and secretaries the least (Sundstrom 1986, 185). Doors do not necessarily have to be closed or locked in order to convey the message of differential power; they merely have to be available for closing and be seen as controlled at the executive's discretion (Steele 1986, 46).

The spatial distribution of employees in an office highlights the complex ways in which spatial segregation contributes to gender stratification. Workers obviously are not assigned space on the basis of sex, but on the basis of their positions within the organization. Theoretically, managers have the most complex jobs and secretaries have the least complex, yet research on secretaries and managers with equal degrees of office enclosure suggests that women's space is still considered more public than men's space. Sundstrom found that "in the workspaces with equivalent enclosure—private offices—[respondents] showed differential ratings of privacy, with lowest ratings by secretaries. This could reflect social norms. Secretaries have low ranks, and co-workers or visitors may feel free to walk unannounced into their workspaces. However, they may knock respectfully at the entrance of the workspaces of managers. . . . *Perhaps a private office is more private when occupied by a manager than when occupied by a secretary*" (Sundstrom 1986, 191; emphasis added). This passage suggests that even walls and a door do not insure privacy for the typical working woman in the same way they do for the typical working man. Features that should allow control of work space do not operate for secretaries as they do for managers.

What of the new "open planning" intended to eliminate all spatial status distinctions in the office? Known by its German name of *Bürolandschaft*, or "office landscape," this design was introduced in the 1960s and featured offices without partitions or walls (Becker 1981; Pile 1978). It was characterized by the extensive use of plants to represent the openness of outdoors and furniture grouped together to "suggest working relationships." Diagrams of such offices at first strike the American eye as chaotic, but these plans were adopted by such corporations as DuPont, Eastman Kodak, Corning Glass, and the Ford Motor Company (Pile 1978).

For all its emphasis on increased communication, easier traffic flow, and an egalitarian environment, there were subtle spatial status distinctions built into the most open of offices. The German Quickborner Team that promoted the plan so vigorously illustrated a design describing an area for the manager "screened by plants, files, and screens" and "assigned extra space to symbolize status and increase[d] sense of privacy" (Pile 1978, 26).

Office landscaping, while apparently creating an environment totally opposite that of the Panopticon, served a similar function. The Quickborner Team explained to executives skeptical of the reduced privacy inherent in open planning that efficiency would be improved by their design, since "most demands for privacy really cover a desire to hide from contacts and from work. An effective manager finds that his performance is enhanced, not hampered, when he moves into well-planned open space" (Pile 1978, 27).

By the end of the 1970s office landscaping had lost its novelty. Many companies had adopted its principles because it was relatively inexpensive and created an image of modernity in a competitive market. But the "new democracy" supposedly characteristic of landscaped office design with more open spaces did not materialize. Those who had power in conventional offices still had it (Becker 1981, 59). The open office facilitates the ability of managers to supervise secretaries by creating greater enclosure for managers

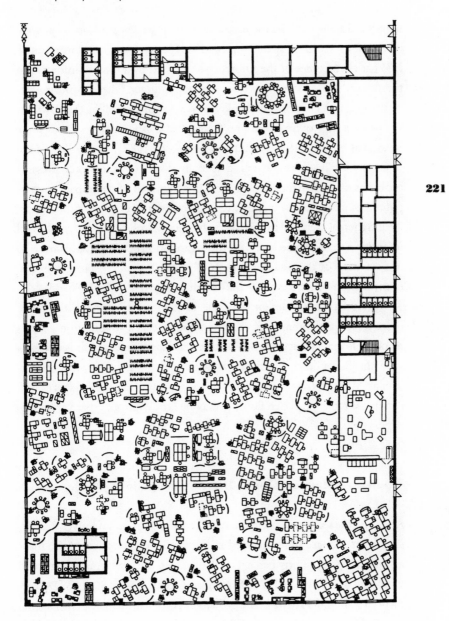

221

Fig. 8.6. This design represents the German Quickborner Team's approach to *Büro-landschaft*. Reproduced from Pile (1978, 12) by permission of Watson-Guptill Publications.

than for clerical staff. To the extent that there are fewer plants to provide privacy for secretaries, spatial segregation reinforces women's lower status.

What of the office of the future, characterized by advanced information technology and a reduced need for spatial proximity? These work arrangements appeal to a minority of employees as a way of controlling their own environments by working at home (fewer than 2 percent of the labor force worked at home in 1980 [Kraut and Grambsch 1987]). Regardless of the costs or benefits to employees, a spatially dispersed labor force presents problems of control for management. In an analysis of the impact of computer technology on the workplace, Ellis observes that "much of the authority and control exercised by managers and supervisors stem from the physical integrity of the organization. . . . If the organization becomes too abstract, so too do many of the traditional tools of management. . . . How does one motivate, control, and evaluate the distant employee?" (Ellis 1986, 46).

Tracing workplace design from the Panopticon up through the home office reveals the common thread of reinforcement of stratification systems through spatial arrangements. Whether the spatial segregation is overt, as with the Panopticon, or covert, as with landscaped offices, the effect is similar. Managers retain control of knowledge by use of enclosed spaces, and secretaries remain on open floors that allow little control of space or knowledge.

Women's Entry to "Closed-Door" Occupations

Although the secretarial occupation has remained almost exclusively female, significant changes have occurred in the gender composition of the managerial profession. Forty percent of all managers are now female, compared with only one in five in 1972 (Bianchi and Rytina 1986, 80; U.S. Department of Labor 1991, 185). The growth in percentage female in managerial occupations was the greatest of thirteen major occupational categories between 1972 and 1980. Between 1980 and 1984, managers experienced the second largest increase in percent female (Bianchi and Rytina 1986, 80). Thus, the gender composition among managers has changed more rapidly than that of any other major occupational grouping since the 1970s.

Part of the explanation for women's increased entry into management is their greater likelihood of receiving degrees in business. In 1965 fewer than one in ten bachelor's degrees in business were awarded to women. By 1980 that proportion had increased to one in three, and by 1988 nearly one-half of all bachelor's degrees in business and management were granted to women (Bianchi and Spain 1986, 120; U.S. Department of Education 1990, 237). Many people in managerial positions do not have degrees in business—indeed, may have no college degree at all—but the changing gender distribution of specialized education indicates a new level of knowledge acquisition for women that did not exist even twenty-five years ago.   **223**

The increase in proportions of master's degrees in business awarded to women is also striking. Until 1970 approximately one in thirty MBA's went to women; between 1975 and 1985, the proportion nearly quadrupled. Approximately one in three master's degrees in business now goes to a woman. The proportion of doctoral degrees in business awarded to women has also increased dramatically and now equals 23 percent (Bianchi and Spain 1986, 120; U.S. Department of Education 1991, 237). However, persons most likely to seek employment in business—as opposed to academia—would do so typically after earning a bachelor's or master's degree rather than a doctorate.

The proportion of all working women who are employed in managerial occupations has also increased over time. Between 1970 and 1990, the proportion of women employed as managers and executives rose from 4 to 11 percent (U.S. Bureau of the Census 1984; U.S. Department of Labor 1991, 163, 183). As women gain entry to "closed-door" jobs, their access to resources increases; as access to resources increases, so should the potential for higher status. This higher status, in turn, increases the likelihood that spatial segregation may be modified to allow women greater interaction with men in the workplace. Spatial proximity promotes both formal and informal cross-gender contact that translates into potentially higher status for women.

Women's Status: Remaining Goals

The twentieth century brought voting rights for American women to accompany their rights to property and labor established during the nineteenth century. Other tangible gains have been the Equal Pay Act of 1963, legalized abortion, and Title 7 of the Civil Rights Act. These legislative actions combined to open additional avenues of public status to women in education and the labor force. However, two areas remain in which few changes have occurred. As we approach the twenty-first century, women are still less likely than men to hold elective office, and working women still earn less than working men.

224

Election to Political Office. Elective offices are considered important positions by Americans. State governors, members of Congress, and city mayors rate some of the highest occupational prestige scores (Hodge, Siegel, and Rossi 1964). Part of the prestige of these occupations reflects their potential for power, compared with jobs held by the majority of workers, and part of it reflects their rarity. There are currently only 50 governors, 100 senators, and 435 congressional representatives (Center for the American Woman and Politics 1989).

Relatively few American women have been elected to political office since their enfranchisement nearly seventy years ago. After the 1988 elections, three out of fifty governors were women, two out of one hundred senators, and 26 of 435 (5.3 percent) congressional representatives. Although the *number* of women holding congressional office has risen steadily throughout the twentieth century (from one in 1919 to twenty-eight in 1989), the *proportion* of congressional members who are female has never exceeded 6 percent (Center for the American Woman and Politics 1989). Representation in Congress is an important source of power for women, since abortion, pay equity, equal rights, and child care are "women's issues" subject to federal legislation.

Plausible explanations for women's low rate of election to public office include the relative scarcity of elective openings and the incumbent's advantage. A traditionally male field tends to remain male, given few turnovers and the expenses associated with running for national office. Sex-role socialization, which traditionally has steered women away from decision-making positions, may also influence women's underrepresentation in political office. Women also are still at an educational disadvantage relative to men in terms of college completion rates. Assuming that a formal education enhances one's opportunities for public office, both through the acquisition of specific knowledge and through social connections, women would not yet have the same preparation as men. Finally, the two occupations most often associated with routes to political office, law and business, have only recently opened to women. The proportion of law degrees granted to women has increased dramatically over the last two decades: 40 percent of all law degrees are now granted to women, compared with just 5 percent in 1970 (Bianchi and Spain 1986, 123; U.S. Department of Education 1991, 248).

The American public appears ready to support more women in elective office. Results from the *1989 General Social Survey* show that 86 percent of respondents said they would vote for a woman for president and 80 percent **225** think women are as qualified for politics as men (National Opinion Research Center 1989). Ironically, as attitudinal, educational, and occupational obstacles to women's political participation have been reduced, incumbents have become more difficult to unseat. Increasing the proportion of women in elective office may therefore be a slow process.

The Earnings Gap. Working women do not earn as much as working men. Between 1955 and 1983, the ratio of women's-to-men's median annual earnings among full-time, year-round workers never exceeded .64; its low point was .57 in the early 1970s (Bianchi and Spain 1986, 170). The wage ratio had risen to .69 by 1989, when women's median annual earnings were slightly below $19,000, compared with approximately $27,000 for their male colleagues (U.S. Bureau of the Census 1990a, table 15).

Controlling for educational differences does not eliminate the gap between women's and men's earnings. In 1987, among full-time, year-round workers with a high-school degree, women's annual median earnings were $16,461, compared with $25,394 for men (a ratio of .65). Among workers who had completed college, women's earnings were $25,645, compared with $37,854 for men (a ratio of .68) (U.S. Bureau of the Census 1989b, table 39).

The gap also persists when occupational classifications are the same. Among year-round, full-time retail sales clerks, women's median annual earnings were $10,592 in 1987, compared with $17,726 for men (a ratio of .60). Among machine operators, women earned $12,395, compared with men's $20,493 (a ratio of .60); among lawyers and judges, women earned an average of $38,650, compared with $54,190 for men (a ratio of .71) (U.S. Bureau of the Census 1989b, table 39).

The classic explanation for women's lower earnings relative to men's is Mincer and Polachek's (1974) human-capital theory. They argue that women invest less than men in acquiring labor-market skills because they expect to work less than men throughout their lives. According to this theory, women anticipate family-related absences from the labor force and choose occupations that can be easily entered and left. These occupations offer little on-the-job training or potential wage growth because employers will invest less in a transitory labor force. Human-capital theory thus emphasizes differences in educational investment as a crucial variable in earnings differences between women and men.

226

Research controlling for work experience and labor force attachment fails to account fully for wage differences by sex (Corcoran and Duncan 1979). Other research focusing on structural aspects of jobs themselves has also failed to completely explain earnings differences (Wolf and Fligstein 1979; Roos 1981). Finally, women's family responsibilities have declined as fertility has declined, while women's labor force attachment (as measured by number of entries and exits) has increased over time, and the earnings gap has remained stable (Bianchi and Spain 1986).

Dwellings and workplaces are connected for women in ways that affect their incomes. Women work closer to home than men, and those journey-to-work patterns are associated with lower earnings (Johnston-Anumonwo 1988; Rutherford and Wekerle 1988). Women's extra commuting time results from the spatial mismatch between their homes and their job opportunities. Not only do husband's jobs determine the family's residential location, but women and men actually work in different parts of the metropolitan area (Hanson and Pratt 1988; Madden 1977). Hayden's (1980a) answer to the disequilibrium between home and workplace is to redesign entire neighborhoods and cities to reduce the demands of time and space on contemporary households.

The necessity of using quantitative data (such as years of school completed, entries and exits from the labor force, and number of years on the job) makes it difficult to incorporate differences in women's and men's motivations to work or employers' possible discriminatory practices when analyzing income differences. In other words, it is impossible to explain completely why differences in women's and men's earnings persist despite women's lower fertility, greater educational attainment, and increased labor force participation and attachment. The constancy of the wage gap in the face of so many other demographic changes for women in contemporary America suggests its importance as an indicator of women's public status.

In sum, many American women now control their own labor, but their returns from that labor are lower than men's. And although women are now granted full political participation through the vote, they are far less likely than men to exercise political power through elective office. These remaining indicators of gender stratification, moreover, are buttressed by the persistence of spatial segregation in the workplace.

227

Conclusion

If job segregation by gender is the "primary mechanism . . . that maintains the superiority of men over women," as Hartmann (1976) argues, spatial segregation is one of the mechanisms reinforcing that job segregation. When women and men do not share the same workplace, women do not receive information that can be translated into higher status—in the form of higher wages, for example.

Unlike other spatial institutions, the workplace has not experienced a significant change in spatial arrangements since the nineteenth century. The meager data available on the physical layout of offices suggest the persistence of separate spheres for women and men to a greater extent than in homes or schools. Women have joined men in the labor force, but many are not working with men in the same place at the same time.

The occupational segregation that concentrates nearly one-third of all working women in teaching, nursing, and secretarial work also results in conditions that make it difficult for women to achieve progress toward higher status. Teachers, nurses, and secretaries have little daily exposure to resources that would raise their wages or elect them to public office. These "open-floor" occupations are characterized by little control of space, resulting in a lack of privacy, lack of control over knowledge, and constant surveillance. Women typically engage in highly visible work—to colleagues, clients, and supervisors—subject to repeated interruptions. The spatial conditions under which women work both reflect and reinforce their lower status relative to men's.

Similarly, the spatial conditions of typical "men's work"—in managerial occupations—reflect and reinforce men's position in the status hierarchy. Closed doors protect privacy and the ability to engage in uninterrupted work. Organizational success is facilitated by the ability to control others' access to knowledge, and that advantage is enhanced by the ability to control space by closing a door.

Is workplace segregation directly associated with women's status in contemporary society? Specifically, are there ways in which spatial segregation affects gender differences in earnings and positions of political power? The lack of quantitative data with which to address these questions means that answers are necessarily speculative. The data on occupational segregation suggest that men's and women's distribution in different occupations contributes to the wage gap. It is more difficult to equate occupational with workplace segregation and still more difficult to link workplace segregation with political power. Yet it appears that the spatial conditions of men's jobs translate more easily into political power than do the spatial conditions of women's jobs; men have greater control of knowledge and resources. Many working men have no control over resources, of course, just as many women now work behind closed doors. Yet the occupations that enhance economic and political power—law, medicine, business—are predominantly "closed door," while those with reduced economic and political power are predominantly "open floor."

Women's entry into traditionally male places of higher education and employment laid the groundwork for their entry into traditionally male occupations. Once women began to major in law and business, for example, opportunities for more highly paid occupations and political careers began to open. As women graduate from law school in greater numbers, their acquisition of legislative knowledge will increase, and with it their election to public office.

Gender stratification, then, should decline as men and women are distributed more evenly between open-floor and closed-door occupations. The greater the contact between the sexes in the workplace, the higher women's status relative to men's. Just as with other social changes that alter existing status hierarchies, however, workplace integration may meet with resistance. Men working in sexually integrated settings report significantly lower job satisfaction and more job related depression than men in predominantly

228

male or female work settings. The greater dissatisfaction is not related to lower economic returns or poorer working conditions. Rather, as with other minority group relations, the minority is perceived as more threatening when their numbers approach a balance with the majority. Thus, women are more threatening to men when their representation in the workplace is approximately equal to men's (Wharton and Baron 1987). These results suggest that integration of the workplace may proceed slowly and with numerous setbacks similar to those that accompanied the coeducation movement in colleges.

229

9

Degendering Spaces

We should not only properly understand society (theory), but use such understanding as a basis for a program of action (practice) to change society. If we succeed in changing the position of women, this requires a reassessment of the situation (theory) and so on.—Women and Geography Study Group of the Institute of British Geographers, *Geography and Gender*

Members of the Women and Geography Study Group recognized the reciprocity of theory and action when they observed that achieving feminist goals depends on the constant interplay between ideas and policies. Society is a changing entity which shapes, and is shaped by, individual actions.

Space and status are linked in much the same way as theory and action. Just as theory both directs and is modified by practice, spatial arrangements produce and are produced by status distinctions. Space is organized in ways that reproduce gender differences in power and privilege. Status is embedded in spatial arrangements, so that changing space potentially changes the status hierarchy and changing status potentially changes spatial institutions. In the terms of the dialectical approach introduced in chapter 1, gendered spaces provide the concrete, everyday-life grounding for the production, reproduction, and transformation of status differences.

By now it should be clear that my argument does *not* assume that women's status automatically will improve if they enter the same rooms as men. Rather, spatial arrangements are but one of many factors contributing to gender stratification. In addition to economic, political, technological, demographic, or ideological changes, changes in gendered spaces potentially influence gender stratification. If knowledge (of technology, for example) is one of the resources by which men maintain a status advantage (Chafetz 1990, 18, 38–39; Cockburn 1983, 138), then spatial arrangements represent one of the conditions perpetuating that advantage. Degendering spaces in the home, school, and workplace will improve women's status only to the extent that it also improves their acquisition of knowledge valued by society.

This book began with the premise that social institutions are characterized by spatial arrangements between women and men that are associated with gender stratification. The term "spatial institution" designates the concrete, physical context in which women's and men's activities occur. Thus, actions within the family are carried out in the dwelling, activities associated with education occur in schools, and labor force participation occurs in the workplace. I have tried to demonstrate that 1) spatial segregation between the sexes exists to varying degrees in these institutions over time and across cultures; 2) greater spatial segregation is associated with lower status for women in many cultures and at many points in history; and 3) the negative association is greatest when segregation reduces women's access to knowledge highly valued in the public realm.

The data presented for nonindustrial societies and for America during the nineteenth and twentieth centuries support the argument. They are not unequivocal, however, nor do they allow for direct empirical investigation **234** of the relationships among spatial segregation, knowledge acquisition, and gender stratification. The point of the research has been to examine seemingly disparate instances of segregation between women and men and to connect those diverse threads through the perspective of the spatial institution. Geographic and architectural concepts have been brought to bear on abstract sociological concepts to form an argument about space and status that can serve as a departure for more methodologically sophisticated quantitative and qualitative analyses. Nonetheless, the findings are convincing: gendered spaces are associated with the position of women in society.

Complexities of Race and Class

The discussion about space and status refers to women as a group and men as a group. In reality, of course, gender stratification is cross-cut by racial and class distinctions as well. The experience of gendered spaces differs within homes, schools, and workplaces depending on the influence of other statuses.

Only the very wealthy, for example, can afford homes that spatially segregate women and men. In purdah societies, affluence buys *anderuns* and *biruns*; among the nineteenth-century British gentry, it bought gentlemen's suites and separate staircases for female and male servants. Poverty, on the other hand, often demands gender integration out of necessity. When black colleges emerged in the United States during the nineteenth century, they were rarely single-sex, as were their white counterparts, because the black community did not have the resources to support a dual system. Finally, workplaces may be segregated by race as well as by sex. Long after Emancipation, certain factory, shop, and clerical occupations were closed to blacks. Spatial barriers to racial integration (in the form of separate entrances, for example) persisted after barriers to gender integration in workplaces had disappeared (Kessler-Harris 1982).

Chafetz (1990, 196) points out that gender status inequalities within disadvantaged groups may be reduced, not because women have greater status, but because men's access to resources is also limited. It is necessary to expand the inquiry about space and status to include the effects of class and race. To paraphrase Cockburn (1983, 195), people do not live three lives, **235** one as a man or woman, one as black or nonblack, and one as upper or lower class. The three systems are connected in ways that affect daily activities.

Degendering Spatial Institutions

The ways in which spaces may become degendered vary with the spatial institution. Likewise, the importance (or centrality) of knowledge varies with the type of institution.

Dwellings. The home is the spatial institution containing the least amount of socially valued knowledge. In America, for example, dwellings are rarely the locus of religious, economic, or political knowledge. Domestic information conveyed within the home is devalued, at least partially because it is possessed by women. A tautological argument is hard to escape. Nevertheless, because less valued knowledge exists in the dwelling, the premise about space and status is less effective for dwellings than for other spatial institutions. Because the home is one of the arenas in which gender relations are reproduced, however, variations in spatial segregation are significant.

Women and men have tried to change the spatial institution of the family before. In *The Grand Domestic Revolution*, Dolores Hayden traces the history of nineteenth-century "material feminists" who advocated communal cooking, dining, laundry, and child-care facilities as a way to free women from domestic tasks. Robert Owen and Charles Fourier were the intellectual pioneers behind this movement to erase gender inequalities through collectivized housing design. About 5,000 American women and men participated in these experiments between 1857 and 1917 (Hayden 1980b, 5).

Their efforts achieved little national prominence because their numbers were so small and the ventures less than profitable (communal enterprises never having enjoyed great popularity in the United States). It is interesting, however, that Owen and Fourier perceived housing changes to be an integral part of their egalitarian social order.

Others have suggested housing modifications as avenues of change for women's status. Feminist architects of the 1920s and 1930s (like Alice Austin and Ruth Adams) argued for kitchenless houses to spare women the
236 drudgery of cooking. In a foreshadowing of Christopher Alexander's "pattern language," Elisabeth Coit proposed in 1938 that the names of rooms be changed or eliminated to avoid potentially restrictive uses. Thus, kitchens would incorporate eating and study areas, and children's bedrooms could be used for sleeping and playing (Rock, Torre, and Wright 1980, 93–94). More recently, Hayden (1984) has proposed "redesigning the American dream" to meet the needs of changing families; Wekerle (1988) has documented the creation of housing cooperatives by and for female householders. All of these proposals stress the importance of multipurpose rooms open to all members of a household, whether that household consists of a traditional nuclear family, an elderly person living alone, or a single parent with children. The ideal contemporary house would be a "rich kaleidoscope of options" reinforcing shared space and domestic tasks (Rock, Torre, and Wright 1980, 95).

Modifying the interior of houses may be the least important form of spatial intervention because less time is spent in the home now than in the past. Several demographic trends have been operating to replace the "home as haven" with the "empty nest." First, lower fertility means there are fewer children at home. In 1988 only one-third of all households included children under eighteen (U.S. Bureau of the Census 1989a, table 21). Second, over one-half of all women are employed outside the home. When both women and men work, and children are at school, homes are inhabited for far fewer hours than when women stayed home to care for large families. Thus, gendered spaces within the dwelling typically are occupied for fewer waking hours than spaces in other institutions. By comparison with schools and workplaces, then, spatial segregation in the home now may be less relevant to gender stratification than it once was.

Schools. Schools are of central importance to an argument about space and status because their raison d'être is the transfer of knowledge from those who possess it to those who do not. In contemporary American society, the vast majority of colleges and universities are coeducational. Women now constitute more than 50 percent of all college students.

The gendered spaces that remain on campuses arise from separate living arrangements (as in the single-sex dorms) or from separate social groupings (in single-sex fraternities and sororities, for example). These types of gender segregation are less relevant to women's status, however, than the separation **237** that still occurs in some classrooms. Those fields of study most closely related to technology are those with the fewest female majors. Fewer than one-third of undergraduate degrees in engineering, architecture, and the physical sciences were granted to women in 1987 (U.S. Department of Education 1989). Until the classrooms in which the most socially valued information is taught are degendered, women's acquisition of knowledge will be less than men's.

The case of architecture is particularly interesting because it, among all disciplines, deals with spatial concepts. Enrollment in undergraduate architecture programs is now 50 percent female, yet women represent only 16 percent of architecture faculty (ACSA Task Force on the Status of Women in Architecture Schools 1990). Perhaps because architecture professors traditionally have been men, gender issues have only recently been introduced into the curriculum in some schools. Once the design professions responsible for the built environment become more aware of the power of spatial arrangements for gender differences in status, degendering spaces in homes, schools, and workplaces may become easier to accomplish.

Workplaces. After schools, workplaces are the spatial institutions containing the greatest amount of valued knowledge. For those who do not attend college or vocational school, on-the-job training is the only mechanism by which knowledge is transferred among those in the labor force. That makes the workplace particularly important from the standpoint of gendered spaces and women's status. Its design has the potential to either inhibit or facilitate the exchange of information between women and men.

The type of knowledge available in the workplace varies with the service or good being produced. In the textile industry it might be information about setting up a frame, putting it in trim, adjusting it for different fabrics and stitches, and repairing it (Bradley 1989, 135). In the fishing industry it might be netmaking or processing the catch (Bradley 1989, 102), and in printing it would be typesetting and composition (Cockburn 1983). Offices contain information on financial markets, banking practices, corporate strategies, or political agendas. If men have appropriated the technology necessary for the control of many jobs, as Cockburn (1983) asserts, then workplace design has helped reinforce that control by limiting women's training **238** in technological knowledge.

Redesigning workplaces to minimize barriers to cross-sex interaction would help reduce gendered spaces and improve women's status. A large insurance company, for example, has eliminated office walls so that managers, professionals, and clerical staff work side by side in shoulder-high cubicles (Baran and Teegarden 1987, 209). The Steelcase furniture manufacturer of Grand Rapids, Michigan, has supplemented closed-door offices with "beverage centers" equipped with sketch boards. Employees are encouraged to draw as they drink coffee and talk (Flanagan 1990, 113). Occupational segregation potentially can be changed if women are exposed to the entire array of organizational issues and managerial responses. The "shine and show them" technique depends on constant interaction among super- and subordinates in the workplace.

If the task of the organization results in constant noise, the space needed for private conferences or preparation of reports could be allocated on a needs-priority basis. Closed doors would still exist, but their use would rotate among various occupants; in this way managers and secretaries would have respite from constant interruptions. Rotating people through stable spatial arrangements is thus another way of reducing segregation in the workplace. Fritz Steele calls this the "cave and commons" approach to office planning. He proposes that workers shuttle between their "caves"—small, private workstations—and common areas that include team and project rooms, sitting lounges, and vending and copy areas. A variety of informal contacts among employees leads to greater productivity (Flanagan 1990, 115). A side effect is that gendered spaces are eliminated and the potential for knowledge transfer between men and women is thus enhanced.

In businesses that cater to the public—such as retail stores—efforts can be made to mix male and female sales personnel in the same departments. The lack of knowledge that presumably keeps women from selling big-ticket items such as appliances and cars would soon be reduced by on-the-job training with more experienced men. Such training is only possible when women and men are in the same place at the same time.

In factories, a reduction in occupational segregation could result in a reduction in spatial segregation. When the manual dexterity that suits women so well for the nonunionized microelectronics industry (O'Connor 1987) also qualifies them to work in unionized auto plants, women and men **239** will share the same space and job benefits. This is an example of the reciprocity between space and status. Once occupational changes occur, workplace modifications become possible which in turn create potentially higher status for women. It would be interesting to discover, for example, if wage comparability for women and men varies by the degree of spatial segregation in their work organizations.

Cockburn (1983, 211) argues that people are "blinkered by their material circumstances." These include the spaces within which paid work is carried out. Cockburn targets labor unions as one mechanism by which the distribution of knowledge can be altered, thereby degendering the workplace: "In the past it has been the practice of a certain group of trade unions, predominantly men, to sequester the technical knowledge arising from the labour process. But knowledge is not property. In future, trade unions must surely become educators . . . deepening and passing on knowledge . . . to those formerly defined as unskilled, particularly to women. Ultimately, men and women together, we have to ensure that technical knowledge becomes common knowledge" (Cockburn 1983, 233).

Opposition to Gendered Spaces

"Degendering" spaces requires work: first, to make gendered spaces and their links with knowledge visible, and second, to oppose their persistence. Women often have been ready to perform the work necessary to oppose gendered institutions. Exclusion from the 1840 World's Anti-Slavery Convention, for example, confronted Elizabeth Cady Stanton and Lucretia Mott with the realities of men's control of the public political sphere. By 1848 they had organized the Seneca Falls Convention in New York. This conference marked the beginning of the American feminist movement (Schneir 1972, 76).

The Declaration of Sentiments produced by conference participants pinpointed education and religion as institutions segregated by gender. Feminists argued that by preventing women entry to colleges and the church, man closed to woman "the avenues of wealth and distinction which he considers most honorable to himself. As a teacher of theology, medicine, or law [woman] is not known" (Schneir 1972, 79). In this single document, Stanton and Mott drew connections between spatial segregation, access to knowledge, and women's status. They also proposed ways in which the resulting inequalities could be addressed.

American labor history is interspersed with examples of women forming unions to challenge the division of paid labor. Even before the Seneca Falls Convention, female textile workers in New England and seamstresses in New York and Philadelphia went on strike to protest unfair wages and working conditions (Kessler-Harris 1982, 40). In 1869 women shoebinders organized the Daughters of St. Crispin to demand pay equity with men (Bradley 1989, 157). Although most of these efforts eventually failed, they are examples of women's early militancy over entry to the same workplaces as men.

A more recent example of women's opposition to gendered spaces is the push to integrate all-male social clubs. Called "bastions of male homosociality" by sociologist Jean Lipman-Blumen (1976), clubs like the Century and University in New York and the Cosmos and Metropolitan in Washington, D.C., bear a certain resemblance to all-male colleges of the nineteenth century. Women kept outside their walls claimed that important business and political contacts were established among men within those walls. The crusade to integrate both colleges and clubs was led by feminists, and the battles fought over the legal right of men's clubs to exclude women were reminiscent of those surrounding coeducation (Kamen 1988; Feinberg 1987; Pressley 1988). However, such clubs were restricted to a small elite membership of men before a Supreme Court decision required them to admit women (Kamen 1988; Starr 1987); now they are restricted to a small elite membership of men *and* women (Barker 1988; Feinberg 1988). Thus, the actions of relatively few men and women—no matter how powerful and influential—have less impact on gender stratification than the routine separation of women and men in daily tasks. Nevertheless, the legal victory over these elite gendered spaces was a result of organized opposition by women (and some men).

The fervor with which the elite try to protect their spatial advantage was recently demonstrated by the alumni of Skull and Bones at Yale University. Identified by the media with such words as "powerful," "secretive," "ritualistic," "clandestine," and "furtive," this society includes President George Bush and several members of Congress among its ranks. In 1991, when seniors at Yale admitted women to Skull and Bones for the first time in the club's history, the alumni board padlocked the building where the organization meets. The *Washington Post* ran a picture of the imposing "Tomb" from which women had been excluded. The symbolism of an actual place thus continues to play an important role both for the members of Skull and Bones and for the public (Specter 1991).

241

Further Research

Other Spatial Institutions. Other institutions, such as the military and religion, have spatial components as well. Some places of worship historically have segregated men and women, for example, and organized religion often reinforces women's lower status. Jewish women traditionally were relegated to the balconies of synagogues; Catholics send male clergy to monasteries and female clergy to convents; Muslim women do not enter the mosque. Unlike less-segregated Protestant religions, the Orthodox Jewish, Catholic, and Muslim religions still limit their most prestigious positions (rabbi, priest, and mullah) to men; thus, sacred forms of knowledge are reserved for men. When religious beliefs extend to other institutions, as when the Koran dictates purdah in the home or when Catholic dioceses administer single-sex parochial schools, the impact of religion on gender stratification is intensified.

The military is another institution traditionally segregated by gender. The relatively few women serving in the armed forces were until recently separated into all-female branches such as the Navy's Women's Appointed Volunteer Emergency Service (WAVES) and the Women's Army Auxiliary Corps (WAACS); none attended West Point or the Naval Academy. Overwhelmingly male throughout history, the military epitomizes masculine control of technology. Weapons, defense, and communication technology are all predominantly male fields supporting the military. Even the content and structure of engineering education in the United States have been heavily influenced by the West Point model (Hacker 1989).

242 Now that women are attending military academies and serving in integrated battalions, some gendered spaces have disappeared. The role of women in the Persian Gulf war is unprecedented and may become a catalyst for change in the postwar military. For those women serving in Saudi Arabia, however, the integrated living arrangements to which they are accustomed have been replaced by separate quarters in deference to Islamic customs (M. Moore 1990).

Socialist and Third World Societies. This examination of the relationship among gendered spaces, valued knowledge, and women's status has focused only on nonindustrial and American societies. We know, of course, that gender stratification is pervasive, independent of the type of economic structure (Beneria and Roldan 1987; Brinton 1989; Roos 1985), but questions about gendered spaces in socialist and Third World societies remain to be answered.

Studies of the division of labor in China, Israel, the Soviet Union, and Cuba suggest patterns of occupational segregation and masculine control of knowledge similar to those in American society. From the communal kibbutz in Israel to the Mondragon workers' cooperative in Spain, women have greater responsibilities for home-based tasks and fewer technology-oriented duties than men (Hacker 1989). Third World countries, with less affluence with which to create gendered spaces, may demonstrate a different relationship among spatial segregation, knowledge, and gender stratification than that in advanced industrial societies.

The Future of Gendered Spaces

Despite persistent wage disparities, despite differences in positions of political leadership—even despite defeat of the Equal Rights Amendment—

American society today is more egalitarian than it was a century ago. From a historical perspective, the degree of gender stratification has declined over time. So, too, has the degree of segregation characteristic of spatial institutions. While homes and schools have become decidedly more integrated, workplaces remain segregated. When workplaces are as sexually integrated as homes and schools, gender will become a less important component of the American stratification system.

Not everyone would agree with the central message of this book. Radical feminists, for example, might argue that segregation works to women's **243** advantage by allowing them to develop power independently of men. Others might contest the idea that men's spaces contain valued knowledge. Often, after all, much of the information traded among men is of little consequence in the status hierarchy. But seemingly trivial talk (about sports, for example), may have implications for the workplace. Sports analogies abound in the business world, where corporations expect their employees to be "team players" who will "go the extra yard" for the company without "making an end run" around the boss. Women's inexperience with—or rejection of— such rules of play has been proposed as one reason for their lower status (Gilligan 1982). On the other hand, few instances of "women's talk" occur in the workplace. It is rare to hear the analogy that an onerous but necessary part of one's job is akin to changing a baby's diaper. Thus, the language of the locker room is more effective in advancing careers than the language of the nursery. Both the content and structure of knowledge, therefore, are shaped by gendered spaces.

This study has made visible the links among spatial arrangements, knowledge, and women's status. The mechanism perpetuating gender stratification is the transfer of knowledge. When that transfer is inhibited by spatial barriers, gender stratification is slow to change. But when the importance of spatial institutions is recognized and barriers to knowledge are reduced, one of the supports of the gender stratification system is removed. The twenty-first century could well see a decline in the number of gendered spaces, accompanied by improvements in women's status.

Appendix A: Data and Methods

The effort to understand the relationship between space and status has been informed by many disciplines. In addition to architectural history, geography, and sociology, anthropological research was used in Part 1 for the analysis of nonindustrial societies, while American history sources informed the chapters in Part 2.

This book uses both quantitative and qualitative analyses of secondary data sources to integrate the concepts of space and status. The qualitative approach includes efforts to reconcile anthropological and architectural accounts for the same cultures. For example, Murdock's *Africa: Its Peoples and Their Culture History* (1959) contains an especially detailed description of women's status among the Tuareg of the Sahara but does not mention the spatial distribution of women and men within the tent. The architectural history literature on tents yielded descriptions of the internal spatial arrangements of the Tuareg (as opposed to those of the Berbers or Bedouins) but no information on gender relations. Thus, information from two disciplines was pieced together to establish the association between segregated dwellings and gender stratification. This one example involved reference to approximately a dozen references, only five of which were useful (Faegre 1979; Nicolaisen 1963; Murdock 1959; Murphy 1964; Rosaldo and Lamphere 1974). A similar process was repeated for each case study reported in chapters 2 through 4.

Human Relations Area File

In addition to qualitative methods, quantitative analysis of Human Relations Area File (HRAF) data was used to examine the relationship between space and status for nonindustrial societies. Chapters 2, 3, and 4 include descriptive statistics on eighty-one nonindustrial cultures for which data on women's status and spatial segregation were available.*

The data are a subset of Murdock and White's (1969) Standard Cross-Cultural Sample consisting of ninety-three cultures randomly drawn by Whyte (1978a) for his study of gender stratification in nonindustrial societies. Frequencies and a detailed description of the sample are available in *The Status of Women in Preindustrial Societies* (Whyte 1978a), and codes for all measures of status are reproduced in Whyte's *Ethnology* article (1978b). Inability to locate original ethnographies for societies reduced the current sample to eighty-one cultures. The sample of cultures and references consulted for gender segregation are listed in appendix B.

Whyte's coding relied on the original sources and required each variable to meet stringent intercoder reliability standards. Whyte's variables on the existence of separate work groups for women and men were used to create a four-point scale of *segregated labor*, which was then dichotomized as lesser or greater. Additional coding (from the HRAF and from Whyte's original sources) was conducted for the presence of *segregated dwellings* and the presence of a *men's house*. Any reference to a segregated dwelling or men's house was coded as one, while no reference was coded as zero. This procedure tended to underestimate the presence of spatial segregation, since references may have been overlooked. However, ethnographies typically include a description of the physical layout and living arrangements of the village, and oversight of clear gender spatial arrangements would be rare.

246

---

*A note is in order regarding use of the terms "society" and "culture." The HRAF sample consists of *cultural* units of people who share common values, beliefs, language, and activities. These units are typically tribes or villages that may form parts of larger *societies* characterized by political and territorial boundaries (Whyte 1978a, 13). The two words are used interchangeably in this research with the recognition that there are conceptual differences between the terms.

Other independent variables used in the calculation of adjusted averages reflect, as closely as possible, alternate theories of gender stratification (reviewed in chapter 1). *Male domestic responsibility* is an adaptation of Whyte's variable representing total absence (0) and minimal contribution (1). *Female economic contribution to subsistence* consists of Whyte's nine-point scale, ranging from least proportionate contribution by women (1) to greatest (9). *Postmarital residence* is designated as patrilocal (0) or matrilocal (1), and type of economic *subsistence* is represented by a scale of the importance of hunting and gathering, ranging from insignificant (1) to dominant (5). Adjusted **247** averages were calculated by multiplying the slope of each independent variable by its mean and adding all values to the constant within each category of spatial segregation. The technique is a version of analysis of variance. Its results give the value of the dependent variable (women's status), controlling for the effects of all independent variables.

Although the Human Relations Area Files have certain limitations (such as a bias toward reports written in English), they remain the primary source of exhaustive data on nonindustrial societies. Murdock and White's Standard Cross-Cultural Sample improves on previous samples by pinpointing societies by location and date, by relying almost exclusively on reports by trained ethnographers, and by representing all one hundred world sampling provinces (Murdock and White 1969).* Since I am using a subset of Whyte's sample, however, claims to randomness are difficult to sustain. Tests of statistical significance are therefore not used in the analyses. Characteris-

---

*This last criterion, geographic diversity, was incorporated in response to "Galton's problem." Briefly stated, Galton's problem refers to the diffusion of cultural traits (by migration or through borrowing) which tends to obscure correlations in cross-cultural research. Strong correlations between variables may be less a result of functional interdependence than an "artifact of common historical circumstances" (Naroll 1970, 974). Parceling out the effects of common cultural origins is best handled by a variety of "propinquity methods" (Naroll and Cohen 1970). They are all based on the assumption that similarities among neighboring cultures are more likely to reflect diffusion than similarities among more dispersed cultures (Naroll 1970). By sampling from all world regions, Murdock and White avoid Galton's problem. (Readers interested in the detailed methodology of cross-cultural research are referred to F. W. Moore [1961] and Naroll and Cohen [1970].)

tics of all nonindustrial societies cannot be inferred from the current sample. Rather, empirical tests of HRAF data are used as a quantitative supplement to the larger descriptive work.

Part 1 of the book is based on ethnographies of cultures studied primarily in the nineteenth and early twentieth centuries (41 percent of the cultures in the sample refer to time periods before 1900, and 59 percent to cultures studied since 1900). The term "nonindustrial" is meant to identify reliance on hunting and gathering, horticultural, or agricultural economies rather than a specific period of history. (See Schrire [1984] for a review of the anthropological debate on the degree of contact between nonindustrial and industrialized societies.) The majority of the sample reflects the "anthropological present" and thus should *not* be considered evolutionary precedents of advanced industrial societies. I use the present tense in describing nonindustrial societies to emphasize this point. Part 2 is based on qualitative historical information.

248

Women's Status

Women's status is a complex concept in both nonindustrial and industrialized societies. It can include life expectancy, control over sexuality and reproduction, domestic authority, literacy, economic production, and political power. Attempts to construct a cross-cultural index of status for women ideally include indicators of the political, legal, economic, and social aspects of women's well-being (Andrews 1982).

In order to represent this diversity while maintaining a common thread for both parts of the book, I have chosen to emphasize economic and sociopolitical indicators of women's status. Control of property, control of labor, and participation in the public sphere are used as consistently as possible in both quantitative and qualitative analyses. They are operationalized differently depending on the cultural context.

Nonindustrial Societies. Nonindustrial societies show a decided lack of gender variance on traditionally masculine indicators of status such as positions of power or force (Lenski 1966), with some variance on positions of property (Blumberg 1984). Whyte (1978a) concluded that women's status is a multidimensional concept represented by fifty-two different variables (which he subsequently condensed to nine scales). Indeed, almost every cross-cultural study of gender stratification relies on a different dependent variable or set of variables (Blumberg 1984; Coltrane 1988; Sanday 1981; Stover and Hope 1984).

Blumberg (1978) specifies control of the means of production and allocation of surplus as more important to women's status than contribution to production. She identifies economic power as the most important for women, influencing such life options as sexual freedom, marriage and divorce rights, and household authority. The index of *female control of labor and property* used in the current research consists of a four-point scale constructed by Whyte to measure women's control of inheritance, dwellings, and male and female labor. *Control of property* is measured separately as a four-point scale indicating gender preference in the *inheritance* of land, tools, animals, orchards, or produce. *Female participation in the public sphere* is measured by a three-point scale indicating degree of power demonstrated in *kinship networks*. (All three dependent variables are described in table A.1.) Control of property and control of labor and property are strongly correlated, while public participation and control of property are weakly correlated, as are public participation and control of labor and property (see table A.2).

American Society. Because quantitative data comparable to the HRAF are not available for American society, measures of spatial segregation and women's status are not as precise in Part 2 as in Part 1 of the book. Descriptions of dwellings rely on content analyses of books and trade magazines on interior housing design from the nineteenth century up to the present. Descriptions of the geographic and architectural separation between women and men in schools come from secondary historical accounts, as do workplace conditions. Surprisingly, it was more difficult to document spatial arrangements in the contemporary workplace than in Bedouin tents.

Women's status in regard to control of property, control of labor, and participation in public life was determined from women's legal rights. Records of the passage of legislation granting women rights to property, wages, and the vote are readily available from secondary sources. Contemporary information on the wage gap and women's election to public office is

Table A.1. Operationalization of Variables for Nonindustrial Societies

Independent variables	(N)	Percent
Segregated dwelling	(79)	100.0%
Absent (0)	62	78.5
Present (1)	17	21.5
Men's hut	(81)	100.0%
Absent (0)	59	72.8
Present (1)	22	27.2
Sexually segregated work	(66)	100.0%
Lesser (0)	37	56.1
Greater (1)	29	43.9

Dependent variable components	(N)	
Female control of labor and property (range = 1–4)	(81)	
Female inheritance rights		
Female dwelling ownership		
Female control of male labor		
Female control of joint labor		
Female control of female labor		
Inheritance of property (range = 1–4)	(71)	
Predominantly male		
Male preference		
Equal preference		
Female preference		
Female kinship power (range = 1–3)	(81)	
Female kinship leaders		
Monogamous marriage form		
Multiple husbands allowed		
Levirate absent		

Source: Whyte's (1978a) Human Relations Area File data and sources cited in appendix B.

Table A.2. Measures of Association among Variables (Gamma Values)

Independent variables	Men's Hut	Segregated Labor
Segregated dwelling	.30	−.15
Segregated labor	.77	—
Dependent variables	Kinship Power	Inheritance Rights
Control of labor	.06	.85
Inheritance rights	.18	—

251

Source: Calculations based on data from Whyte (1978a) and sources cited in appendix B.

included in the sociological, economic, and government sources cited in the text.

The research method for Part 2 consisted of reviewing parallel sources of data for the time period of interest. Thus, data were gathered for housing design and women's status throughout the nineteenth and twentieth centuries. The same technique was applied to changes in school and workplace design in relation to women's status. In sum, the research methodology can be compared to assembling a jigsaw puzzle. Disparate pieces of data from anthropology, architecture, history, and sociology—which alone convey only limited information—fit together to create a clearly visible picture of the relationship between gendered spaces and women's status.

Appendix B: Cross-Cultural Sample and References for Gender Segregation Data

Abipon

Dabrizhoffer, Martin. *An Account of the Abipones, an Equestrian People of Paraguay*. Vol. 2. London: John Murray, 1822.

Abkhaz

Byhan, Arthur. *Caucasians, East and North Russia, Finland: I. The Caucasian Peoples*. Illustrierte Völkerkunde, edited by Georg Buschan, vol. 2, pt. 2. Stuttgart: Strecker und Schröder, 1926.

Dzhanashvile, M. G. *Abkhazia and the Abkhaz*. Zapiski Kavkazskago Otdiela Imperatorskajo Russkago Geograficheskago Obshchestua [Memoirs of the Caucasus Section of the Imperial Russian Geographical Society], book 16. Tiflis, 1894.

Aleut

Sparks, Jared. *Life of John Ledyard, the American Traveler*. Library of American Biography, ser. 2, vol. 14. Boston: Charles C. Little and James Brown, 1847.

Veniaminov, Ivan Evsîeevich Popov. *Notes on the Islands of the Unalaska District*. St. Petersburg: Russian-American Company, 1840.

Alorese

DuBois, Cora. *The People of Alor: A Social-Psychological Study of an East Indian Island*. Minneapolis: University of Minnesota Press, 1944.

Amhara

Levine, Donald Nathan. *Wax and Gold: Tradition and Innovation in Ethiopian Culture*. Chicago: University of Chicago Press, 1965.

Messing, Simon David. "The Highland-Plateau Amhara of Ethiopia." Ph.D. dissertation, University of Pennsylvania, 1957.

Rey, C. F. *The Real Abyssinia*. 2d ed. Philadelphia: J. B. Lippincott, 1935.

Andamanese

Man, Edward Horace. *On the Aboriginal Inhabitants of the Andaman Islands*. London: Royal Anthropological Institute of Great Britain and Ireland, 1932.

Radcliffe-Brown, A. R. *The Andaman Islanders: A Study in Social Anthropology*. Cambridge: Cambridge University Press, 1922.

Temple, Richard C. *The Andaman and Nicobar Islands*. Census of India, 1901, vol. 3. Calcutta: Office of the Superintendent of Government Printing, 1903.

Aranda

Basedow, Herbert. *The Australian Aboriginal*. Adelaide: F. W. Preece and Sons, 1925.

Spencer, [Walter] Baldwin, and Francis James Gillen. *The Arunta: A Study of a Stone Age People*. London: Macmillan, 1927.

Ashanti

Field, M. J. *Search for Security: An Ethno-Psychiatric Study of Rural Ghana*. Norton Library, no. 508. New York: W. W. Norton, 1970.

Rattray, R. S. *Ashanti Law and Constitution*. Oxford: Clarendon Press, 1929.

Aztec

Bandelier, Adolph F. *On the Distribution and Tenure of Lands, and the Customs with Respect to Inheritance, among the Ancient Mexicans*. Reports of the Peabody Museum of American Archaeology and Ethnology in Connection with Harvard University, vol. 2. Cambridge, 1880.

Díaz del Castillo, Bernal. *The True History of the Conquest of New Spain*. Vol. 2. Translated and edited by Alfred Percival Mandslay. Works issued by the Hakluyt Society, 2d ser., no. 24. London, 1910.

Vaillant, George Clapp. *Aztecs of Mexico: Origin, Rise and Fall of the Aztec Nation*. Garden City, N.Y.: Doubleday, Doran, 1941.

Babylonians
Contenau, Georges. *Everyday Life in Babylon and Assyria*. London: E. Arnold, 1955.

Bemba
Richards, Audrey I. *Land, Labour and Diet in Northern Rhodesia: An Economic Study of the Bemba Tribe*. Oxford: Oxford University Press, 1939.   **255**

Bribri
Gabb, William M. *On the Indian Tribes and Languages of Costa Rica*. Proceedings of the American Philosophical Society, vol. 14. Philadelphia, 1876.
Stone, Doris. *The Boruca of Costa Rica*. Papers of the Peabody Museum of American Archaeology and Ethnology, Harvard University, vol. 26, no. 2. Cambridge, 1949.
————. *The Talamancan Tribes of Costa Rica*. Papers of the Peabody Museum of Archaeology and Ethnology, Harvard University, vol. 43, no. 2. Cambridge, 1962.

Burmese
Orr, Kenneth Gordon. "Field Notes on the Burmese Standard of Living as Seen in the Case of a Fisherman-Refugee Family." Notes of the Burma Community Research Project, Department of Anthropology, University of Rangoon. Rangoon, Burma, 1951.
Scott, James George. *The Burman, His Life and Notions*, 3d ed. Edited by Shway Yoe. London: Macmillan, 1910.

Callinago
Breton, Raymond. *Observations of the Island Carib: A Compilation of Ethnographic Notes*. Selected, organized, and translated by Marshall McKusick and Pierre Verin. Auxerre: Gilles Bouquet, 1775. Facsimile edition, Leipzig: B. G. Teubner, 1892.
DuTertre, Jean-Baptiste. *General History of the Antilles Occupied by the French*. . . . Vol. 2. 2d rev. ed. Paris, 1667.

Rouse, Irving. *The Carib*. Bureau of American Ethnology, bulletin 143, vol. 4. Washington, D.C.: Smithsonian Institution, 1948.

Cayua

Watson, James Bennett. *Caejuá Culture Change: A Study in Acculturation and Methodology*. Memoirs of the American Anthropological Association, no. 73. Menasha, Wisc., 1952.

Chukchee

Borgoraz-Tan, Vladimir Germunovich. *The Chukchee: Material Culture* [Part 1], *Religion* [Part 2], *Social Organization* [Part 3]. Memoirs of the American Museum of Natural History, vol. 11. Leiden: E. J. Brill, and New York: G. E. Stechert, 1904 [Part 1], 1907 [Part 2], 1909 [Part 3].

Nordenskiöld, [Nils] Adolf Erik. *The Voyage of the Vega round Asia and Europe, with a Historical Review of Previous Journeys along the North Coast of the Old World*. New York: Macmillan, 1882.

Wrangell, Ferdinand von. *Narrative of an Expedition to the Polar Sea in the Years 1820, 1821, 1822 and 1823*. London: James Maddin, 1844.

Comanche

Hoebel, E. Adamson. *The Political Organization and Law-Ways of the Comanche Indians*. Memoirs of the American Anthropological Association, no. 54. Menasha, Wisc., 1940.

Wallace, Ernest, and E. Adamson Hoebel. *The Comanches: Lords of the South Plains*. Norman: University of Oklahoma Press, 1952.

Creek

Swanton, John R. *Social Organization and Social Usages of the Indians of the Creek Confederacy*. Forty-second Annual Report of the Bureau of Ethnology, 1924–25. Washington, D.C.: U.S. Government Printing Office, 1928.

Cubeo

Goldman, Irving. *The Cubeo: Indians of the Northwest Amazon*. Illinois Studies in Anthropology, no. 2. Urbana: University of Illinois Press, 1963.

Eastern Pomo

Barrett, Samuel A. *Pomo Buildings*. Holmes Anniversary Volume, Anthropological Essays. Washington, D.C.: James William Bryan Press, 1916.

Gifford, Edward Winslow, and Alfred L. Kroeber. *Culture Element Distributions: IV, Pomo*. University of California Publications in American Archaeology and Ethnology, vol. 37. Berkeley: University of California Press, 1937.

Kroeber, Alfred L. *Handbook of the Indians of California*. Berkeley: California Book Company, 1953.

Loeb, Edwin M. *Pomo Folkways*. University of California Publications in American Archaeology and Ethnology, vol. 19, no. 2. Berkeley: University of California Press, 1926.

Egyptians

Ammar, Hamed. *Growing Up in an Egyptian Village, Silwa, Province of Aswan*. London: Routledge and Paul. 1954.

Fur

Beaton, Arthur Charles. *A Grammar of the Fur Language*. Khartoum, Sudan: Research Unit, Faculty of Arts, University of Khartoum, 1958.

Wilson, Charles Thomas, and R. W. Felkin. *Uganda and the Egyptian Soudan*. London: S. Low. Marston, Scarlo and Rivington, 1882.

Garo

Burling, Robbins. *Rengsanggri: Family and Kinship in a Garo Village*. Philadelphia: University of Pennsylvania Press, 1963.

Playfair, A. *The Garos*. London, David Nutt, 1909.

Gilyak

Schrenck, Leopold von. *The Peoples of the Amur Region in the Years 1854–1856*. Vol. 3. St. Petersburg: Kaiserliche Akademie der Wissenschaften, 1881–95.

Shternberg, Lev Iâkoulevick. *The Gilyak, Orochi, Goldi, Negidal, Ainu: Articles and Materials*. Edited with a preface by Iâ. P. Al'kor [Koshkin]. Khabarovsk: Dal'giz, 1933.

Goajiro

Armstrong, John M., and Alfred Metraux. "The Goajiro." In *Handbook of*

South American Indians, edited by Julian H. Steward. Vol. 4: The Circum-Caribbean Tribes. [Bureau of American Ethnology, bulletin 143]. Washington, D.C.: Smithsonian Institution, 1948.

Simons, F. A. A. *An Exploration of the Goajira Peninsula, U.S. of Colombia.* Proceedings of the Royal Geographical Society, n.s., vol. 7. London, 1885.

Haida

Memoirs of the American Museum of Natural History, vol. 8, pt. 14. New York: Trustees of the American Museum of Natural History, 1903–21.

Hidatsa

Bowers, Alfred W. *Hidatsa Social and Ceremonial Organization.* Washington, D.C.: U.S. Government Printing Office, 1965.

Iban

Freeman, J. Derek. *The Family System of the Iban of Borneo.* Cambridge Papers in Social Anthropology, The Developmental Cycle in Domestic Groups, edited by Jack Goody, no. 1. Cambridge: Cambridge University Press, 1958.

———. *Iban Agriculture: A Report on the Shifting Cultivation of Hill Rice by the Iban of Sarawak.* Colonial Research Studies, no. 18. London: Her Majesty's Stationery Office, 1955.

Gomes, Edwin H. *Seventeen Years among the Sea Dyaks of Borneo: A Record of Intimate Association with the Natives of the Bornean Jungles.* London: Seeley, 1911.

Howell, William. *The Sea Dyak.* The Sarawak Gazette, vols. 38–40. Kuching, Sarawak, 1908–10.

Ibo

Basden, George T. *Among the Ibos of Nigeria: An Account of the Curious and Interesting Habits, Customs and Beliefs of a Little Known African People....* London: Frank Cass, 1966.

Green, Margaret Mackeson. *Ibo Village Affairs: Chiefly with Reference to the Village of Umueke Agbaja.* 2d ed. London: Frank Cass, 1964.

Ottenberg, Phoebe Vestal. "The Afikpo Ibo of East Nigeria." In *Peoples of*

Africa, edited by James L. Gibbs, Jr. New York: Holt, Rinehart and Winston, 1965.

Inca

Rowe, John Howland. *Inca Culture at the Time of the Spanish Conquest.* Bureau of American Ethnology, bulletin 143, vol. 2. Washington, D.C.: Smithsonian Institution, 1946.

Vega, Garcilaso de la. *El Inca*. The Royal Commentaries of the Incas, pt. 1. Hakluyt Society Publications, ser. 1, vols. 41 and 45. Translated by Clements R. Markham. London, 1869 and 1871.

259

Irish

Arensberg, Conrad M., and Solon T. Kimball. *Family and Community in Ireland*. 2d ed. Cambridge: Harvard University Press, 1968.

Japanese

Beardsley, Richard King, John W. Hall, and Robert E. Ward. *Village Japan*. Chicago: University of Chicago Press, 1959.

Javanese

Jay, Robert Ravenelle. *Javanese Villagers: Social Relations in Rural Modjokuto*. Cambridge: MIT Press, 1969.

Koenljaraningrat. *Javanese*. In Frank M. LeBar, comp., Insular Southeast Asia: Ethnographic Studies. Section 2: Java, Lesser Sundas, and Celebes. HRAFlex Books, Ethnography Series, ALI-002. New Haven: Human Relations Area Files, 1976.

Palmier, Leslie H. *Social Status and Power in Java*. London School of Economics, Monographs on Social Anthropology, 20. London: University of London, Athlone Press, 1969.

Jivaro

Dyott, George Miller. *On the Trail of the Unknown in the Wilds of Ecuador and the Amazon*. London: Thornton Butterworth, 1926.

Farabee, William Curtis. *Indian Tribes of Eastern Peru*. Papers of the Peabody Museum of American Archaeology and Ethnology, vol. 10. Cambridge: Peabody Museum, Harvard University, 1922.

Harner, Michael J. *The Jivaro: People of the Sacred Waterfalls*. Garden City, N.Y.: Anchor Books, 1973.

Hermessen, J. L. *A Journey on the Rio Zamora, Ecuador. The Geographical Review*, vol. 9. New York: American Geographical Society, 1917.

Karsten, Rafael. *The Head-Hunters of Western Amazonas: The Life and Cultures of the Jibaro Indians of Eastern Ecuador and Peru.* Societas Scieniarum Fennica: Commentationes Humanarum Litterarum, vol. 7, no. 1. Helsinki: Centraltryckeriet, 1935.

Kaffa

Huntingford, George Wynn B. *The Galla of Ethiopia: the Kingdoms of Kafa and Janjaro.* London: International African Institute, 1955.

Kaska

Honigmann, John J. *The Kaska Indians: An Ethnographic Reconstruction.* Yale University Publications in Anthropology, no. 51. New Haven: Yale University Press, 1954.

Kazak

Hudson, Alfred E. *Kazak Social Structure.* Yale University Publications in Anthropology, no. 20. New Haven: Yale University Press, 1938.

Sedel'nikov, A. N., A. N. Bukukhanov, and S. D. Chadov. *The Kirghiz Krai.* Rossiia. Polnoe Geograficheskoe Opisanie Nashego Otechestua [Russia, a Complete Geographical Description of Our Fatherland], edited by V. P. Semenov. Vol. 18. St. Petersburg: Izdanie A. F. Deuriena, 1903.

Khmer Cambodians

Vincent, Frank, Jr. *The Land of the White Elephant: Sights and Scenes in South-eastern Asia.* New York: Harper and Brothers, 1874.

Kikuyu, 1910

Kenyatta, Jomo. *Facing Mount Kenya: The Tribal Life of the Gikuyu.* London: Secker and Warburg, 1953.

Middleton, John. *The Central Tribes of the North-Eastern Bantu (The Kikuyu, including Embu, Meru, Mbere, Chuka, Mwimbi, Tharaka, and the Kamba of Kenya).* Ethnographic Survey of Africa, East Central Africa, pt. 5. London: International African Institute, 1953.

Kimam

Serpenti, Laurentius M. *Cultivators in the Swamps: Social Structure and Horticulture in a New Guinea Society*. 2d ed. Assen, Netherlands: Van Gorcum, 1977.

Konso

Hallpike. C. R. *The Konso of Ethiopia: A Study of the Values of a Cushitic People*. Oxford: Clarendon Press, 1972.

Kurds

Garnett, Lucy M. J. *Women of Turkey and Their Folk-Lore. II: The Jewish and Moslem Women*. London: David Nutt, 1891.

Hansen, Henry Harold. *The Kurdish Woman's Life: Field Research in a Muslim Society, Iraq*. Copenhagen Ethnographic Museum Record, no. 7. Copenhagen: Nationalmusett, 1961.

Masters, William M. *Rowanduz: A Kurdish Administrative and Mercantile Center*. Ph.D. dissertation, University of Michigan, 1953.

Kwoma

Whiting, John Wesley Mayhew. *Becoming a Kwoma: Teaching and Learning in a New Guinea Tribe*. New Haven: Yale University Press for the Institute of Human Relations, 1941.

———. *Kwoma Journal*. HRAFlex Book OJ13-001. New Haven: Human Relations Area Files, 1970.

Lolo

Lin, Yueh-kioa. *The Lolo of Liang-shan*. Shanghai: The Commercial Press, 1947.

Tseng, Chao-lun. *The Lolo District in Liang-Shan: A Selection from an Account of Investigation Trip to Liang-Shan*. Chungking, 1945.

Marquesans

Handy, E. S. Craighill. *The Native Culture in the Marquesas*. Bernice P. Bishop Museum, bulletin no. 9. Honolulu, 1923.

Linton, Ralph. *The Material Culture of the Marquesas Islands*. Memoirs of the Bernice P. Bishop Museum, vol. 8, no. 5. Honolulu, 1923.

Mbundu

Childs, Gladwyn Murray. *Ovimbundu Kinship and Character*. London: International African Institute and Witwatersrand University Press, 1949.

Hambly, Wilfred D. *The Ovimbundu of Angola*. Publications of the Field Museum of Natural History, Anthropological Series, vol. 21, no. 2. Chicago, 1934.

McCulloch, Merran. *The Ovimbundu of Angola*. Ethnographic Survey of Africa, West Central Africa, pt. 2. London: International African Institute, 1952.

Mbuti

Turnbull, Colin M. *The Mbuti Pygmies: An Ethnographic Survey*. American Museum of Natural History, Anthropological Papers 50. New York: American Museum of Natural History, 1965.

———. *Wayward Servants: The Two Worlds of the African Pygmies*. Garden City, N.Y.: Natural History Press, 1965.

Montagnais

Lips, Julius E. *Naskapi Law: Law and Order in a Hunting Society*. Transactions of the American Philosophical Society, n.s., vol. 37, pt. 4. Philadelphia, 1947.

Tanner, V. *Outlines of the Geography, Life and Customs of Newfoundland-Labrador*. Acta Geographica, vol. 8, no. 1. Helsinki: Societas Geographica Fennia, 1944.

Nama Hottentot

Schapera, Isaac. *The Khoisan Peoples of South Africa: Bushmen and Hottentots*. London: George Routledge and Sons, 1930.

Ten Rhyne, William. *A Short Account of the Cape of Good Hope, and of the Hottentots Who Inhabit That Region*. Translated by B. Farrington. Cape Town: Van Riebeeck Society, 1933.

New Irelanders

Powdermaker, Hortense. *Life in Lesee: The Study of a Melanesian Society in New Ireland*. New York: W. W. Norton, 1933.

North Vietnamese

Gourou, Pierre. *Outline of a Study of the Annamese House in Northern and*

Central Annam, from Thanh Hoa to Binh Dinh. Paris: Editions d'Art et d'Histoire, 1936.

————. *The Peasants of the Tonkin Delta: A Study in Human Geography*. Paris: Editions d'Art et d'Histoire, 1936.

Robequain, Charles. *Than-Hoa: Geographical Study of an Annamese Province*. Paris: G. Van Oest, 1929.

Tran-Van-Trai. *The Annamese Patriarchal Family*. Paris: P. Lapagesse, 1942.

Omaha

Dorsey, Rev. J. Owen. *Omaha Sociology*. Smithsonian Institution, Bureau of Ethnology, Third Annual Report, 1881–82. Washington, D.C.: U.S. Government Printing Office, 1884.

Fletcher, Alice C., and Francis La Flesche. *The Omaha Tribe*. Twenty-seventh Annual Report of the Bureau of American Ethnology, 1905–6. Washington, D.C.: U.S. Government Printing Office, 1911.

Palauans

Barnett, H. S. *Being a Palauan*. New York: Hold, 1960.

Papago

Joseph, Alice, Rosamond B. Spicer, and Jane Chesky. *The Desert People: A Study of the Papago Indians*. Chicago: University of Chicago Press, 1949.

Underhill, Ruth Murray. *The Autobiography of a Papago Woman*. Memoirs of the American Anthropological Association, no. 46. Menasha, Wisc., 1936.

Romans

Carcopino, Jerome. *Daily Life in Ancient Rome: The People and the City at the Height of the Empire*. New Haven: Yale University Press, 1940.

Salteaux (and Pekangekum)

Hilger, Inez M. *A Social Study of One Hundred Fifty Chippewa Indian Families of the White Earth Reservation of Minnesota*. Washington, D.C.: Catholic University of America Press, 1939.

Kinietz, W. Vernon. *Chippewa Village: The Story of Katikitegon*. Cranbrook Institute of Science, bulletin no. 25. Bloomfield Hills, Mich.: Cranbrook Press, 1947.

Skinner, Alanson. *Notes on the Eastern Cree and Northern Salteaux*. Anthropological Papers of the American Museum of Natural History, vol. 9, pt. 1. New York, 1912.

Saramacca

Herskovits, Melville J., and Frances S. Herskovits. *Rebel Destiny: Among the Bush Negroes of Dutch Guiana*. New York: McGraw-Hill, 1934.

Semang

Schebesta, Paul. *The Negritos of Asia*. Vol. 2, *Ethnography of the Negritos*; Half-vol. 1, *Economy and Sociology*. Studio Instituti Anthropas, vol. 12. Vienna-Mödling: St.-Gabriel-Verlag, 1954.

Shavante

Maybury-Lewis, David. *Akwē-Shavante Society*. Oxford: Clarendon Press, 1967.

Shilluk

Dempsey, James. *Mission on the Nile*. London: Burns and Oates, 1955.
Seligman, C. G., and Brenda Z. Seligman. *Pagan Tribes of the Nilotic Sudan*. London: George Routledge and Sons, 1932.

Siriono

Holmberg, Allan R. *Nomads of the Long Bow: The Siriono of Eastern Bolivia*. Smithsonian Institution, Institute of Social Anthropology Publications, no. 10. Washington, D.C.: U.S. Government Printing Office, 1950.

Siuai

Oliver, Douglas L. *A Solomon Island Society: Kinship and Leadership among the Siuai of Bougainville*. Cambridge: Harvard University Press, 1955.

Tallensi

Fortes, Meyer. *The Web of Kinship among the Tallensi: The Second Part of an Analysis of the Social Structure of a Trans-Volta Tribe*. London: Oxford University Press for the International African Institute, 1949.
Rattray, Robert Sutherland. *The Tribes of the Ashanti Hinterland*, vol. 2. Oxford: Clarendon Press, 1932.

Tanala

Linton, Ralph. *The Tanala: A Hill Tribe of Madagascar*. Publications of the

Field Museum of Natural History, Anthropological Series, vol. 22. Chicago, 1933.

Tehuelche

Cooper, John M. *Patagonian and Pampean Hunters*. Handbook of South American Indians, Bureau of American Ethnology, bulletin no. 143, vol. 1. Washington, D.C.: Smithsonian Institution, 1946.

Thonga

Junod, Henri A. *The Life of a South African Tribe*, vols. 1 and 2. London: Macmillan, 1927.

Toda

Breeks, James Wilkinson. *An Account of the Primitive Tribes and Monuments of the Nilagiris*. London: India Museum, 1873.

Marshall, William E. *A Phrenologist amongst the Todas*. London: Longmans, Green, 1873.

Rivers, W. H. R. *The Todas*. London: Macmillan, 1906.

Toradja

Kruyt, Adriani N., and Albert C. Kruyt. *The Bare'e-speaking Toradja of Central Celebes (the East Toradja)*, vol. 1. 2d ed. Koninklijke Nederlandse Akademie van Wetenschappen, Verhandelingen, Afdeling Letterkunde, Nieuwe Reeks, Deel 54. Amsterdam: Noord-Hollandsche Vitgevers Maatschappij, 1950.

Trukese

Goodenough, Ward H. *Property, Kin and Community on Truk*. Yale University Publications in Anthropology, no. 46. New Haven: Yale University Press, 1951.

Trumai

Murphy, Robert F., and Buell Quain. *The Trumai Indians of Central Brazil*. Monographs of the American Ethnological Society, no. 24. Locust Valley, N.Y.: J. J. Augustin, 1955.

Tuareg

Lhote, Henri. *The Hoggar Tuareg*. Paris: Payot, 1944.

Nicolaisen, Johannes. *Ecology and Culture of the Pastoral Tuareg*. Copenhagen Ethnographic Museum Record, no. 9. Copenhagen: National-musett, 1963.

Tupinamba

Abbeville, Claude d'. *History of the Mission of the Capuchin Fathers on the Isle of Maragnan and the Surrounding Lands*. Paris: François Huby, 1614.

Staden, Hans. *The True Story of His Captivity*. Translated and edited by Malcolm Letts. London: George Routledge and Sons, 1928.

266   Turks

Morrison, John A. Alisor. *A Unit of Land Occupance in the Kanak Su Basin of Central Anatolia*. Chicago: University of Chicago Libraries, 1939.

Pierce, Joe E. *Life in a Turkish Village*. New York: Holt, Rinehart and Winston, 1964.

Sterling, Paul. *Turkish Village*. London: Weidenfeld and Nicolson, 1965.

Twana

Eells, Myron. *The Indians of Puget Sound: The Notebooks of Myron Eells*. Seattle: University of Washington Press, 1985.

Uttar Pradesh

Wiser, Charlotte V., and William H. Wiser. *Behind Mud Walls*. New York: Richard R. Smith, 1930.

West Punjabi

Darling, Malcolm Lyall. *The Punjab Peasant in Prosperity and Debt*. New Delhi: Manchar Book Service, 1977.

Wodaabe Fulani

Stenning, Derrick J. *Savannah Nomads: A Study of the Wodaabe Pastoral Fulani of Western Bornu Province*. London: Oxford University Press for the International African Institute, 1959.

Wolof

Gamble, David P. *Contributions to a Socio-Economic Survey of the Gambia*. London: Research Department, Colonial Office, 1949.

———. *The Wolof of Senegambia*. Ethnographic Survey of Africa, Western Africa, pt. 14. London: International African Institute, 1957.

Yanomamo

Becker, Hans. *The Surana and Pakidai, Two Yanomamo Tribes in Northwest Brazil*. Hamburg, Museum für Völkerkunde, Mitteilungen, vol. 26. Hamburg: Kommissionsverlag Cram, De Gruyter, 1960.

Chagnon, Napoleon Alphonseau. *Yanomamo Warfare, Social Organization and Marriage Alliance*. Ph.D. dissertation, University of Michigan, 1967.

Wilbert, Johannes. *The Sanema*. In *Indias de la Región Orinoco-Ventuari*. Fundación La Salle de Ciencias Naturales, monografía no. 8. Caracas, 1963.

Yurak Samoyed

Hajdu, Peter. *The Samoyed Peoples and Languages*. Indiana University, Uralic and Altaic Studies, vol. 14. Bloomington and the Hague, Indiana University and Mouton, 1963.

Kopytoff, Igor. *The Samoyed*. Indiana University. Graduate Program in Uralic and Altaic Studies. Subcontractor's Monograph, HRAF-B, Indiana-49. New Haven: Human Relations Area Files, 1955.

Popov, A. A. *The Nganason: The Material Culture of the Tavgi Samoyeds*. Translated by Elaine K. Ristinen. Indiana University Publications, Uralic and Altaic Series, vol. 56. Bloomington: Indiana University, 1966.

Zuni

Smith, Watson, and John M. Roberts. *Zuni Law: A Field of Values*. Papers of the Peabody Museum of American Archaeology and Ethnology, Harvard University, vol. 43, no. 1 (Reports of the Rimrock Project Value Series, no. 4). Cambridge, 1954.

Stevenson, Matilda Coxe. *The Zuni Indians: Their Mythology, Esoteric Fraternities and Ceremonies*. Twenty-third Annual Report of the Bureau of American Ethnology to the Secretary of the Smithsonian Institution, 1901–2. Washington, D.C.: U.S. Government Printing Office, 1904.

References

Abbott, Edith. 1906. "Harriet Martineau and the Employment of Women in 1836." *Journal of Political Economy* 14 (December): 614–26.

———. [1910] 1969. *Women in Industry: A Study in American Economic History.* Reprint. New York: Arno Press.

ACSA Task Force on the Status of Women in Architecture Schools. 1990. "Status of Faculty Women in Architecture Schools." Washington, D.C.: Association of Collegiate Schools of Architecture.

Alcott, William. 1838. *The Young Wife, or Duties of Woman in the Marriage Relation.* Boston: George W. Light.

———. [1839] 1972. *The Young Husband, or Duties of Man in the Marriage Relation.* Reprint. New York: Arno Press.

Alexander, Christopher, S. Ishakawa, and Murray Silverstein. 1977. *A Pattern Language: Towns/Building/Construction.* New York: Oxford University Press.

Andersen, Margaret. 1988. *Thinking about Women.* 2d ed. New York: Macmillan.

Anderton, Frances. 1989. "Learning from Jaipur." *Journal of Architectural Education* 42 (Summer): 15–24.

Andrews, Alice C. 1982. "Toward a Status-of-Women Index." *Professional Geographer* 34 (1): 24–31.

Ardener, Shirley, ed. 1981. *Women and Space.* London: Croom Helm.

Aron, Cindy. 1987. *Ladies and Gentlemen of the Civil Service.* New York: Oxford University Press.

Astin, Alexander. 1977. *Four Critical Years.* San Francisco: Jossey-Bass.

Awe, Bolanle. 1977. "The Iyalode in the Traditional Yoruba Political System." Chap. 7 in *Sexual Stratification*, edited by Alice Schlegel. New York: Columbia University Press.

Bacdayan, Albert S. 1977. "Mechanistic Cooperation and Sexual Equality among the Western Bantoc." Chap. 12 in *Sexual Stratification*, edited by Alice Schlegel. New York: Columbia University Press.

Baran, Barbara, and Suzanne Teegarden. 1987. "Women's Labor in the Office of the Future: A Case Study of the Insurance Industry." In *Women, Households, and the Economy*, edited by Lourdes Beneria and Catharine R. Stimpson, pp. 201– 24. New Brunswick, N.J.: Rutgers University Press.

Barker, Karlyn. 1988. "4 Nominated as Cosmos Goes Coed." *Washington Post*, June 22, p. B1.

Barnett, H. G. 1960. *Being a Palauan*. New York: Holt, Rinehart, and Winston.

Baron, James N., and William T. Bielby. 1985. "Organizational Barriers to Gender Equality: Sex Segregation of Jobs and Opportunities." Chap. 12 in *Gender and the Life Course*, edited by Alice Rossi. New York: Aldine.

Bascom, William. 1955. "Urbanization among the Yoruba." *American Journal of Sociology* 60 (March): 446–54.

Bateson, Gregory. 1958. *Naven*. 2d ed. London: Wildwood House.

Becker, Franklin D. 1981. *Workspace: Creating Environments in Organizations*. New York: Praeger.

Becker, Gary S. 1981. *A Treatise on the Family*. Cambridge: Harvard University Press.

Beecher, Catharine. 1842. *Treatise on Domestic Economy, for the Use of Young Ladies at Home and at School*. Boston: Thomas H. Webb.

Beecher, Catharine, and Harriet Beecher Stowe. [1869] 1975. *The American Woman's Home*. Reprint. Hartford, Conn.: Stowe-Day Foundation.

Belker, Loren. 1981. *The Successful Secretary*. New York: American Management Associations.

Beller, Andrea. 1984. "Trends in Occupational Segregation by Sex and Race, 1960–1981." In *Sex Segregation in the Workplace: Trends, Explanations, Remedies*, edited by Barbara Reskin, pp. 11–26. Washington, D.C.: National Academy Press.

Beneria, Lourdes, and Martha Roldan. 1987. *The Crossroads of Class and Gender*. Chicago: University of Chicago Press.

Benson, Mary Summer. 1935. *Women in Eighteenth-Century America*. New York: Columbia University Press.

Berger, Peter, and Thomas Luckmann. 1967. *The Social Construction of Reality: A Treatise on the Sociology of Knowledge*. Garden City, N.Y.: Anchor Books.

Berk, Sarah Fenstermaker. 1985. *The Gender Factory*. New York: Plenum Press.

Bianchi, Suzanne, and Nancy Rytina. 1986. "The Decline in Occupational Sex Segregation during the 1970s: Census and CPS Comparisons." *Demography* 23 (February): 79–86.

270

Bianchi, Suzanne, and Daphne Spain. 1986. *American Women in Transition*. New York: Russell Sage Foundation.

Bielby, Denise, and William T. Bielby. 1988. "She Works Hard for the Money: Household Responsibilities and the Allocation of Work Effort." *American Journal of Sociology* 93 (March): 1031–59.

Bielby, William, and James Baron. 1984. "A Woman's Place Is with Other Women: Sex Segregation within Organizations." In *Sex Segregation in the Workplace: Trends, Explanations, Remedies*, edited by Barbara Reskin, pp. 27–55. Washington D.C.: National Academy Press.

———. 1986. "Men and Women at Work: Sex Segregation and Statistical Discrimination." *American Journal of Sociology* 91 (January): 759–99.

Biermann, Barrie. 1971. "Indlu: The Domed Dwelling of the Zulu." In *Shelter in Africa*, edited by Paul Oliver, pp. 96–105. New York: Praeger.

Bigglestone, W. E. 1971. "Oberlin College and the Negro Student, 1865–1940." *Journal of Negro History* 56 (July): 198–219.

Black, J. Thomas, Kelly S. Roark, and Lisa S. Schwartz, eds. 1986. *The Changing Office Workplace*. Washington, D.C.: Urban Land Institute.

Blake, Robert, Jane S. Mouton, and Artie Stockton. 1983. *The Secretary Grid*. New York: American Management Association.

Blau, Francine. 1977. *Equal Pay in the Office*. Lexington, Mass.: Lexington Books.

Blaxall, Martha, and Barbara Reagan, eds. 1976. *Women and the Workplace*. Chicago: University of Chicago Press.

Blumberg, Rae Lesser. 1978. *Stratification: Socioeconomic and Sexual Inequality*. Dubuque, Iowa: William C. Brown.

———. 1984. "A General Theory of Gender Stratification." In *Sociological Theory, 1984*, edited by Randall Collins, pp. 23–101. San Francisco: Jossey-Bass.

Bonvillain, Nancy. 1980. "Iroquoian Women." In *Studies on Iroquoian Culture*, edited by Nancy Bonvillain. Occasional Publications in Northeastern Anthropology, no. 6. Rindghe, N.H.: Franklin Pierce College.

Boserup, Ester. 1970. *Woman's Role in Economic Development*. New York: St. Martin's Press.

Boulding, Elise. 1976. "Familial Constraints on Women's Work Roles." In *Women and the Workplace*, edited by Martha Blaxall and Barbara Reagan, pp. 95–117. Chicago: University of Chicago Press.

Bourdieu, Pierre. 1971. "The Berber House." Chap. 18 in *Rules and Meanings: The Anthropology of Everyday Knowledge*, edited by Mary Douglas. Harmondsworth: Penguin.

———. 1977. *Outline of a Theory of Practice*. Cambridge: Cambridge University Press.

Bowlby, S. R., J. Foord, L. McDowell. 1986. "The Place of Gender in Locality Studies." *Area* 18 (4): 327–31.

Bowlby, S. R., J. Foord, S. Mackenzie. 1982. "Feminism and Geography." *Area* 14 (1): 19–25.

Bradley, Harriet. 1989. *Men's Work, Women's Work*. Cambridge: Polity Press.

Brandt, Elizabeth A. 1980. "On Secrecy and the Control of Knowledge: Taos Pueblo." Chap. 5 in *Secrecy: A Cross-Cultural Perspective*, edited by Stanton Tefft. New York: Human Sciences Press.

Brinton, Mary C. 1988. "The Social-Institutional Bases of Gender Stratification: Japan as an Illustrative Case." *American Journal of Sociology* 94 (September): 300–334.

———. 1989. "Gender Stratification in Contemporary Urban Japan." *American Sociological Review* 54 (August): 549–64.

Brown, Clair, and Joseph Pechman, eds. 1987. *Gender in the Workplace*. Washington, D.C.: Brookings Institution.

Brown, Judith K. 1970. "Economic Organization and the Position of Women among the Iroquois." *Ethnohistory* 17:151–67.

———. 1975. "Iroquois Women: An Ethnohistoric Note." In *Toward an Anthropology of Women*, edited by Rayna Reiter, pp. 235–51. New York: Monthly Review Press.

Buenaventura-Posso, Elisa, and Susan Brown. 1980. "Forced Transition from Egalitarianism to Male Dominance: The Bari of Colombia." Chap. 5 in *Women and Colonization*, edited by Mona Etienne and Eleanor Leacock. New York: Praeger.

Calloway, Helen. 1981. "Spatial Domains and Women's Mobility in Yorubaland, Nigeria." Chap. 9 in *Women and Space*, edited by Shirley Ardener. London: Croom Helm.

Caplan, Patricia. 1985. *Class and Gender in India*. London: Tavistock Publications.

Caplow, Theodore. 1964. *The Sociology of Work*. New York: McGraw-Hill.

Card, Emily. 1981. "Women, Housing Access, and Mortgage Credit." In *Women and the American City*, edited by Catharine Stimpson, Elsa Dixler, Martha Nelson, and Kathryn Yatrakis, pp. 212–16. Chicago: University of Chicago Press.

Center for the American Woman and Politics. National Information Bank on Women in Public Office. 1988. "Women in Elective Office 1988." New Brunswick, N.J.: Eagleton Institute of Politics, Rutgers University.

———. 1989. "Women in Elective Office 1989." New Brunswick, N.J.: Eagleton Institute of Politics, Rutgers University.

Chafetz, Janet. 1984. *Sex and Advantage*. Totowa, N.J.: Rowman and Allanheld.

———. 1990. *Gender Equity*. Newbury Park, Calif.: Sage.

Chance, Norman. 1966. *The Eskimo of North Alaska*. New York: Holt, Rinehart, and Winston.

Charpentier, Sophie. 1982. "The Lao House: Vientiane and Louang Prabang." In *The House in East and Southeast Asia*, edited by K. G. Izikowitz and P. Sorensen, pp. 49–61. London: Curzon Press.

Chodorow, Nancy. 1978. *The Reproduction of Mothering*. Berkeley: University of California Press.

Clark, Clifford Edward. 1986. *The American Family Home: 1800 to 1960*. Chapel Hill: University of North Carolina Press.

Clawson, Mary Ann. 1980. "Early Modern Fraternalism and the Patriarchal Family." *Feminist Studies* 6 (Summer): 368–91.

Clement, Pierre. 1982. "The Lao House among the Thai Houses: A Comparative Survey and a Preliminary Classification." In *The House in East and Southeast Asia*, edited by K. G. Izikowitz and P. Sorensen, pp. 71–80. London: Curzon Press.

Cockburn, Cynthia. 1983. *Brothers: Male Dominance and Technological Change*. London: Pluto Press.

Collins, Randall. 1971. "A Conflict Theory of Sexual Stratification." *Social Problems* 19:3–21.

———. 1986. "Is 1980s Sociology in the Doldrums?." *American Journal of Sociology* 91 (May): 1336–55.

———. 1988. "Women and Men in the Class Structure." *Journal of Family Issues* 9 (March): 27–50.

Coltrane, Scott. 1988. "Father-Child Relationships and the Status of Women: A Cross-Cultural Study." *American Journal of Sociology* 93 (March): 1060–95.

Coolidge, John Phillips. 1942. *Mill and Mansion: A Study of Architecture and Society in Lowell, Massachusetts, 1820–1865*. New York: Columbia University Press.

Cooper, Elizabeth. 1916. *The Harim and the Purdah*. New York: Century.

Corcoran, Mary, and Greg Duncan. 1979. "Work History, Labor Force Attachment, and Earnings Differences between the Races and Sexes." *Journal of Human Resources* 14 (Winter): 3–20.

Corlin, Claes. 1982. "The Organization of Space in a Tibetan Refugee Settlement." In *The House in East and Southeast Asia*, edited by K. G. Izikowitz and P. Sorensen, pp. 173–80. London: Curzon Press.

Cott, Nancy F. 1977. *The Bonds of Womanhood: "Woman's Sphere" in New England, 1780–1835*. New Haven: Yale University Press.

Cowan, Ruth Schwartz. 1983. *More Work for Mother*. New York: Basic Books.

Crompton, Rosemary. 1986. "Women and the 'Service Class.'" In *Gender and Stratification*, edited by Rosemary Crompton and Michael Mann, pp. 119–36. Cambridge: Polity Press.

Crompton, Rosemary, and Michael Mann, eds. 1986. *Gender and Stratification*. Cambridge: Polity Press.

Crompton, Rosemary, and Kay Sanderson. 1990. *Gendered Jobs and Social Change*. London: Unwin Hyman.

Crook, J. Mordaunt. 1972. Introduction to *The Gentleman's House; or How to Plan English Residences*, by Robert Kerr. New York: Johnson Reprint Company.

Damas, David. 1972a. "The Structure of Central Eskimo Associations." In *Alliance in Eskimo Society*, edited by Lee Guemple, pp. 40–55. Seattle: University of Washington Press.

———. 1972b. "The Copper Eskimo." Chap. 1 in *Hunters and Gatherers Today*, edited by M. G. Bicchieri. New York: Holt, Rinehart, and Winston.

Daniels, Arlene Kaplan. 1975. "Feminist Perspectives in Sociological Research." In *Another Voice*, edited by Marcia Milman and Rosabeth Moss Kanter, pp. 340–80. New York: Anchor Books.

Dear, Michael, and Jennifer Wolch. 1989. "How Territory Shapes Social Life." In *The Power of Geography*, edited by Jennifer Wolch and Michael Dear, pp. 3–18. Boston: Unwin Hyman.

Douglas, Mary. 1966. *Purity and Danger: An Analysis of Concepts of Pollution and Taboo*. London: Routledge and Kegan Paul.

Downing, Andrew Jackson. [1873] 1981. *Victorian Cottage Residences*. Reprint. New York: Dover Publications.

Downs, James F. 1972. *The Navajo*. New York: Holt, Rinehart, and Winston.

Draper, Patricia. 1975. "!Kung Women: Contrasts in Sexual Egalitarianism in Foraging and Sedentary Contexts." In *Toward an Anthropology of Women*, edited by Rayna Reiter, pp. 77–109. New York: Monthly Review Press.

Dublin, Thomas. 1979. *Women at Work: The Transformation of Work and Community in Lowell, Mass., 1826–1860*. New York: Columbia University Press.

Duffy, Francis, Colin Cave, and John Worthington, eds. 1976. *Planning Office Space*. London: Architectural Press.

Dupire, Margaret. 1963. "The Position of Women in a Pastoral Society." In *Women of Tropical Africa*, edited by Denise Paulme, pp. 47–92. Berkeley: University of California Press.

Durkheim, Émile. 1915. *The Elementary Forms of the Religious Life*. London: Allen and Unwin.

Eastwood, Mary. 1978. "Legal Protection against Sex Discrimination." In *Women Working*, edited by Ann Stromberg and Shirley Harkess, pp. 108–23. Palo Alto, Calif.: Mayfield.

Eisenstein, Zillah. 1979. "Developing a Theory of Capitalist Patriarchy and Socialist Feminism." In *Capitalist Patriarchy and the Case for Socialist Feminism*, edited by Zillah Eisenstein, pp. 5–40. New York: Monthly Review Press.

Ellis, Peter. 1986. "Office Planning and Design: The Impact of Organizational Change Due to Advanced Information Technology." In *The Changing Office Workplace*, edited by J. Thomas Black, Kelly S. Roark, and Lisa S. Schwartz, pp. 37–52. Washington, D.C.: Urban Land Institute.

Engels, Friedrich. [1884] 1942. *The Origin of the Family, Private Property, and the State*. Reprint. New York: International Publishers.

England, Paula, George Farkas, Barbara Kilbourne, and Thomas Dou. 1988. "Explaining Occupational Sex Segregation and Wages: Findings from a Model with Fixed Effects." *American Sociological Review* 53 (August): 544–58.

Evans, Robin. 1982. *The Fabrication of Virtue: English Prison Architecture, 1750–1840*. Cambridge: Cambridge University Press.

Evans-Pritchard, Edward Evan. 1965. "The Position of Women in Primitive Societies and in Our Own." In *The Position of Women in Primitive Societies and Other Essays in Social Anthropology*, edited by Edward Evan Evans-Pritchard, pp. 37–58. London: Faber and Faber.

Fadipe, N. A. 1970. *The Sociology of the Yoruba*. Nigeria: Ibadan University Press.

Faegre, Torvald. 1979. *Tents: Architecture of the Nomads*. Garden City, N.Y.: Anchor Books.

Feinberg, Lawrence. 1987. "Cosmos Club to Fight D.C. Bias Finding." *Washington Post*, November 14, p. G2.

———. 1988. "18 Women End Cosmos Club's 110-Year Male Era." *Washington Post*, October 12, p. B3.

Fenton, William N. [1951] 1985. "Locality as a Basic Factor in the Development of Iroquois Social Structure." Reprinted in *An Iroquois Sourcebook*, edited by Elizabeth Tooker, vol. 1, *Political and Social Organization*. New York: Garland Publishing.

Flanagan, Barbara. 1990. "The Office that (Almost) Does the Work for You." *Working Women*, October, pp. 112–15.

Flax, Jane. 1987. "Postmodernism and Gender Relations in Feminist Theory." *Signs* 12 (Summer): 621–43.

Fletcher, Robert Samuel. 1943. *A History of Oberlin College*. 2 vols. Oberlin, Ohio: Oberlin College.

Flexner, Eleanor. 1975. *Century of Struggle*. 2d ed. Cambridge: Harvard University Press.

Foner, Eric. 1988. *Reconstruction: America's Unfinished Revolution: 1863–1877*. New York: Harper and Row.

Force, Roland W., and Maryanne Force. 1972. *Just One House*. Honolulu: Bishop Museum Press.

Foucault, Michel. 1977. *Discipline and Punish: The Birth of the Prison*. Translated by Alan Sheridan. New York: Vintage Books.

———. 1980. *Power/Knowledge*. New York: Pantheon Books.

Fox-Genovese, Elizabeth. 1988. *Within the Plantation Household: Black and White Women of the Old South*. Chapel Hill: University of North Carolina Press.

Franklin, Jill. 1981. *The Gentleman's Country House and Its Plan, 1835–1914*. London: Routledge and Kegan Paul.

Friedl, Ernestine. 1975. *Women and Men: An Anthropologist's View*. New York: Holt, Rinehart, and Winston.

Gauldie, Enid. 1974. *Cruel Habitations: A History of Working Class Housing, 1700–1918*. London: Unwin University Books.

Geertz, Hildred, and Clifford Geertz. 1975. *Kinship in Bali*. Chicago: University of Chicago Press.

Gerth, H. H., and C. Wright Mills. [1946] 1972. *From Max Weber: Essays in Sociology*. New York: Oxford University Press.

Giddens, Anthony. 1979. *Central Problems in Social Theory: Action, Structure, and Contradiction in Social Analysis*. Berkeley: University of California Press.

Gilligan, Carol. 1982. *In a Different Voice*. Cambridge: Harvard University Press.

Girouard, Mark. 1979. *The Victorian Country House*. New Haven: Yale University Press.

Goffman, Erving. 1959. *The Presentation of Self in Everyday Life*. New York: Doubleday/Anchor.

———. 1977. "The Arrangement between the Sexes." *Theory and Society* 4:301–36.

Goldberg, Steven. 1974. *The Inevitability of Patriarchy*. New York: William Morrow.

Goldin, Claudia. 1977. "Female Labor Force Participation: The Origin of Black and White Differences, 1870 and 1880." *Journal of Economic History* 37 (March): 87–108.

Goodman, Ellen. 1990. "All-Women Colleges: Are They Necessary?." *Philadelphia Inquirer*, May 26.

Gordon, Larry. 1990. "Decision to Go Coed Prompts Tears at Calif. Women's College." *Philadelphia Inquirer*, May 5.

Gray, Francine du Plessix. 1990. "Reflections: Soviet Women." *New Yorker*, February 19, pp. 48–81.

Gross, Edward. 1968. "Plus Ça Change . . . ? The Sexual Structure of Occupations over Time." *Social Problems* 16:198–208.

Guemple, Lee. 1972. "Kinship and Alliance in Belcher Island Eskimo Society." In *Alliance in Eskimo Society*, edited by Lee Guemple, pp. 56–78. Seattle: University of Washington Press.

Gutek, Barbara. 1985. *Sex and the Workplace*. San Francisco: Jossey-Bass.

Gutentag, Marcia, and Paul Secord. 1983. *Too Many Women?*. Beverly Hills: Sage.

Hacker, Sally. 1989. *Pleasure, Power, and Technology: Some Tales of Gender, Engineering, and the Cooperative Workplace*. Boston: Unwin Hyman.

Hallet, Stanley, and Rafi Samizay. 1980. *Traditional Architecture of Afghanistan*. New York: Garland STPM Press.

Hanson, Susan, and Geraldine Pratt. 1988. "Spatial Dimensions of the Gender Division of Labor in a Local Labor Market." *Urban Geography* 9 (March–April): 180–202.

Hareven, Tamara. 1982. *Family Time and Industrial Time*. Cambridge: Cambridge University Press.

Hartmann, Heidi. 1976. "Capitalism, Patriarchy, and Job Segregation by Sex." In *Women and the Workplace*, edited by Martha Blaxall and Barbara Reagan, pp. 137–69. Chicago: University of Chicago Press.

———. 1981. "The Unhappy Marriage of Marxism and Feminism: Towards a More Progressive Union." In *Women and Revolution*, edited by Lydia Sargent, pp. 1–42. Boston: South End Press.

Harvey, David. 1972. "Society, the City, and the Space-Economy of Urbanism." Association of American Geographers Resource Paper no. 18. Washington, D.C.

———. 1973. *Social Justice and the City*. Baltimore: Johns Hopkins University Press.

Hasell, Mary Joyce, and Frieda D. Peatross. 1990. "Exploring Connections between Women's Changing Roles and House Forms." *Environment and Behavior* 22 (January): 3–26.

Hayden, Dolores. 1980a. "What Would a Non-Sexist City Look Like?" In *Women and the American City*, edited by Catharine Stimpson, Elsa Dixler, Martha Nelson, and Kathryn Yatrakis, pp. 167–84. Chicago: University of Chicago Press.

———. 1980b. *The Grand Domestic Revolution*. Cambridge: MIT Press.

———. 1984. *Redesigning the American Dream: The Future of Housing, Work, and Family Life*. New York: W. W. Norton.

Herdt, Gilbert H. 1981. *Guardians of the Flutes: Idioms of Masculinity*. New York: McGraw-Hill.

———. 1982. *Rituals of Manhood: Male Initiation in Papua New Guinea*. Berkeley: University of California Press.

———. 1987. *The Sambia: Ritual and Gender in New Guinea*. New York: Holt, Rinehart, and Winston.

Hill, Joseph A. 1929. *Women in Gainful Occupations, 1870 to 1920*. Washington, D.C.: U.S. Bureau of the Census.

Hillier, Bill, and Julienne Hanson. 1984. *The Social Logic of Space*. New York: Cambridge University Press.

Hitchcock, Henry-Russell. 1942. *In the Nature of Materials, 1887–1941: The Buildings of Frank Lloyd Wright*. New York: Duell, Sloan and Pearce.

Hodge, Robert, Paul Siegel, and Peter Rossi. 1964. "Occupational Prestige in the United States: 1925–1963." *American Journal of Sociology* 70 (November): 290–92.

Hogbin, Ian. 1970. *The Island of Menstruating Men*. London: Chandler Publishing.

Holden, Karen, and W. Lee Hansen. 1987. "Part-time Work, Full-time Work, and Occupational Segregation." In *Gender in the Workplace*, edited by Clair Brown and Joseph Pechman, pp. 217–46. Washington, D.C.: Brookings Institution.

278 Horowitz, Helen Lefkowitz. 1984. *Alma Mater: Design and Experience in the Women's Colleges from Their Nineteenth Century Beginnings to the 1930s*. Boston: Beacon Press.

House Beautiful. 1955. "Frank Lloyd Wright: His Contribution to the Beauty of American Life." November.

Huber, Joan. 1990. "Macro-Micro Links in Gender Stratification." *American Sociological Review* 55 (February): 1–10.

Huber, Joan, and Glenna Spitze. 1983. *Sex Stratification*. New York: Academic Press.

Hugh-Jones, Christine. 1979. *From the Milk River: Spatial and Temporal Processes in Northwest Amazonia*. Cambridge: Cambridge University Press.

Hugh-Jones, Stephen. 1979. *The Palm and the Pleiades: Initiation and Cosmology in Northwest Amazonia*. Cambridge: Cambridge University Press.

Humphrey, Caroline. 1974. "Inside a Mongolian Tent." *New Society* 31 (October): 273–75.

Izikowitz, K. G., and P. Sorensen, eds. 1982. *The House in East and Southeast Asia*. London: Curzon Press.

Jacobs, Jerry A. 1989. "Long-term Trends in Occupational Segregation by Sex." *American Journal of Sociology* 95 (July): 160–73.

Jencks, Christopher, and David Riesman. 1968. *The Academic Revolution*. Garden City, N.Y.: Doubleday.

Jennings, Eugene Emerson. 1971. *Routes to the Executive Suite*. New York: McGraw-Hill.

Jensen, Joan. 1980. "Cloth, Butter, and Boarders. Household Production for the Market." *Review of Radical Political Economics* 12 (Summer): 14–24.

Jett, Stephen C., and Virginia Spencer. 1981. *Navajo Architecture: Forms, History, Distributions*. Tucson: University of Arizona Press.

Johnson, George, and Frank Stafford. 1974. "The Earnings and Promotion of Women Faculty." *American Economic Review* 64 (December): 888–903.

Johnston-Anumonwo, Ibipo. 1988. "The Journey to Work and Occupational Segregation." *Urban Geography* 9 (March–April): 138–514.

Kamen, Al. 1988. "Law against Club Bias Is Upheld." *Washington Post*, June 21, p. A1.

Kanter, Rosabeth Moss. 1977. *Men and Women of the Corporation*. New York: Basic Books.

Kaplan, Susan Romer. 1978. "Women's Education: The Case for the Single-Sex College." In *The Higher Education of Women*, edited by Helen Astin and Werner Hirsch, pp. 53–67. New York: Praeger.

Katzman, David M. 1978. *Seven Days a Week: Women and Domestic Service in Industrializing America*. New York: Oxford University Press.

Kendall, Elaine. 1975. *Peculiar Institutions: An Informal History of the Seven Sister Colleges*. New York: G. P. Putnam's Sons.

Kerr, Robert. [1871] 1972. *The Gentleman's House; or How to Plan English Residences*. New York: Johnson Reprint Company.

Kessler-Harris, Alice. 1982. *Out to Work: A History of Wage-Earning Women in the United States*. New York: Oxford University Press.

Khatib-Chahidi, Jane. 1981. "Sexual Prohibitions, Shared Space, and Fictive Marriages in Shi'ite Iran." Chap. 6 in *Women and Space*, edited by Shirley Ardener. London: Croom Helm.

Kitchen and Bath Ideas. 1988. Spring.

Kluckhohn, Clyde, and Dorothea Leighton. 1946. *The Navaho*. New York: Anchor Books.

Kraditor, Aileen S., ed. 1968. *Up from the Pedestal*. Chicago: Quadrangle Books.

Kraut, Robert, and Patricia Grambsch. 1987. "Home-Based White Collar Employment: Lessons from the 1980 Census." *Social Forces* 66 (December): 410–26.

Lamphere, Louise. 1987. "The Struggle to Reshape Our Thinking about Gender." In *The Impact of Feminist Research in the Academy*, edited by Christie Farnham, pp. 11–33. Bloomington: Indiana University Press.

Lawrence, Roderick J. 1982. "Domestic Space and Society: A Cross-Cultural Study." *Comparative Studies in Society and History* 24 (January): 104–30.

———. 1984. "Transition Spaces and Dwelling Design." *Journal of Architectural and Planning Research* 1:261–71.

Lee, Richard B. 1972. "The !Kung Bushmen of Botswana." Chap. 8 in *Hunters and Gatherers Today*, edited by M. G. Bicchieri. New York: Holt, Rinehart, and Winston.

Lenski, Gerhard. 1966. *Power and Privilege*. New York: McGraw-Hill.

Lerner, Gerda. 1971. *The Woman in American History*. Menlo Park, Calif.: Addison-Wesley.

———. 1986. *The Creation of Patriarchy*. New York: Oxford University Press.

Levinson, Harry. 1968. *The Exceptional Executive: A Psychological Conception*. Cambridge: Harvard University Press.

————. 1981. *Executive*. Cambridge: Harvard University Press.

Lipman-Blumen, Jean. 1976. "Toward a Homosocial Theory of Sex Roles: An Explanation of the Sex Segregation of Social Institutions." In *Women and the Workplace*, edited by Martha Blaxall and Barbara Reagan, pp. 15–31. Chicago: University of Chicago Press.

————. 1984. *Gender Roles and Power*. Englewood Cliffs, N.J.: Prentice-Hall.

Lloyd, P. C. 1965. "The Yoruba of Nigeria." Chap. 15 in *Peoples of Africa*, edited by James L. Gibbs. New York: Holt, Rinehart, and Winston.

Luker, Kristen. 1984. *Abortion and the Politics of Motherhood*. Berkeley: University of California Press.

Maccoby, Eleanor E., and Carol N. Jacklin. 1974. *The Psychology of Sex Differences*. Stanford, Calif.: Stanford University Press.

McDowell, Linda. 1983. "City and Home: Urban Housing and the Sexual Division of Space." In *Sexual Divisions: Patterns and Processes*, edited by Mary Evans and Clare Ungerson, pp. 142–63. London: Tavistock.

Mackenzie, Suzanne, and Damaris Rose. 1983. "Industrial Change, the Domestic Economy and Home Life." In *Redundant Spaces in Cities and Regions?*, edited by J. Anderson, S. Duncan, and R. Hudson, pp. 155–200. London: Academic Press.

Madden, Janice Fanning. 1977. "A Spatial Theory of Sex Discrimination." *Journal of Regional Science* 17:369–80.

Mandelbaum, David. 1988. *Women's Seclusion and Men's Honor*. Tucson: University of Arizona Press.

Marshall, Lorna. 1965. "The !Kung Bushmen of the Kalahari Desert." Chap. 7 in *Peoples of Africa*, edited by James L. Gibbs. New York: Holt, Rinehart, and Winston.

Massey, Doreen. 1984a. "Introduction: Geography Matters." In *Geography Matters!*, edited by Doreen Massey and John Allen, pp. 1–11. Cambridge: Cambridge University Press.

————. 1984b. *Spatial Divisions of Labor: Social Structures and the Geography of Production*. London: Macmillan.

Maududi, S. Abul a'la. 1972. *Purdah and the Status of Woman in Islam*. Lahore, Pakistan: Islamic Publications.

Maybury-Lewis, David. 1967. *Akwē-Shavante Society*. Oxford: Clarendon Press.

Mead, Margaret. 1949. *Male and Female*. New York: William Morrow.

Mennerick, Lewis. 1975. "Organizational Structuring of Sex Roles in a Nonstereotyped Industry." *Administrative Science Quarterly* 20 (December): 570–86.

Metropolitan Home. 1988. March.

Meyerowitz, Joanne J. 1988. *Women Adrift: Independent Wage Earners in Chicago, 1880–1930*. Chicago: University of Chicago Press.

Milkman, Ruth. 1987. *Gender at Work*. Urbana: University of Illinois Press.

Mill, John Stuart. [1869] 1970. *The Subjection of Women*. Reprint. Cambridge: MIT Press.

Mincer, Jacob, and Solomon Polachek. 1974. "Family Investment in Human Capital: Earnings of Women." In *Marriage, Family Human Capital, and Fertility*, edited by Theodore Schultz, pp. 576–1008. Chicago: University of Chicago Press.

Mogulescu, Maurice. 1970. *Profit through Design: Rx for Effective Office Space Planning*. New York: American Management Associations.

Moore, Frank W. 1961. *Readings in Cross-Cultural Methodology*. New Haven: HRAF Press.

Moore, Henrietta. 1986. *Space, Text, and Gender*. Cambridge: Cambridge University Press.

Moore, Molly. 1990. "Desert Culture Shock: For Female Soldiers, Different Rules." *Washington Post*, August 23, sec. D1, pp. 1–2.

Morgan, Lewis H. 1962. *League of the Iroquois*. New York: Corinth Books.

Moughtin, J. C. 1985. *Hausa Architecture*. London: Ethnographica.

Murdock, George Peter. 1934. *Our Primitive Contemporaries*. New York: Macmillan.

———. 1937. "Comparative Data on the Division of Labor by Sex." *Social Forces* 15 (May): 551–53.

———. 1959. *Africa: Its Peoples and Their Culture History*. New York: McGraw-Hill.

Murdock, George P., and Caterina Provost. 1973. "Factors in the Division of Labor by Sex: A Cross-Cultural Analysis." *Ethnology* 12 (April): 203–25.

Murdock, George P., and Douglas White. 1969. "Standard Cross-Cultural Sample." *Ethnology* 8 (October): 329–69.

Murgatroyd, L., M. Savage, D. Shapiro, J. Urry, S. Walby, A. Warde, with J. Mark-Lawson. 1985. *Localities, Class, and Gender*. London: Pion.

Murphy, Robert. 1964. "Social Distance and the Veil." *American Anthropologist* 66:1257–74.

Murphy, Yolanda, and Robert Murphy. 1985. *Women of the Forest*. 2d ed. New York: Columbia University Press.

Naroll, Raoul. 1970. "Galton's Problem." Chap. 47 in *A Handbook of Method in Cultural Anthropology*, edited by Raoul Naroll and Ronald Cohen. Garden City, N.Y.: Natural History Press.

Naroll, Raoul, and Ronald Cohen, eds. 1970. *A Handbook of Method in Cultural Anthropology*. Garden City, N.Y.: Natural History Press.

National Opinion Research Center. 1989. *1989 General Social Survey*. Made available through the Inter-University Consortium for Political and Social Research.

281

Newcomer, Mabel. 1959. *A Century of Higher Education for American Women*. New York: Harper and Brothers.

Newman, Phillip L. 1965. *Knowing the Gururumba*. New York: Holt, Rinehart, and Winston.

Newmark, Norma L., and Patricia J. Thompson. 1977. *Self, Space, and Shelter*. San Francisco: Canfield Press.

Nicolaisen, Johannes. 1963. *Ecology and Culture of the Pastoral Tuareg*. Copenhagen: National Museum of Copenhagen.

Noble, Jeanne. 1956. *The Negro Woman's College Education*. New York: Columbia University.

Oates, Mary J., and Susan Williamson. 1978. "Women's Colleges and Women Achievers." *Signs* 3 (Summer): 795–806.

———. 1980. "Comment on Tidball's 'Women's Colleges and Women Achievers Revisited.'" *Signs* 6 (Winter): 342–45.

O'Connor, David. 1987. "Women Workers and the Changing International Division of Labor in Microelectronics." In *Women, Households, and the Economy*, edited by Lourdes Beneria and Catharine Stimpson, pp. 243–67. New Brunswick, N.J.: Rutgers University Press.

Ojo, G. J. Afolabi. 1966. *Yoruba Culture: A Geographical Analysis*. London: University of London Press.

Oliver, Douglas. 1955. *A Solomon Island Society*. Cambridge: Harvard University Press.

Oliver, Paul. 1987. *Dwellings: The House across the World*. Austin: University of Texas Press.

Ortner, Sherry. 1974. "Is Female to Male as Nature Is to Culture?" In *Women, Culture, and Society*, edited by Michelle Z. Rosaldo and Louise Lamphere, pp. 67–88. Stanford, Calif.: Stanford University Press.

Palliser, George, and Charles Palliser. [1878] 1978. *The Palliser's Late Victorian Architecture*. Facsimile of *Model Homes* and *American Cottage Homes*. Watkins Glen, N.Y.: American Life Foundation.

Papanek, Hanna. 1973. "Purdah: Separate Worlds and Symbolic Shelter." *Comparative Studies in Society and History* 15 (June): 289–325.

Parsons, Talcott, and Robert Bales. 1955. *Family, Socialization, and Interaction Process*. Glencoe: Free Press.

Philo, Chris. 1989. "Enough to Drive One Mad: The Organization of Space in 19th-Century Lunatic Asylums." In *The Power of Geography*, edited by Jennifer Wolch and Michael Dear, pp. 258–90. Boston: Unwin Hyman.

Pile, John. 1978. *Open Office Planning: A Handbook for Interior Designers and Architects*. London: Architectural Press.

Pinxten, Rik, Ingrid van Dooren, and Frank Harvey. 1983. *Anthropology of Space*. Philadelphia: University of Pennsylvania Press.

Pleck, Elizabeth. 1978. "A Mother's Wages: Income Earning among Married Italian and Black Women, 1896–1911." In *The American Family in Social-Historical Perspective*, edited by Michael Gordon, pp. 490–511. New York: St. Martin's Press.

Pond, Jean Sarah. 1930. *Bradford: A New England Academy*. Bradford, Mass.: Bradford Academy Alumnae Association.

Pred, Allan. 1981. "Power, Everyday Practice and the Discipline of Human Geography." In *Space and Time in Geography*, edited by Allan Pred, pp. 30–55. Lund, Sweden: CWK Gleerup.

Pressley, Sue Anne. 1988. "Metropolitan Club Ends Ban on Women Members." *Washington Post*, June 26, p. B1.

Rapoport, Amos. 1969. *House Form and Culture*. Englewood Cliffs, N.J.: Prentice-Hall.

Read, Kenneth. 1965. *The High Valley*. New York: Charles Schribner's Sons.

Reskin, Barbara, ed. 1984. *Sex Segration in the Workplace: Trends, Explanations, Remedies*. Washington, D.C.: National Academy Press.

———. 1988. "Bringing the Men Back In: Sex Differentiation and the Devaluation of Women's Work." *Gender and Society* 2 (March): 58–81.

Reskin, Barbara, and Heidi Hartmann, eds. 1986. *Women's Work, Men's Work*. Washington, D.C.: National Academy Press.

Richards, Audrey. 1939. *Land, Labour and Diet in Northern Rhodesia*. London: Oxford University Press.

———. 1956. *Chisungu*. London: Faber and Faber.

Robinson, Harriet. [1898] 1976. *Loom and Spindle or Life among the Early Mill Girls*. Reprint. Kailua, Hawaii: Press Pacifica.

Rock, Cynthia, Susana Torre, and Gwendolyn Wright. 1980. "The Appropriation of the House: Changes in House Design and Concepts of Domesticity." In *New Space for Women*, edited by Gerda Wekerle, Rebecca Peterson, and David Morley, pp. 83–99. Boulder, Colo.: Westview Press.

Roos, Patricia. 1981. "Sex Stratification in the Workplace: Male-Female Differences in Economic Returns to Occupation." *Social Science Research* 10 (September): 195–224.

———. 1985. *Gender and Work: A Comparative Analysis of Industrial Societies*. Albany: State University of New York Press.

Rosaldo, Michelle Zimbalist. 1974. "Woman, Culture, and Society: A Theoretical Overview." In *Woman, Culture, and Society*, edited by Michelle Z. Rosaldo and Louise Lamphere, pp. 17–42. Stanford, Calif.: Stanford University Press.

———. 1980. "The Use and Abuse of Anthropology: Reflections on Feminism and Cross-Cultural Understanding." *Signs* 5 (Spring): 389–417.

Rosaldo, Michelle Z., and Louise Lamphere. 1974. *Woman, Culture, and Society*. Stanford, Calif.: Stanford University Press.

Rosenberg, Rosalind. 1982. *Beyond Separate Spheres*. New Haven: Yale University Press.

Rosenfeld, Rachel. 1984. "Job Changing and Occupational Sex Segregation: Sex and Race Comparisons." In *Sex Segregation in the Workplace*, edited by Barbara Reskin, pp. 56–86. Washington, D.C.: National Academy Press.

Rosenfeld, Rachel, and Arne Kalleberg. 1990. "A Cross-National Comparison of the Gender Gap in Income." *American Journal of Sociology* 96 (July): 69–106.

Ross, Marc Howard. 1986. "Female Political Participation: A Cross-Cultural Explanation." *American Anthropologist* 88 (December): 843–58.

Rossi, Alice. 1969. "Sex Equality: The Beginnings of Ideology." *The Humanist* 29 (September–October): 3–6.

———. 1973. *The Feminist Papers*. New York: Columbia University Press.

Rotella, Elyce J. 1981. *From Home to Office: U.S. Women at Work, 1870–1930*. Ann Arbor, Mich.: UMI Research Press.

Rothenberg, Diane. 1980. "The Mothers of the Nation: Seneca Resistance to Quaker Intervention." Chap. 3 in *Women and Colonization*, edited by Mona Etienne and Eleanor Leacock. New York: Praeger.

Rothman, David, and Sheila Rothman, eds. 1987. *The Dangers of Education: Sexism and the Origin of Women's Colleges*. New York: Garland Publishing.

Rothman, Sheila. 1978. *Woman's Proper Place*. New York: Basic Books.

Rowbotham, Sheila. 1973. *Woman's Consciousness, Man's World*. Baltimore: Penguin Press.

Rutherford, Brent, and Gerda Wekerle. 1988. "Captive Riders, Captive Labor: Spatial Constraints and Women's Employment." *Urban Geography* 9 (March–April): 116–37.

Ryan, Mary P. 1981. *Cradle of the Middle Class: The Family in Oneida County, New York, 1790–1865*. Cambridge: Cambridge University Press.

Rytina, Nancy, and Suzanne Bianchi. 1984. "Occupational Reclassification and Changes in Distribution of Gender." *Monthly Labor Review* 107 (March): 11–17.

Sack, Robert David. 1980. *Conceptions of Space in Social Thought*. Minneapolis: University of Minnesota Press.

Saegert, Susan. 1980. "Masculine Cities and Feminine Suburbs: Polarized Ideas, Contradictory Realities." In *Women and the American City*, edited by Catharine Stimpson, Elsa Dixler, Martha Nelson, and Kathryn Yatrakis, pp. 93–108. Chicago: University of Chicago Press.

Salmon, Lucy. [1897] 1972. *Domestic Service*. Reprint. New York: Arno Press.

Sanday, Peggy. 1974. "Female Status in the Public Domain." In *Woman, Culture, and Society*, edited by Michelle Rosaldo and Louise Lamphere, pp. 189–206. Stanford, Calif.: Stanford University Press.

———. 1981. *Female Power and Male Dominance*. Cambridge: Cambridge University Press.

Saphier, Michael. 1968. *Office Planning and Design*. New York: McGraw-Hill.

Schlegel, Alice. 1977. *Sexual Stratification: A Cross-Cultural View*. New York: Columbia University Press.

Schneir, Miriam, ed. 1972. *Feminism: The Essential Historical Writings*. New York: Vintage Books.

Schrire, Carmel, ed. 1984. *Past and Present in Hunter Gatherer Studies*. New York: Academic Press.

Sciama, Lidia. 1981. "The Problem of Privacy in Mediterranean Anthropology." Chap. 5 in *Women and Space*, edited by Shirley Ardener. London: Croom Helm.

Scoresby, Rev. William. [1845] 1968. *American Factories and Their Female Operatives*. Reprint. New York: Burt Franklin.

Scott, Alison MacEwen. 1986. "Industrialization, Gender Segregation and Stratification Theory." In *Gender and Stratification*, edited by Rosemary Crompton and Michael Mann, pp. 154–89. London: Polity Press.

Scott, Joan Wallach. 1982. "The Mechanization of Women's Work." *Scientific American* 247 (September): 167–87.

Sergeant, John. 1975. *Frank Lloyd Wright's Usonian Houses*. New York: Watson-Guptill Publications.

Shalala, Donna, and JoAnn McGeorge. 1981. "The Women and Mortgage Credit Project: A Government Response to the Housing Problems of Women." In *Building for Women*, edited by Suzanne Keller, pp. 39–45. Lexington, Mass.: D. C. Heath.

Shanley, Mary Lyndon. 1986. "Suffrage, Protective Labor Legislation, and Married Women's Property Laws in England." *Signs* 12 (Autumn): 62–77.

Shaw, Jenny. 1976. "Finishing School: Some Implications of Sex-Segregated Education." In *Sexual Divisions and Society: Process and Change*, edited by Diana Leonard Barker and Sheila Allen, pp. 133–49. London: Tavistock.

Shoppell, Robert. [1887] 1978. *Shoppell's Modern Houses*. Reprint. Rockville Center, N.Y.: Antiquity Reprints.

Sizer, Theodore, ed. 1964. *The Age of the Academies*. New York: Teachers College, Columbia University.

Sklar, Kathryn Kish. 1973. *Catharine Beecher: A Study in American Domesticity*. New Haven: Yale University Press.

Soja, Edward. 1971. *The Political Organization of Space*. Washington, D.C.: Association of American Geographers.

———. 1989. *Postmodern Geographies: The Reassertion of Space in Critical Social Theory*. London: Verso.

Solomon, Barbara. 1985. *In the Company of Educated Women*. New Haven: Yale University Press.

Sopher, David E. 1980. "Sex Disparity in Indian Literacy." Chap. 4 in *An Exploration of India*, edited by David E. Sopher. Ithaca, N.Y.: Cornell University Press.

Specter, Michael. 1991. "Skull and Bones at Yale: First No Women, Now No Club." *Washington Post*, April 16, p. A1.

Spencer, Robert F. 1972. "The Social Composition of the North Alaskan Whaling Crew." In *Alliance in Eskimo Society*, edited by Lee Guemple, pp. 110–20. Seattle: University of Washington Press.

Starr, Roger. 1987. "Men's Clubs, Women's Rights." *The Public Interest* 89 (Fall): 57–70.

Steele, Fritz. 1986. "The Dynamics of Power and Influence in Workplace Design and Management." In *Behavioral Issues in Office Design*, edited by Jean D. Wineman, pp. 43–64. New York: Van Nostrand Reinhold.

Stenning, Derrick. 1965. "The Pastoral Fulani of Northern Nigeria." Chap. 10 in *Peoples of Africa*, edited by James L. Gibbs. New York: Holt, Rinehart, and Winston.

Stickley, Gustav. [1909, 1912] 1979. *The Best of Craftsman Homes*. Reprint. Santa Barbara, Calif.: Peregrine Smith.

Stirling, M. W. 1938. "Historical and Ethnographic Material on the Jivaro Indians." Smithsonian Institution Bureau of American Ethnology, Bulletin 117. Washington, D.C.: U.S. Government Printing Office.

Stockard, Jean, and Miriam M. Johnson. 1980. *Sex Roles: Sex Inequality and Sex Role Development*. Englewood Cliffs, N.J.: Prentice-Hall.

Stover, Ronald, and Christine Hope. 1984. "Monotheism and Gender Status: A Cross-Societal Study." *Social Forces* 63 (December): 335–48.

Sundstrom, Eric. 1986. "Privacy in the Office." In *Behavioral Issues in Office Design*, edited by Jean Wineman, pp. 177–202. New York: Van Nostrand Reinhold.

Sundstrom, Eric, Robert Burt, and Douglas Kemp. 1980. "Privacy at Work: Architectural Correlates of Job Satisfaction and Job Performance." *Academy of Management Journal* 23 (March): 101–17.

Talbert, Joan, and Christine Bose. 1977. "Wage-Attainment Processes: The Retail Clerk Case." *American Journal of Sociology* 83 (September): 403–24.

Tefft, Stanton K. 1980. "Secrecy, Disclosure, and Social Theory." Chap. 2 in *Secrecy: A Cross-Cultural Perspective*, edited by Stanton Tefft. New York: Human Sciences Press.

Thorne, Barrie. 1989. "Girls and Boys Together . . . But Mostly Apart: Gender Arrangements in Elementary Schools." In *Feminist Frontiers II*, edited by Laurel Richardson and Verta Taylor, pp. 73–84. New York: Random House.

Tidball, M. Elizabeth. 1973. "Perspective on Academic Women and Affirmative Action." *Educational Record* 54:130–35.

————. 1980. "Women's Colleges and Women Achievers Revisited." *Signs* 5 (Spring): 504–17.

Tidball, M. Elizabeth, and Vera Kistiakowsky. 1976. "Baccalaureate Origins of American Scientists and Scholars." *Science* 193:646–52.

Tiger, Lionel. 1969. *Men in Groups*. New York: Random House.

Treiman, Donald, and Heidi Hartmann, eds. 1981. *Women, Work, and Wages: Equal Pay for Jobs of Equal Value*. Report of the Committee on Occupational Classification and Analysis. Washington, D.C.: National Academy Press.

Tryon, Rolla Milton. [1917] 1966. *Household Manufactures in the U.S., 1640–1680: A Study in Industrial History*. Reprint. New York: Augustus M. Kelley.

Twombly, Robert C. 1979. *Frank Lloyd Wright: His Life and His Architecture*. New York: John Wiley and Sons.

Urry, John. 1985. "Social Relations, Space and Time." In *Social Relations and Spatial Structures*, edited by Derek Gregory and John Urry, pp. 20–48. London: Macmillan.

U.S. Bureau of the Census. 1907. *Statistics of Women at Work*. Washington, D.C.: U.S. Government Printing Office.

————. 1975. *Historical Statistics of the United States, Colonial Times to 1970, Bicentennial Edition, Part 1*. Washington D.C.: U.S. Government Printing Office.

————. 1984. *1980 Census of Population*. Supplementary Report, Detailed Occupation of the Experienced Civilian Labor Force by Sex for the U.S. and Regions: 1980 and 1970. PC80-S1-15. Washington, D.C.: U.S. Government Printing Office.

————. 1986. *Statistical Abstract of the United States: 1987*. 107th ed. Washington, D.C.: U.S. Government Printing Office.

————. 1989a. "Household and Family Characteristics: March 1988." *Current Population Reports*, ser. P-20, no. 437. Washington, D.C.: U.S. Government Printing Office.

————. 1989b. "Money Income of Households, Families, and Persons in the United States: 1987." *Current Population Reports*, ser. P-60, no. 162. Washington, D.C.: U.S. Government Printing Office.

————. 1990a. "Money Income and Poverty Status in the United States: 1989". *Current Population Reports*, ser. P-60, no. 168. Washington, D.C.: U.S. Government Printing Office.

————. 1990b. *Statistical Abstract of the United States: 1989*. 110th ed. Washington, D.C.: U.S. Government Printing Office.

U.S. Department of Education. 1991. *Digest of Education Statistics 1990*. 26th ed. Washington, D.C.: National Center for Education Statistics.

U.S. Department of Labor. 1991. *Employment and Earnings* 38 (January). Washington, D.C.: Bureau of Labor Statistics.

Varanda, Fernando. 1982. *Art of Building in Yemen*. Cambridge: MIT Press.

Verity, Paul. 1971. "Kababish Nomads of Northern Sudan." In *Shelter in Africa*, edited by Paul Oliver, pp. 25–35. New York: Praeger.

Walby, Sylvia. 1986. *Patriarchy at Work*. Cambridge: Polity Press.

Ware, Caroline F. 1931. *The Early New England Cotton Manufacture: A Study in Industrial Beginnings*. Boston: Houghton Mifflin.

Waterson, Roxana. 1990. *The Living House: An Anthropology of Architecture in South-East Asia*. New York: Oxford University Press.

Watson, Joellen. 1977. "Higher Education for Women in the United States: A Historical Perspective." *Educational Studies* 8 (Summer): 133–46.

Weber, Max. [1921] 1978. *Economy and Society*. Reprint, edited by Guenther Roth and Claus Wittich. Berkeley: University of California Press.

Weeks, John R. 1988. "The Demography of Islamic Nations." *Population Bulletin* 43, no. 4. Washington, D.C.: Population Reference Bureau.

Wekerle, Gerda. 1988. "Canadian Women's Housing Cooperatives: Case Studies in Physical and Social Innovation." In *Life Spaces*, edited by Caroline Andrew and Beth Moore Milroy, pp. 102–40. Vancouver: University of British Columbia Press.

Wekerle, Gerda, Rebecca Peterson, and David Morley. 1980. *New Space for Women*. Boulder, Colo.: Westview Press.

Welter, Barbara. 1966. "The Cult of True Womanhood, 1820–1860." *American Quarterly* 18 (Summer): 151–74.

Wharton, Amy, and James Baron. 1987. "So Happy Together? The Impact of Gender Segregation on Men at Work." *American Sociological Review* 52 (October): 574–87.

Whyte, Martin. 1978a. *The Status of Women in Preindustrial Societies*. Princeton, N.J.: Princeton University Press.

———. 1978b. "Cross-Cultural Codes Dealing with the Relative Status of Women." *Ethnology* 17 (April): 211–37.

Wolf, Wendy, and Neil Fligstein. 1979. "Sex and Authority in the Workplace: The Causes of Sexual Inequality." *American Sociological Review* 44 (April): 235–52.

Wolff, Kurt, ed. 1950. *The Sociology of Georg Simmel*. New York: Free Press.

Women and Geography Study Group of the Institute of British Geographers. 1984. *Geography and Gender*. London: Hutchinson.

Woody, Thomas. [1929] 1974. *A History of Women's Education in the United States*. 2 vols. Reprint. New York: Octagon Books.

Woolf, Virginia. 1929. *A Room of One's Own*. New York: Harcourt, Brace and World.

Wright, Gwendolyn. 1980. *Moralism and the Model Home*. Chicago: University of Chicago Press.

———. 1985. "Women's Aspirations and the Home: Episodes in American Feminist Reform." Chap. 9 in *The Unsheltered Woman*, edited by Eugenie Ladner Birch. New Brunswick, N.J.: Rutgers University Center for Urban Policy Research.

Wulff, Inger. 1982. "Habitation among the Yakan, a Muslim People in the Southern Philippines." In *The House in East and Southeast Asia*, edited by K. G. Izikowitz and P. Sorensen, pp. 137–50. London: Curzon Press.

Zelinsky, Wilbur, Janice Monk, Susan Hanson. 1982. "Women and Geography: A Review and Prospectus." *Progress in Human Geography* 6 (September): 317–66.

Index

293